I HAVE SEEN THE
WORLD BEGIN

Also by Carsten Jensen in English translation

EARTH IN THE MOUTH
Translated by Anne Born

Carsten Jensen

I HAVE SEEN THE
WORLD BEGIN

Translated from the Danish by
Barbara Haveland

HARCOURT, INC.
NEW YORK   SAN DIEGO   LONDON

Requests for permission to make copies of any part of the work should
be mailed to the following address: Permissions Department, Harcourt, Inc.,
6277 Sea Harbor Drive, Orlando, Florida 32887-6777.

www.HarcourtBooks.com

First published in Danish by Munksgaard/Rosinante as *Jeg har set verden begynde*.
First published in English by The Harvill Press.

Library of Congress Cataloging-in-Publication Data
Jensen, Carsten.
[*Jeg har set verden begynde*. English]
I have seen the world begin/Translated from the Danish by Barbara Haveland.
p.   cm.
ISBN 0-15-100768-3
1. Jensen, Carsten—Journeys—Asia.   2. Asia—Description and travel.
I. Haveland, Barbara.   II. Title.

DS10.J4713 2002
915.04'429—dc21   2001039736

Printed in the United States of America
First U.S. edition
A C E G I K J H F D B

"And who are you?" he asked.
"A common traveller," I replied, "a traveller who pays his way.
    And who are you?"

HANS CHRISTIAN ANDERSEN, In Sweden

Contents

Maps:

China   ix

Cambodia   x

Vietnam   xi

A Brief Prologue   I

China: The Highest Mountains

Days of Glass   5

A Man with a Shopping Bag   12

Night on the Shanghai Express   17

An Unbelievable Number of People   20

The Joy of the Stunted   23

A Clown in the Arena of Words   25

Big Bang   28

The Long River   34

A Fight in Chinese   43

Nature's Stop Sign   48

The Artistry of Violation   54

Upwards, Ever Upwards   62

A Shameful Rebel   66

In the Heart of Civilization   83

Partisans of Love   85

The Music of Old Men   92

The Biggest Tiger in the World   95

As the Wall in Space, So the Book Pyre in Time   101

Out of the Clay Pit   105

A Blessing for the Traveller   107

Cambodia: Hour of the Tiger

Invention of a Nation 111

A Scar on the Landscape 123

Propaganda with a Stammer 132

S-21: Where the World Vanishes 134

The Children's Revolution 139

With Greetings from a Tree 149

Confession of a Fratricide 154

Black Spaces on the Globe 160

River Patrol to the End of the Earth 180

Pure Evil 193

The Woman under the Rain Tree 198

Vietnam: Arrival on Earth

Motorized Flowers 203

A Chink in the Wall 205

Victor Hugo and the Coconut Monk 220

Man is Like a Bamboo Shoot 227

Would I Could Own the Face of Eternity 247

Land of Women 254

A Garden City 259

Ask the Immortals about the Meaning of Life 265

The Snow behind Thien Mu Pagoda 272

The Eunuchs' Graveyard 276

Remote-controlled Death and Murderous
    Innocence 282

Scent of Spring and Harvest Moon 293

Intimacies between Strangers 302

Embroidery is their Native Land 313

The Simplest of all Gifts 322

Parting is the Little Sister of Death 333

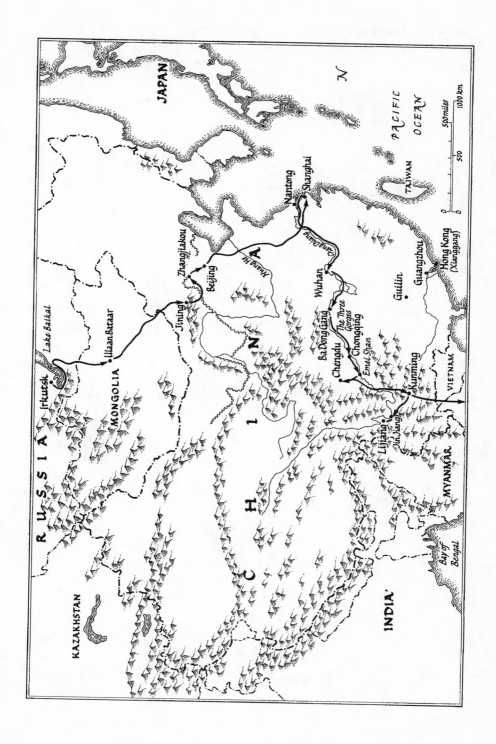

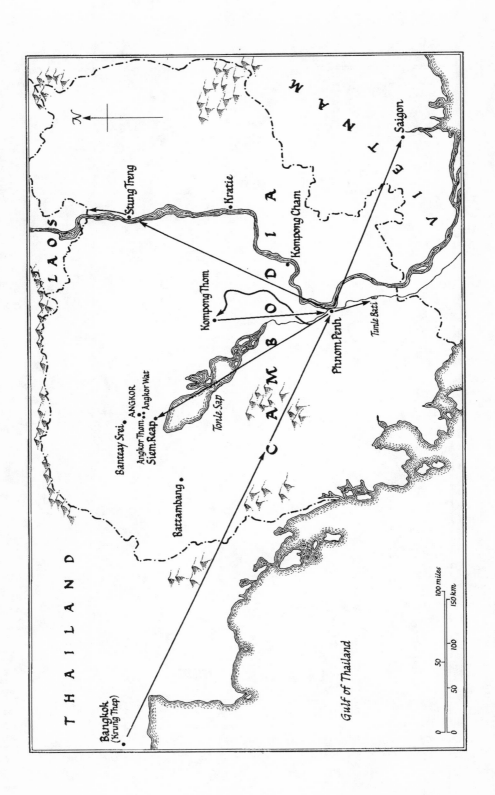

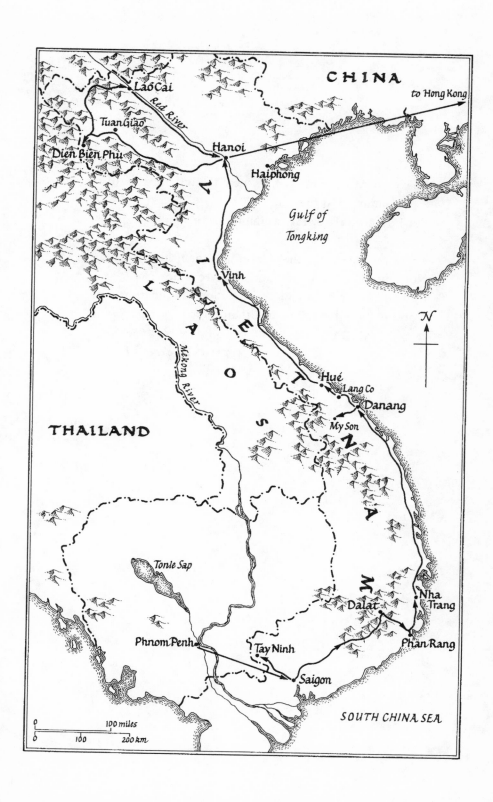

CHINA

Lao Cai

Red River

Tuan Giao

Dien Bien Phu

Hanoi

Haiphong

to Hong Kong

Gulf of Tongking

N

Vinh

THAILAND

L A O S

Mekong River

V I E T N A M

Hué

Lang Co

Danang

My Son

Tonle Sap

Dalat

Nha Trang

Phnom Penh

Tay Ninh

Phan Rang

Saigon

SOUTH CHINA SEA

0   100 miles
0   100   200 km

I have heard what the talkers were talking, the talk of the
    beginning and the end;
But I do not talk of the beginning or the end.

There was never any more inception than there is now,
Nor any more youth or age than there is now;
And will never be any more perfection than there is now,
Nor any more heaven or hell than there is now.

WALT WHITMAN, Leaves of Grass

A Brief Prologue

WHILE THIS BOOK DEPICTS A JOURNEY THROUGH COUNTRIES which in recent years have been the scene of cataclysmic events, it is not a political or a historical work, since all I know about the history of the world is what I have learned from witnessing the birth of a child. When at long last the infant emerged, coated in blood and vernix, and proclaimed with a little whimper that it was alive, both its mother and I knew that all the pain leading up to that moment had been no more than an adjunct to a process which, at heart, we could neither comprehend nor control. Unseen hands had shaped the child in the womb, in response to a force which is familiar only if one considers the frequency with which children come into the world, but which has remained a mystery when it comes to considering the origin and purpose of such a will. Surely there is no other time in the life of a human being when he or she is more aware of how little their so-called ownership of their bodies amounts to than when they become the source of a new life. We are but instruments of nature, and the moment we hold a fragile newborn infant in our arms we discover the inadequacy of words such as "I" and "we". Because it is not we who have created the child. We have simply allowed it to be created. Some unknown power has a hand in it and in us. And yet the child is helplessly dependent on us, our individual abilities and willingness to guide it through life. The breast to which it is laid for the first time, the arm in which it first finds repose are none other than that very boundary between impotence and omnipotence along which all human life is played out.

CHINA

The Highest Mountains

Some day I must ascend the summit
And see how small other mountains are.

TU FU

Days of Glass

IT WAS A DAY OF GLASS. I, TOO, WAS MADE OF GLASS. Handle with care!

I could allow nothing to get close to me, not even impressions. It was as if I had only just learned to walk and might fall down at any minute. The womblike security of the Trans-Siberian train compartment was gone. I wrapped myself up in my old Boss overcoat and Johnston scarf. I had brought them all the way to China with the intention of jettisoning them. Farther south, when I had outrun winter, they would be given away, free to continue their own travels around the shoulders of others, perhaps taking a part of my soul with them.

I felt the burden of the tremendous mental alertness this journey demanded. I was not big enough, I was not receptive or self-confident enough; it was just me against a billion people. I wanted to shout it out across the rooftops of Beijing: I'm too little!

A silver-grey winter sky hung over Beijing. Everything that first day was silver-grey. Hard-packed snow on grey pavements. Asphalt. Grey-clad people on bicycles. The apartment blocks were grey. I left the Hotel Long Tan on a sturdy, rented bicycle. It made a funny noise as I pedalled and the rusty chain turned only under protest. I have ridden bicycles all my life, but my attitude to them is much the same as my attitude to my internal organs: a sense of helplessness, because I have no idea what to do when they cease to function properly. I am powerless in the face of coughing fits, stomach aches, punctures and loose chains. For me, the bicycle mechanic is as revered an authority as the doctor. And here I was, landed with a bicycle of which I was only nominally in command.

I peddled off down a road leading to the city centre. Here the traffic was confined to bicycles and the occasional bus. There were even round-abouts for bicycles and for a moment it seemed as if China was a cyclist's paradise – but the roundabout lay under the concrete supports of a motorway flyover. According to my guide book, which was a couple of years old, there were no more than a few hundred private cars in China. So where had all the thousands of cars come from that were now zooming towards the city centre along the multi-lane motorway above my head?

Had the cars been there in the days when Mao provided a compass-bearing for the dreams of a generation of young people, it would not have been so easy to dream such innocent dreams of the Cultural Revolution. For then, in a salutary way, Chinese society would have been compromised in the eyes of an all too romantic youth. Cars and motorways – they called for level-headedness, not daydreaming.

Although the bicycles were still in the majority, they did not overrun the streets, which were as wide as runways. There remained room enough on the main thoroughfares of Beijing for another couple of million cyclists. It felt very safe to be cycling on them, carried along almost automatically by the smooth-flowing stream of bicycles. One was never alone in the battle against the cars, there was always this massive river of hunched figures slowly forging ahead. Having joined the stream you felt no inclination to leave it again. The most you could get away with was the odd little maverick solo sprint, zig-zagging ahead at a speed marginally greater than that of everyone else. But then, why bother?

When you are used to weaving through big-city traffic – which, even in bicycle-friendly Copenhagen, is a notoriously risky business – this was like coming home to the mother country of the bicycle. But I was falling into a romanticism that always lay in wait for me in China, as in all places where there is not too much knowledge standing in the way of one's dreams.

There were lots of delivery bicycles, the trailer trundling along behind a lean, round-shouldered coolie, his straining back muscles visible through a threadbare quilted jacket. At one point the cycle lane ran uphill and the coolie jumped off to push his bicycle, its trailer filled with bulky sacks. They looked as if they must together weigh several hundredweight. Even in minus ten degrees the sweat was pouring down his prominent cheekbones. I use the word "coolie" advisedly, believing that such displays of superhuman effort and lone desperation have been there to see in China since time began.

Another coolie came cycling along with a batch of imitation leather sofas piled up into a large sculpture on his trailer. He took a tight bend the wrong way and the next moment bicycle and trailer had careened over onto the asphalt. The hapless cyclist got to his feet and rubbed a bruised knee. Then he simply stood there, arms hanging by his sides, staring helplessly at the toppled furniture mountain, his face glazed with embarrassment. He looked as if he longed to vanish into the crowd.

That evening I ate at the Hotel Long Tan. The dining room was a vast, high-ceilinged hall in the basement, unheated and with bare walls that threw back the ice-cold light from rows of fluorescent tubes. The place was almost empty. A fair-haired American in his forties, with a beard and round, steel-rimmed spectacles, was pointing at the menu, speaking slowly and with suppressed irritation. The waitress, who was small and deft in her movements, took his order with a smile. Then she turned to me.

"May I?" the American asked, then seated himself across from me without waiting for a reply.

"I've been here for two months. The Chinese are driving me crazy." He complained so bitterly about the Chinese that I wondered why he had stayed so long. "I won't be back, that's for sure," he said.

The waitress brought his meal. He peered at the plate and called her back.

"This isn't what I ordered. Why can't I just get what I asked for? What's the matter with you Chinese?"

His slouched figure radiated disgust. His lips, red and moist, squirmed like worms in the thick of his dishevelled beard as he enunciated his dismay with pedantic precision.

The waitress smiled and reached for his plate. He pushed her arm aside. He was blatantly hostile, but in a condescending manner, as though he lacked a target worthy of his indignation.

"No, leave it. You Chinese, you're all hopeless anyway."

Reluctantly he began to eat while entertaining me with stories of his exploits. Earlier that day he had visited Tiananmen Square and laid a flower at the foot of the monument to the Chinese revolution. He had intended to take a photograph of his little set piece, although he did not explain why. Neither did he to the two policemen who had required him to accompany them, subjecting him to an hour-long interrogation during which they informed him that dropping litter in Tiananmen Square was against the law. They confiscated the flower but let him go.

Clearly he had wanted to pay his respects to those killed at Tiananmen Square, but I found it difficult to sympathise with this egocentric and self-righteous demonstration. The flower on the paving stones where the students had died was a tableau destined only for his own photograph album.

Besides, how could he feel any sympathy with rebels in a country all of whose people he despised? It was after all for democracy, for the people, that the rebels had given their lives. The American was simply cultivating his self-conscious nobility. That was all he had wanted to document in the image of a lonely flower in a world of stone.

The following day I moved to the Hotel Lu Song Yuan, a small hotel in a *hútóng*, one of the narrow streets which were all that remained of old Beijing. The building was all on one floor around an open courtyard. On the bed was a quilt of emerald-green silk embroidered with a red and gold dragon.

In the morning the pleasant girl at reception was pale with tiredness as she huddled, shivering, inside her down jacket.

"We work for 36 hours without a break," she said. "Yes, I am very tired. If we don't do our job well, we are sacked. I'll be going off duty soon. I'll just have time to catch some sleep before I have to get back to work."

Also staying at the Hotel Lu Song Yuan were a young French couple, Valerie and Fabrice. He was tall, with lips like Jean-Paul Belmondo, fleshy and sensitive. He had bought himself a dark blue Mao jacket which he wore with a Chinese balaclava. It was all a game, complete with props and poses, and he carried it off with the same effortless elegance that nature had exercised in casting his features which combined a distinctly French masculinity with a disarming vulnerability. Valerie was freckled, blonde and blithe. They made a lovely, harmonious couple.

They had been travelling in China for a month and were now heading home to Paris. They would not be coming back. As a country they found it too difficult to get around, but there was one place they recommended.

They unearthed a cutting from *Marie Claire*. A photographer had

8

visited the obscure Dong tribe, one of China's numerous ethnic minorities, who inhabited a region not far from Guilin in the south.

The cutting showed pictures of terraces on which flooded rice paddies mirrored the clouds, while water buffalo plodded nose to tail along the line where the sky greeted its reflection. There were ingeniously constructed wooden huts, laughing faces and grubby children carried around in baskets. These were the Dong people, forgotten by progress. Even the heavy-handed Communist regime had let them preserve their culture. The Iron Age had not yet touched them (they used no nails in their buildings) and this made them unique. The Dong people could neither read nor write. They expressed themselves chiefly in song and as children they ate flowers tasting of strawberries to sweeten their voices. Anyone wishing to experience their song-filled, nail-less existence would have to be quick about it.

In their room Valerie and Fabrice had a red-painted cardboard Chinese suitcase crammed with objects they had picked up on their visit to the Dong people. There was a small, three-legged stool, its seat shiny from use, a rake attached to a long wooden handle, spoons, a sieve, long tongs made from pig iron for lifting burning coals. (So iron was not, after all, entirely unheard of among the Dongs.) They were the kind of objects you might see in a folk or rural museum, except that they were primitive and clumsy and bore no sign of craftsmanship. Yet they were unlikely holiday souvenirs, household implements snatched from the hands of farmers, workmen and housewives who, if they wished to see their own future, did not need to look in any crystal ball, but simply take a peek in Valerie and Fabrice's suitcase. Here they would find that what they took to be their life was already in the past tense, all set for an afterlife as *objets d'art* on the wall of an *appartement* in Paris's *sixième*.

The Dong people had been too small and politically insignificant to be disturbed by the dogmatists of Communist progress. No one could even be bothered to educate them. The true heralds of their decline were not political commissars but romantics such as Valerie and Fabrice who, out of sheer infatuation with their unique way of life, plundered it and left them with a wad of banknotes in exchange.

As time went on I was to meet many visitors to China who loathed the country, but who were enamoured of its colourful ethnic minorities, whose unavoidable submersion in China's sea of people they bemoaned even as they helped themselves to the few remaining treasures. Presumably the Dong people did not know that they had a culture until someone had put a price on it. Only then was their desire for progress awakened; a desire that in the eyes of their romantic benefactors was forbidden because it heralded the demise of their way of life. Such was the relationship between the ethnic minorities and their fans. The latter ended up as the guardians of the former. That longing for freedom which drove these young romantics to set off on their travels was something they denied their captors. The ethnic minorities were only extras in somebody else's dream and they were not allowed to leave the Middle Ages behind in pursuit of their own liberty.

The fondness that many youthful travellers from the West feel for China's ethnic minorities might be attributed to the fact that they were one of the few opportunities in China for them to feel culturally superior. The Chinese, for their part, behaved as equals and refused to respond with fawning gratitude to the amiable condescension of Westerners.

Visiting hours for Mao began at eight o'clock on Sunday mornings, but since I could not get myself out of bed that early I abandoned the idea, even though I – who had just managed in Moscow to catch a glimpse of the embalmed Lenin before it was too late – had in fact been determined to work my way through Asia viewing the rest of the Communist mummies. This ambition was obviously not strong enough, however, or perhaps I was not as much of a political necrophiliac as I had thought.

Instead I went to see the temple erected to ancient China's great master of philosophy, Confucius. One could only visit the courtyard, bounded by the red temple buildings with bricked-up entrances at every turn; the temple itself, unlike Mao, was outside all visiting hours. In the courtyard stood some Chinese pines. They must have been centuries old, perhaps as old as the temple itself and they looked as if they drew their nourishment from the very paving stones through massive trunks stripped of their bark and grey as fossils. From their ghostly, near-dead tops bare branches poked through blue-grey needles, standing out in gnarled silhouette against a frosty sky.

A flock of birds flew high over the temple courtyard, a swirling cloud of black specks. And from up above a note floated down, as though someone were practising on a flute; a long-drawn-out prelude to a piece of music that refused to take shape. The sound faded away, only to return a moment later, the same hesitant refrain, wavering yet insistent. I recognized the sound, but from where I could not say. Then there it was again, and I realized how in some way it was connected to the appearance and disappearance of the flock of birds.

No, I had not heard it before, or perhaps only in my head with the inner ear of the imagination. I recognized it from the stories of my childhood. I had read about it in one of Johannes V. Jensen's "myths", a little piece entitled "On Java". He had heard that sound three-quarters of a century earlier in a town by the name of Maglang where the natives tied bamboo flutes to the undersides of doves' wings. Now I was listening to it here, in Beijing. It was the wind, composing its own monotonous little melody high in the sky. I associated it with a world that was gone forever and now here it was, a thin, sustained chord in Beijing, the city where Mao had once ordered the extermination of all the sparrows, with the result that the town almost fell to a plague of insects.

Beijing was reaching out to the future with tower blocks, cranes, busy highways and crowded markets, but it had also reached out to the past and brought back this little melody. It was the sound of the wind's flight of fancy, the sigh of gravity conquered.

A Man with a Shopping Bag

IN MY MIND WAS A PICTURE FROM THE FILM FOOTAGE OF the prelude to the Tiananmen Square massacre, at the Gate of Heavenly Peace, on that day in the summer of 1989 when the army launched an attack on student demonstrators: the lone figure on a wide boulevard who stopped a column of oncoming tanks.

The massive armoured vehicles tried to sidle round him. The man sidestepped with them. The leading tank tried again. Again he blocked its path. Back and forth. The little man and the war machine feeling its way forwards blindly, feebly, beetle-like and mindless, but by no means heartless, because behind that steel sat a human being: the insect's vulnerable heart. Was the tank's driver acting under orders? Was his irresolution deliberate?

It had all the makings of the classic image of individual heroism and indomitability: the individual confronting the totalitarian State, vulnerable flesh defying armour-plated steel. Or it could be a picture of something else again: the State hesitating.

Miraculously the lone man halted a phalanx of tanks. In there, behind the steel were people exactly like him, and perhaps what we were actually witnessing here was the moment of recognition, the only true and democratic moment in all revolutions, that of fraternization, as the soldiers lay down their arms and give themselves up to the unarmed rebels.

Mao got by without tanks. Which was how he was able to beguile a whole generation of Western youth that had seen through Stalinism and felt nothing but abhorrence for all symbols of power.

Mao broke with the State's monopoly on violence and turned hatred into a citizen's right. He liberated oppression from its uniforms and institutions and rendered it universal and mutual as self-imposed subjugation. Instead of the KGB and the "thought police" one had daughters who informed on mothers, sons who publicly ridiculed and denounced fathers, neighbours who beat up neighbours and reduced them to cripples, all in the name of "The Correct Line".

Maoism was Stalinism from below, in the form of a grass-roots movement, the privileges of a dictator, his whims and paranoia evenly distributed among the masses. The straightforward democracy of hate and evil became an anti-authoritarian massacre in which the symbols of authority were conspicuous by their absence, because the democratically liberated forces of hate, fear and envy were capable of doing far greater damage than any secret service agency or squadron of tanks. And behind it all the power remained undisturbed, unaltered, having with one masterstroke succeeded in getting the people to turn their rebellion inwards in a frenzy of self-mutilation which knew no bounds because there was no institution to stem the flow or set the water mark of the flood that resulted from this boiling sea of bitterness.

A day or two – or was it only an hour or two? – after the solitary young man's confrontation with the advancing column of tanks, the massacre on Tiananmen Square began: barricades in flames, gunfire, people fleeing, all caught in the spotlight of the omnipresent film crews.

By morning the square was strewn with the scattered belongings of the dead, the imprisoned and the fugitive. It was the mangled bicycles – squashed flat, their frames smashed and disabled – that had the most impact. After all, Maoism had ridden straight into the naïve hearts of the West on bicycles. The bicycle was the symbol of Maoism – that was as far as the infatuation and insight of Western sympathizers went. Murderers did not ride bicycles. How to come to terms with a nation of bike-lovers? Ghandi might have ridden a bicycle. If Jesus had ridden along his Via Dolorosa on a bicycle he might have had more success in filling the churches of today. The bicycle stood for innocence, disarming in all its banal reliability, a nice way for nice people to get around.

And now here the crushed bicycles lay on the paving stones of Tiananmen Square in that grainy news footage from a grey morning in history, symbols of shattered dreams and the dawning of a new and more ruthless age. We never did see the dead. We still do not know their numbers. Perhaps 300, maybe 10,000. Their abandoned bicycles seemed like a memorial to them, a monument to an innocence that spoke directly to the heart, something like a doll left on a motorway by the small victim of a road accident.

We never saw the victims of Maoism's massacres. We did not even hear about them until the Cultural Revolution was over. The Cultural Revolution was an enigma, which invited speculation, even fascination in the West, but never concrete protest. Its brand of terrorism was based on psychological subversion rather than the firing squad. Its instruments of execution were not in the hands of policemen, but of skinny teenagers. It was possibly the first mass slaughter in history that was able to maintain its innocuous facade for decades. I blame it on the bicycle.

But perhaps the bicycle was also responsible for the fact that the international response to Tiananmen Square was far more intense than any reaction to Mao's regime, even though the number of victims was relatively small beside the millions who lost their lives in the Cultural Revolution.

The Chinese government gave no sign on the occasion of the Tiananmen Square massacre – or at any time since then – that it was sensitive to pressure from the outside world. But, with this blatant act of violence the murderers had shown their faces. And their faces were not those of the people. For the first time in modern Chinese history there was something tangible to oppose.

Reading Jung Chang's eye-witness description of the Cultural Revolution had revealed to me how little I knew about China. In *Wild Swans* Jung Chang maintains that by the time the Cultural Revolution had come to an end China was an ugly country. Whereas Europe had entrepreneurs and architects, China had the Red Guard. That same reaction against the old, against history and tradition, which had cleared the cities of Europe, creating instead motorways and suburban wildernesses; the steady depopulation of rural areas; the opening up of the job market to include both sexes – the reshaping of the psyche which marked the advent of what is known as the modern world, took the form in China of rampaging teenagers whose confused instincts seemed able, for a moment, to dictate the course of history.

In Europe history was spurred on by machinery, in China by hand still; in Europe by a covert brutality inherent in the dictates of progress, in China with actual brutality in an open dictatorship; in Europe a new type of individual was shaped and moulded into existence by the unseen pressure of a thousand outside influences, in China it was terrorized into being in one concerted roar of hate issuing from millions of young people.

Europe had steamrollers, cement-mixers and cranes, China had vandalism. In Europe the churches, those symbols of the past, were not torn down, but simply bypassed until their influence was diminished. In China the temples were desecrated and the seated Buddhas lost their heads or had their serene expressions chiselled away in a frenzy of youthful rage. In both places history was seen to renew itself, but in China that element of destruction which is contained within every process of renewal was laid bare to the bone.

There was a detail easily overlooked on the reel of film showing the prelude to the massacre on Tiananmen Square. It was something about the lone man himself just as he stepped into the path of those tanks. The heroic element in this picture was provided by his ordinariness. A slightly built man in shirt and trousers. No Freedom leading the people to the barricades as in Delacroix's painting here, because there were no barricades. Nor were there any bayonetted rifles as at the storming of the Winter Palace, no Molotov cocktails as in the uprising in Hungary, no sea of people as in Prague which had tried to halt an advancing tank by sheer weight of numbers. But there was one detail, apart from the man himself and the squadron of tanks, and the man held it in his hand. It was a shopping bag. He was a man with a shopping bag disturbed on his way home from market because history had a rendezvous with him.

There were two ways of interpreting the situation: the man with the shopping bag arrested the tanks' advance. Or, the tanks got in the way of the man with the shopping bag. The question as to which was the stronger was only one part of a much greater question: which of them was the agent of History?

This situation could be viewed as a classic confrontation: lone man against tyranny. In which case what the man was testing by dodging back and forth was the scale of man, his significance and his potential for influencing events.

Or one could focus on the shopping bag and see the man as a representative of progress, the impending consumer society. Then he becomes not a timeless figure, but a very contemporary one, since the modern age has swapped the banner and the barricade for the shopping bag.

One could also regard him as a man who was not trying to write history at all. As far as he was concerned the squadron of tanks was not his adversary, merely a bothersome element encountered on his way from market to home. For him, the daily round was the only reality, and that which we know as History was to him nothing more than an unwelcome interruption.

Then the film presented no political confrontation, but a clash between history and what lay outside and underneath it, the foundation of life itself.

It is impossible to say which of these interpretations is the right one, if, indeed, any one of them. Or perhaps it is all three at once.

Night on the Shanghai Express

THE COLOURS IN THE INTERIOR OF THE SHANGHAI EXPRESS
perfectly complemented those of the glorious winter's day outside. In first
class – "Soft Sleeper" as it was called – there were dark-blue plush seats
with starched white covers and a lace cloth on the table by the window.
A conductor handed out raffia slippers to the passengers, while another
served green tea in blue-patterned china cups. Soap, toothbrush, tooth-
paste and a collapsible coathanger were also provided.

Opposite me sat an elderly gentleman, a professor of medicine, with
a strong chin and a mane of grey hair. Indeed, he was not merely a professor, he was a famous professor, as my two other travelling companions
confided to me when he left the compartment for a moment. In Beijing he
had once operated on a government minister, but see, they said, how freely
and easily he talks to us just the same.

For their part, they worked at a large, newly opened hotel in
Shanghai and they quizzed me with scientific thoroughness on what I
needed and expected from such an establishment. The older one treated
me to a long monologue on the hotel's two-year history and the staff's
heroic struggle to raise their standards. The younger one offered me a
discount.

"We have made some mistakes," said the elder man, "but we have
been critical of ourselves. We have succeeded in making improvements
in all the vital areas. We now lead the field on those points which the
foreigner values. Cleanliness, above all cleanliness. And the hotel staff
have to smile. At the Hotel Longmen we smile as nowhere else."

I asked Qian Hai, the younger man, about the boom in the Chinese
economy. He quoted me China's annual growth rate of 10.87 per cent and
his expression, a combination of servile politeness and cool intelligence,
glowed with satisfaction. He appeared to entertain the same feelings for
his country as for his place of work, regarding both quite unsentimentally

as nothing more than sources of income. This was the modern equivalent of patriotism.

I asked him how much he earned. "Hard to say," he said. "It varies." A friend in Shanghai had offered him a job as the manager of a newly opened restaurant. He could earn four times as much there as in his present job, besides pocketing a fair amount. Opening his jacket he pointed to an inside pocket to make sure that I understood. But that was not his vision of the future. He was going to use his head. He had a degree in economics and English, he was 24 years old and the way he saw it, with his gifts, he would one day be sitting in front of a computer screen playing the stock market.

I asked if he was married. "Guess," he said.

I guessed no. He was too skinny, too unfinished and servile to be married. Or perhaps I was wrong about his servility. Perhaps it masked a hard-nosed sense of purpose. But it boiled down to the same thing. In neither case had the romantic in him been aroused.

Qian Hai nodded.

Then it was his turn to ask the questions and apparently I made my first blunder.

"I'm divorced," I said.

Qian Hai gasped, as if he were fighting for breath. He had gone bright red and seemed quite overcome by the awkwardness of the situation.

"Oh, that is dreadful," he moaned, putting his hands to his head.

"That's the way things are in the West," I told him soothingly. "It's perfectly normal."

I decided it might be better to change the subject and committed my second *faux pas* by asking Qian Hai what he thought about "the events" in Tiananmen Square.

He gave a short peal of laughter, then lapsed into his gasping act once more.

"I do not concern myself with politics," he said, once he had composed himself. "I was taken up with my studies and thought of nothing but my career. The students were naïve. They were exploited by someone who wanted things to move in another direction."

I wanted to ask what other direction, but refrained from doing so, feeling that I had put my foot in it enough already.

"They were naïve," Qian Hai repeated broodily, as if he were trying to convince himself of something. "Progress cannot be achieved in leaps and bounds. They were too impatient."

Then he brightened up. "I am for whatever government will improve my standard of living. Year by year earnings in China are climbing."

We were back to the annual growth rate of 10.87 per cent, an incontrovertible argument even in a Communist country, presented by a young-executive type whom one would as likely have found in Hong Kong, Singapore, New York or London.

Qian Hai said a polite good-night and clambered up into the top bunk. Preparatory to settling for the night he stretched right out and then set his abdomen rippling violently, an exercise which induced three loud burps. Then he snuggled down and opened a magazine sporting colour photographs of willowy Chinese girls in enormous white brassières on its front cover.

The famous professor of medicine who had once operated on a government minister let rip a resounding fart.

It was night on the Shanghai Express.

An Unbelievable Number of People

THE HOTEL PU JIANG HAD BEEN THE ASTOR HOTEL AND THE name could still be made out on its facade. The hotel's enormous bathrooms were fitted with the gleaming white tiles of an old-fashioned hospital. The door to my room a portal, the room itself a ballroom. The clothes stand had the dimensions of a caber. The battered wooden bed was so vast and sturdy that elephants could have copulated in it.

Of bygone elegance only the rudiments remained. All that was wanting was the smell of cleaning fluid and I could have been cooped up in any old institution.

The floor maid asked for a deposit for the room key.

"How much?" I asked.

"How much?" she replied.

"You understand English?"

"You understand English?"

"Now listen –"

"Now listen."

I handed her my wallet. She took ten yuan and gave me a receipt.

I had arrived in Shanghai at nine o'clock in the morning. There were no rooms vacant at the Hotel Pu Jiang and I was told to come back around noon. I spent the interval strolling along Shanghai's waterfront, The Bund, and up and down some of the nearby streets, and was struck by the strangest feeling of having already seen everything there was to see in Shanghai.

There was panic in this feeling; a gut-wrenching hollowness as if there was nothing left to experience, as if there were something inside one that could never be satisfied. It was my arrival anxiety. Everything seemed too big, too daunting and I responded to this by belittling it all, to the point where I lost sight of the world and was overwhelmed by a childlike sense of having been abandoned.

Shanghai gave me a headache. It was the combination of the noise and the foul air. It was true what I had read: there were an unbelievable number of people here. And all so close to one that it felt as though the top of one's head were being sliced off to leave the brain exposed and defenceless.

One sound stood out: the hooting of the freighters on the river, that deep bass note bursting with foreboding and wanderlust, so sure and so questing. Ferries went back and forth across the river, huge cargo ships, and everywhere the workhorses of the river, the low-lying barges – roped together, battling upstream and then heading off up some tributary, passing under low-arched concrete bridges as they went. The muddy, grey water slopped across their decks and lapped against hatch coamings. The bows of these doughty beasts of burden were rounded and bulging with fenders and car tyres. Astern, the wheelhouse was so low that even a diminutive Chinese would have found it difficult to stand upright.

The sailors on the river all wore grimy, fluorescent orange life jackets which, while they were no doubt compulsory, they rather diminished the air of self-sufficient, introverted clannishness which those who have chosen a life on the water always exude. A patronising State had intervened and left its mark. Their identical life jackets made the sailors look like civil servants. It was as if there were an eye somewhere, keeping them all under surveillance.

I decided to take a look first of all at the back of Shanghai and proceeded to walk along a tributary which my guide book told me was Suzhou Creek, but which was referred to on the map I had bought at the hotel as the Wusong River.

No more than 20 metres from the water, where barges lay in their moorings several rows deep, the residential neighbourhoods began. There were so many people that it was impossible to tell where the houses stopped and the street started. Every house seemed to have been stripped of its front wall, and the street appeared to serve as an extra room for homes which had long since burst at the seams under the strain of growing families. The kitchen was set up in the middle of the pavement. The ingredients for the evening meal had already been laid out: filleted fish and cabbage, its fresh green and yellow leaves adding a bright touch of colour to the earthy hues of poverty. Quilts had been hung out to air, along with the oldest member of the family who sat slumped in his wicker chair in a patch of sunlight.

Tower blocks reared up behind the narrow streets with their low buildings, while vast building sites stood in readiness, waiting for more. The residents of Shanghai's slums were about to go up in the world, to live one on top of the other in a rectangular version of the self-same poverty, the only difference being that all four walls would be intact, as in a prison cell.

The Joy of the Stunted

I HAVE HEARD IT SAID THAT CIRCUS ARTISTS OFTEN COME from backward, oppressed societies. This is why they are no longer recruited from the West, but from further and further east, at one time from Eastern Europe and Russia, nowadays from China. Why, one is tempted to ask, can neither Africa nor Latin America lay claim to a great circus tradition?

Poverty and oppression play less of a role in shaping a circus artist than feudal society, the embodiment of a highly refined and specialized tradition of craftsmanship passed on from father to son. The circus artist is akin to the makers of Chinese porcelain, to the carvers of virtuoso landscapes out of ivory; to the nimble-fingered watchmakers and even to the ballet dancers who also have to start early if they are to school their limbs in suppleness. All of their skills can only be developed by sacrificing what a modern society considers most inviolable: the carefree, irresponsible, spontaneous play of the child.

Today, the schools of a democratic society do not go in for early specialization. Children are taught to be all-rounders. There can be no doubt that the child performer has to suffer for his or her art. But you cannot say of a person that it is a shame that he or she has been trained to do something in the way that you can of an animal. If an animal "can do something", then its essential nature has been violated. Not so with a human being whose nature is enhanced.

I was struck by this distinction when I spent an evening at the Shanghai Acrobatics Theatre and saw an elephant lurching on two legs around the ring of the unheated circus building, with an uncomprehending but long-suffering expression in its tiny eyes.

A young woman sitting on the sparsely populated benches burst into tears. She looked like an American, with a woolly hat and strawberry-blonde pigtails hanging down the back of a checked lumberjacket. Her boyfriend put his arm round her and kept looking ahead, in sheepish helplessness at being faced with such an outburst of grief, the cause of which appeared to be philosophical, much like Nietzsche sobbing in the streets of Turin with his arms around the neck of a horse.

No doubt others might also weep with pity for those child performers, for they could not have been much more than 13 or 14 years old and yet already they were in perfect command of every muscle in their childish bodies; bodies which, in the case of the girls, had not yet lost their puppy fat. But there was an energy about them, a mischievousness, as they poked fun at the inflexibly strict law of gravity.

One adolescent girl ascended a flight of steps while balancing a tall triangular crown decked with full cognac glasses on her head, a headdress of potential disasters. Having reached the top she then turned and came back down, and as she set foot on the bottom step her face beamed with triumph. She was far too young to dissemble.

There was another girl who stood on one hand on her partner's head. On her own head she later carried a pile of china bowls which she removed one by one – with her feet. She did not slip up once, everything was perfectly balanced in that impossible stack, that frail, teetering human sculpture in which arms and legs had moved beyond the laws of anatomy.

But she was not some pathetic, stunted child, forced to grow up into a deformed human being thanks to one talent being overdeveloped to the detriment of all the rest; she was no freak of the sort once put on show at travelling fairs. No, she was a fully-fledged human being who, through the development of this one talent had developed them all. It was not only her performance that caused her to shine, there was also an inner fulfilment which endowed her with a beauty far beyond both the natural-ness of the child and the sweetness of the young woman. She had been given the chance to do her utmost. It was this which gave her such a luminous presence.

And I left the place full of gratitude, feeling that a human being had found fulfilment – on my behalf, as well.

A Clown in the Arena of Words

I HAD THE IDEA OF SAILING UP THE YANGTSE RIVER AS FAR as I could go. The river ran into the sea near Shanghai and from there boats sailed up to Chongqing: seven days' journey.

Not far from the harbour lay an old quarter which – even in colonial times when Shanghai was divided up into a number of "concessions", each in the hands of its own colonial power – had been very much China's domain. It was quite clearly a slum district, now merely waiting for the bulldozer to arrive, but still its narrow streets were teeming with life. The houses were built on two storeys with the ground floor open to the street. The upper floor was wooden, with tiny windows, galleries and oriels jutting out over pavements littered with refrigerators and fireplaces. Washing hung everywhere, with very few cars around to soil it. Cyclists in blue quilted work jackets wove in and out among the pedestrians. The old women wore trousers and black jackets drawn tight across their chests. Their miniature faces were ravaged and wizened like parchment with two slits for eyes.

I was surprised by the number of public toilets, always denoted by the same two symbols: a man's head in profile and a woman's with rather softer features. Then it dawned on me: there were no lavatories inside the houses.

I wandered into a labyrinthine park full of pavilions and small rockeries linked together by footpaths, little hump-backed bridges and curving flights of steps. The paths made unexpected twists and turns, providing constant novelty for the eye, like a vast and bountiful maze. One could not really explore it, since everything was too carefully ordered. It was a feat of illusion, the artfulness of which was brought home to me only when I found myself coming out of the park just a few metres from the gate through which I had entered.

I felt as though I had been walking for hours, when in fact I had been conducted around what was a very small plot of land that had simply been exploited to the full, like a hall of mirrors.

It was possible to walk from the Chinese quarter all the way back to Europe in a couple of hours, by heading towards what had once been the French concession. Here, peaceful, almost deserted avenues were lined by pollarded plane trees, steep, tiled roofs and pointed, half-timbered gable ends that reared up behind high walls. The overcast sky and grey winter light lent a very northern European feel to the whole setting and the few Chinese cycling past gave no impression of experiencing any culture clash, but rather of having gone back in time: weary workers on their way home from the factory at some point early in the twentieth century with faces which, as in a painting by Edvard Munch, had grown Oriental only through exhaustion and introversion.

There were other places where the contrast between the architecture and the people was more dramatic. This must have been the locality of the French lower-classes, or at any rate a lower middle-class consigned to a life with no sheltering garden walls, in terraced houses with narrow passageways leading to tall staircases and heavy, still stylish, wooden front doors. The Chinese had been closer still and how great the fear must have been here, where the shabby-genteel titles of *Monsieur* and *Madame* took the place of garden walls.

Now, of course, the Chinese, not the French, were everywhere and even from the outside one could see how overcrowded the houses were. The result was like something out of science fiction, as if I had found myself in an occupied Europe in which the descendents of Attila the Hun and Ghengis Khan had at long last succeeded in digging themselves in.

The French quarter petered out and the number of soot-blackened Chinese-built apartment blocks increased. It was late in the afternoon, I had been walking for six or seven hours and was worn out. I tried to find my way back to the river on the map, only to discover after half an hour that all this time I had been walking in the opposite direction. Huang Pu lay to the east, but I had continued west.

The sky was still overcast and there was no afternoon sun by which I might take my bearings. My map did not give the bus routes and the crammed and swaying rush-hour buses that careered past, tightly packed with people squashed up against the windows, gave no clue as to where they were heading. The passengers stared out through the grimy panes, their pale faces seeming almost disconnected from the solid mass of dark-coated bodies. I stared back. We were as alien to one another as the fish in the aquarium are to the visitors on the other side of the glass and I was not entirely certain which of us was which.

Exhausted, I felt like sitting down and giving up, as if I had strayed from more than just a street map.

Not once in Shanghai had I seen a taxi for hire. On my arrival in the town I had paid almost $10 to a pirate minicab driver in order to avoid the long, unmoving queues at the sparsely-manned taxi ranks. It had to be something like a two to three hour walk back to the hotel. I simply couldn't face it.

And then it hit me, this metaphysical weariness that seemed to strike at the very will to live. I could walk and walk, but my legs were never going to carry me anywhere. I could open my mouth to ask directions, but I knew it was no use. Nothing intelligible would come out. Because, if no one understands you, it is you who are dumb, not they who are deaf. Language has always been the dictatorship of the majority. If you are in the minority where language is concerned then you either become mad or lonely, invisible and inaudible; and that is what I was, confronted by those impassive faces and the solipsistic movement of the traffic: powerless.

It is at such moments that one realizes how much one is a social animal, desperately dependent on everyone else. There is no greater lie than to think that one travels alone. The lone traveller is the most dependent of all, because he has need of everybody and no one has need of him. It was a sobering moment to feel so helpless.

Then, as the twilight deepened above the road, I spied a tiny, flickering light in the windscreen of a car cruising past.

The FOR HIRE sign on a taxi!

Big Bang

AN OBLONG TABLE WITH STOOLS AROUND IT. A BLACK LACQUERED table top bearing twelve porcelain cups each with a crane motif. A teapot and an extra cup on a little tray, an empty flower vase, two matching ashtrays each with a holder for a box of matches. That is what history looks like.

It was here the Chinese Communist Party was founded in 1920. A room so neat, so tidy, fragile even, with its porcelain cups and unassuming stools. And yet a colossal drama began here – over a cup of tea.

On the walls were group photographs of young men with faces which to an observer blessed with hindsight, seemed to shine with a superior knowledge of the historic mission that awaited them. The eye immediately homed in on pictures of Deng Xiao Ping and Zhou En Lai during their student days in 1920s Paris. The poor reproductions rendered their faces grave and foreboding. Their eyes receded into the shadows of their sockets as if their innermost thoughts had to be kept hidden.

Even so, their faces were also open and clean-lined, for their youth could not be denied or airbrushed out of existence. There they stood, so untried and at the same time so prepared, captured a moment before they outgrew themselves, and all human proportion, to become myths, monsters, spectres, shadows on celluloid and words in history books; more real there, in the picture and in the myth, even to themselves, than in flesh and blood. In the end, their flesh was merely an embarassing envelope, of no more than anecdotal importance.

It was this anecdotal flesh which would be publicly presented many years later, when they had grown old, but were more powerful than ever, slumped in an enormous armchair, or being pushed onto the world stage in a wheelchair. But to them the flesh meant nothing; what mattered was the name, the will, the analysis, the concept. These old men of China refused to recognize the dominion of nature or the passage of time.

Maybe that was where the Marxist philosophers went wrong, in tracing their materialism to constants such as the so-called forces of production: steel and coal, the conducting metals, electricity, but never to the one place where it is actual and active, our inconstant flesh.

As I left the building and walked through the streets, I came across a market full of freshly slaughtered animals. Entrails flared red and blue. Chicken feet, bound together with blood-soaked cotton twine stuck up in the air while their owners, heads upside-down, awaited their unavoidable fate. Live fish flopped about in huge plastic tubs; a few had turned belly-up and floated around dead among their kin. When they were eventually carried off down the street with a string through their cheeks, they left behind them a long trail of blood.

On The Bund I met an elderly gentleman, a French speaker, who began talking about food, prompted by the Spring Festival, the Chinese New Year which was to fall a couple of days later. Did I realize the Chinese pictograph for fish was very like the pictograph for wealth? he asked.

That was why, at the Spring Festival, the most important night of the year, the Chinese ate fish: to ensure prosperity in the years to come. And bamboo shoots, the most significant characteristic of the bamboo shoot being its prodigious rate of growth; in other words, wealth again. On New Year's morning the Chinese ate dumplings stuffed with a variety of delicacies. The number of dumplings represented the number of people in the family, along with the wish to have many children and many generations living under the same roof. Thus, he explained, food was a system of symbols pertaining to the central values of Chinese society: wealth and the family.

I thought of his words as I walked in the twilight along Nanjing Dong Lu, the neon signs lighting up the way ahead and the street growing black with people. Maybe the gathering crowd was a sort of anti-metaphysical communion, the closest an irreligious culture can come to a religious ceremony. It was certainly a transformation of sorts, a kind of erasure; like the lines on a face being smoothed away, allowing an inner, purifying acquiescence to shine through.

I searched for words to describe it and kept coming back to something bordering on the sacramental; the sentiment aroused when you feel you are seeing humanity distilled, its naked hope, its raw dynamism, and indeed it was moving, this baring of something within yourself which left you with no choice but to join in and be swallowed up by the crowd because, like them, you were human, nothing else, nothing more, nothing less.

This sense came from the enormous size of the Chinese population, which you were very rarely, if ever, allowed to forget. Its density was so physically present and unsettling to anyone used to having a bit of space around them. You either had to go on the defensive or surrender. Your humanity was made clear to you when every single gesture was echoed by a thousand others; a life so basic, its invitations so irresistible.

Nanjing Dong Lu in the twilight: the banality of the consumer society, albeit at the hour of its birth. A vulcanic eruption of life: Chinese calligraphy in blazing neon, glowing faces igniting spontaneously beneath advertising slogans in red, green and yellow, a forest fire of people under a flinty winter sky.

It was (in the truest sense) a free-and-easy scene, like prisoners at long last finding themselves outside the prison gates.

That was what one was supposed to grasp, a vibration in the air which had to be construed: in the shadow of a century of Chinese history fraught with disaster and war, revolutions and prison camps, famine and executions, each purchase – be it cameras, curling tongs, patent-leather shoes, Walkmans, food mixers, refrigerators or tights – was a symbol, not a question of need, but of hope.

As with the food, so with all of these consumer goods which the shoppers clutched to their chests and ran off with under the winter sky in a moment of fragile freedom: the freedom of the consumer combining with traditional Chinese values, the symbolism of the fish, the bamboo shoot, the dumpling; the values of the family and of wealth. Here was a new world beginning and an old one continuing.

There were men in suits with mobile telephones pressed to their ears. All the young women sported the same hairstyle: a little quiff teased back over the right temple and held in place with lashings of hair spray. In a parfumerie window display *Voilà Paris* stood alongside Johnson's cockroach poison; the dream and the reality, sharing the same consumerist world. The street sweepers plodded along, pushing their dustpans on wheels, constantly on the move, as if the mass of consumers were an enormous animal that they were forever having to muck out.

A sense of buoyancy, of anticipation, bound together the crowds on the broad pavements and the footbridges criss-crossing the streets. I had never seen so many people at one time, even in India. There had to be millions of them, or so it seemed to me, standing high up on one of the footbridges and looking down on the constant stream of people, its common course lost to view in a succession of never-ending whirlpools. The multitude beat against the shop fronts like surf against cliffs until one almost expected to see the buildings erode and come crashing down. The tension here was greater than in any revolutionary storm or street riot, so great was the power of hope. The very framework of life looked set to burst.

I was being given a glimpse of China, today's China; here the circuit closed and I was in some way a part of it.

On the way back I stopped for a coffee at the bar of the Peace Hotel and read a copy of *Newsweek* that I had picked up in the hotel's small bookshop. It contained an article on China. "No country has ever developed so rapidly," it said.

It was as if the myth of the mysterious Orient was being supplanted by new myths: first, the poverty-stricken Orient, then the politically uniform Orient, and now the Orient of economic growth, populated by efficient robots.

Colonialism, whose interest in the Orient was of a strictly financial nature, preferred to surround itself with riddles rather than confront the inhumanity of its own exploitation. Now we entrusted our image of the Orient to the economists and the political scientists – and were still none the wiser. The mystery of the Orient had been replaced by that of the robots; the enigma of the East by that of efficiency; the image we had conjured up was of the absence of any humanity, as in the worker ant.

On Nanjing Dong Lu I had just seen something different.

It was the eve of the Chinese New Year and my last day in Shanghai. For purely literary reasons I had moved from the Hotel Pu Jiang to the Peace Hotel. Noel Coward had written one of his plays here. The Austro-American writer Vicki Baum had stayed there in 1937, when the hotel was hit by a Japanese bomb, and wrote a novel about the incident. I found Baum's book in the hotel bookshop. There, too, I came across a novel by Jules Verne about a journey through China. André Malraux's *La Condition humaine*, which deals with the massacre of the Shanghai Communists in 1927 was, however, nowhere to be seen. Sympathizing as it did with the Communists one would have thought it would have been an obvious choice, but perhaps it did not coincide with the official version of history.

In the evening I ate in the restaurant on the eighth floor, where the hotel's well-preserved Art Deco had given way to a Chinese-style decor in turquoise and red lacquer. On my plate was a duck egg, the yolk shot through with blue and ringed by an amber border of jellied stock.

On the other side of the Huang Pu river the first fireworks were shooting up into the sky. There were so many that their explosions in the dusk created a new skyline of red and green and dazzling white stars over Shanghai's jagged ridge of cranes and half-finished tower blocks. Directly below blazed a wall of advertising signs and neon Chinese calligraphy. Barges and river boats glided like black chevrons through the reflection of the fireworks in the water.

I left the hotel towards midnight. All was quiet down on the Bund, nor was there anyone to be seen near the shops. Nevertheless a colossal din swelled up like a dome over Shanghai. That was what I had stepped out into, not a city but a sound, the indescribable noise of millions of maroons being let off; neither a rumbling nor a banging, more of a ringing sound – as if the night sky were an immense bronze bell giving the maroons an amplified and much deeper echo.

As I walked behind the Hotel Pu Jiang I saw a cloud of gunpowder smoke come rolling across the river. The streets were shrouded in mist, making it impossible to see more than a few feet ahead. The locals stood with their backs to the walls of the houses. Low-flying rockets careered through the streets, fireworks were shot from open windows at the houses opposite, strings of exploding firecrackers were thrust out on broom handles, making a sound like machine-guns. Showers of sparks flew from every balcony and roof terrace, the walls flared red, then green. A lone cyclist zig-zagged, panic-stricken, down the street, hesitated for an instant, then was off again, weaving his way around the bangers. On either side of him dark silhouettes leapt out of the way. Flakes of ash and embers rained down. In one explosive moment the fireworks appeared to have taken on a life of their own, spontaneously igniting in an orgy of light and deafening thuds.

It was obvious what was going on here, in the eyes of all of those Chinese who stood with their backs to the walls, filled with blissful terror and delight, constantly wondering anew at the forces that they themselves had unleashed: one night of rebellion, against everything, for everything, with light and colours the only actors. Who but the followers of Confucius could have invented the firework? All that self-discipline engendered a longing for explosions.

Deafened, I walked back to the Bund. The gunpowder cloud had overwhelmed the waterfront. The lighted windows of the skyscrapers and the neon slogans on the rooftops could only just be made out. For one night China had wiped out its present and given itself up to the chaos that existed before Time began. The Big Bang, the beginning of all things, the end of all things.

The Long River

THE FERRY WHICH WAS TO CARRY ME OVER THE FIRST TWO-DAY stretch up the Yangtse River was a low-lying barge-like vessel on three decks, battered and filthy and painted a drab green. Most of the cabins were a tight squeeze, sleeping twelve passengers stacked one on top of the other in silver enamelled bunks. At the stern, between decks, was a dining room of sorts, furnished with tiny stools and vinyl-clad tables.

I was travelling first class, but since in communist China there was no such thing as first class, this had been rechristened second class; and so I sailed most democratically with no one above me and many below.

My cabin was on the top deck, with a window overlooking a corridor. I was instantly struck by a feeling of claustrophobia which was not lessened by the appearance of an elderly, corpulent gentleman with an inscrutable bulldog face who proceeded to install himself in the bunk across from me without so much as a nod or a smile. A while later the sound of his snoring reached me from behind the bed curtain. I tried to read, but found it impossible to ignore the spasmodic fits and starts of sound. Whenever there was a lull I found myself hoping the din would stop, but the next minute it was there again, growling and booming.

Finally I wrenched open the door and ran off to find the stewardess. When I imitated my travelling companion's snores she burst out laughing and with charming zeal proceeded to find me a larger and brighter cabin all to myself, though the small aluminium-coated radiator was just as cold as the clammy bulkhead.

"*Meio*," said the stewardess, when I patted the icy radiator. "There is none."

One has to sail through Shanghai harbour to have any conception of its size. Hour after hour we stole along the banks of the Huang Pu, which were thick with cranes, warehouses and storage depots, while the river itself seemed to be in the grip of a permanent rush hour, swarming with cargo boats of every description, many of them anchored in the middle of the stream.

After a couple of hours the height of the buildings along the banks decreased. Traditional Chinese houses with curving roofs came into view, as the interminable run of docks stretched on and on. Around the anchored freighters swarmed the barges. Derricks swung palettes piled high with sacks out across the water before the loads were manoeuvred with ropes over the open hatches of the barges. On the docks, huge cranes were unloading container ships.

Tugs nudged barges upstream, the latter roped together, two by two, so heavily laden that only the bows were visible above the water; these, and the mound of gravel or coke protruding from the hatch.

This was a world of raw materials.

On the outskirts of Shanghai a gigantic and as yet uncompleted bridge thrust its carriageways out into thin air. From down on the river the piers of the bridge looked to be hundreds of metres high, but the roads had long since shaken off any form of support and hovered giddily aloft, restrained only by steel cables that seemed to shoot straight up into the clouds.

I had never seen anything like it. It was not simply an impressive piece of engineering. In all its grandeur it was also a great work of poetry, stretching out across the Huang Pu; an immense Aeolian harp with steel cables for strings. Here, modernisation had indeed found a worthy instrument and far up the Yangtse River in the days that followed I would hear the Chinese speak with pride of the bridge, not as though they had personally had a hand in the building of it, but as if it were an expression of something within themselves, a greatness for which they too had the inherent potential.

At its mouth the Yangtse was so wide that it was almost impossible to see from one bank to the other. The water was muddy, a yellow sea patchily reflecting a blue sky. In the pale winter light every colour took on a pastel hue. The temperature, hovering just around freezing, was something I was familiar with from Danish winters, but here there was no leaden winter sea with sluggish, oleaginous waves. Instead one met a clash of season and colour, and I sailed through a winter that was light and airy.

35

Most of the passengers disembarked at Nantong, our first port of call. The boat had been only half full to begin with. It was the first day of the Chinese New Year, the biggest holiday of the year, and not a day to set out on a lengthy journey. A bell in a tower somewhere began to chime a plaintive Chinese melody, as slow as the vessels slipping through the last ray of afternoon sun.

Junks with spindly masts and high sterns sailed past. A fishing fleet headed down-river in the sunset, the steady throb of their engines filling the air. Far in the distance the opposite bank could only just be made out, like a shadow, a drifting cloud in the pale tones of evening.

Darkness fell. Two barges swept by, roped together, slate-grey in the impenetrable darkness and barely distinguishable from the black river. A firework sputtered on one of the decks.

Back in my ice-cold cabin I curled up in my thermal underwear under the blanket. I could hear the ferry's warning horn and the waves washing along the hull. It was the sound of motion, the breath of travel.

In the morning sunlight the Yangtse river, also known to the Chinese as Chang Jiang or "The Long River", was like a watercolour rendered in limpid washes of white and blue. Pink sandbanks stood delineated in delicate brush strokes unable to keep sky and river apart. At the point where the Yangtse forks and the coast falls away, the water seemed to run directly into the sky.

Later the colours changed; everything faded away from a warm yellow into tones of purple. Dock after dock went by: mountains of coal, gravel and pebbles; cranes; barges being unloaded; a pagoda between two mounds of rubble. I had settled on deck in the watery winter sunlight. The frozen puddles on the red-painted boards were gradually thawing out. I warmed my hands round a cup of tea, a book resting in my lap. Just for a second I had the marvellous feeling of being alone in China, between the far-off banks of the river, on the long, deserted sunlit deck, and already I had spent enough time in this overpopulated country to appreciate what a rare moment it was.

I fell into conversation with a young couple later that day. They were students of biology from Shanghai and had been married for six months. Both were small in stature; he with a broad head and buck teeth. They were keen to hear what I thought of their country. I gave them my impressions of Shanghai.

"Ah, but China is a poor country," they countered, "we have need of heavy industry."

I did not know whether to laugh or cry. They stood there, repeating the discredited Soviet development model in which "heavy industry" was the panacea for all ills. Could they really still be living on the legacy of that bankrupt ideology?

Another young man came along. His skin was darker than that of the other two, his features sculpted and classically Chinese, with slanting eyes and no discernible eyelids. He was an engineer, working for a Shanghai branch of Siemens. He spoke fluent English and a little German.

"Oh yes," he said, "China was a poor country," but then added, more deliberately, "compared to the West."

Again I mentioned Shanghai. It was an odd, inverted situation. I was drawing attention to the good points of their country. The young Chinese kept stressing how poor it was.

True, the engineer, whose name was Wang Yongjun, conceded China was developing at a tremendous rate. "Five years ago what is happening now would have been described as capitalism. Now companies can be privately owned. Restrictions on foreign investment are nowhere near as tight as they used to be. Today we have a number of Chinese millionaires with annual incomes of more than 100 million yuan."

He put up a hand: "Five millionaires – at least. But farther up the river you will see many signs of poverty."

During the journey I had read books about China by Colin Thubron and Paul Theroux, written in the mid-1980s when this country, which had until then been so cut off, first opened its borders and the traveller was once more able to move about freely. At that time there was one major, and awkward, question which all travel writers felt compelled to ask the Chinese. It was about the hidden tragedies of the once so romantically applauded and, subsequently, politically condemned Cultural Revolution.

When I brought up the subject of Tiananmen Square I received the same reaction as I had on the Shanghai Express. All three of my interlocutors tittered nervously.

The young wife glanced diffidently at her husband.

"I was in Shanghai," the engineer said evasively.

"Yes, but weren't there demonstrations in Shanghai?" I asked.

"How much were you told in the West?"

"We saw some of it. The tanks, buses in flames, dead bodies. The Western television networks were right there."

"The Western television networks," they echoed. "In China we do not get to hear a great deal."

"When the demonstrations were banned they closed the universities for three months," said the engineer. "We went back to five months of political re-education. Many Chinese live in poverty we were told. Democracy cannot be made in one day. Afterwards we were ordered to write a report about our innermost thoughts."

"And did you?"

All three of them nodded and again laughed inanely.

"Chinese people no longer talk about Tiananmen," continued the engineer, who had now completely taken over the conversation.

The young couple smiled politely and said nothing.

"For us it is a bad memory." He looked thoughtful. "The government is right. Democracy and prosperity go hand in hand."

"And do you believe democracy will come?"

"Yes," he replied confidently, "things are moving in that direction. People are better off. They are becoming better educated. Democracy will follow as a matter of course."

The ferry had pulled alongside a dock. Here, again, were the cranes, the mounds of coal, the grimy buildings of urine-coloured cement; industrialism in an archaic phase. But did that necessarily mean democracy in the making?

There can hardly have been any totalitarian regime this century – with Nazism as the prime exception – which has not invoked democracy as its ideal and goal; although always a deferred democracy, sometime in the future; a democracy for which the country or its people were not quite ready. Totalitarian rule always presents itself as something like a waiting room for democracy; a forecourt, indistinguishable from a prison yard, under the surveillance of guards with hourglasses in one hand and automatic rifles in the other; tragic figures, these guardians, if one were to take their word for it; democrats at heart, but having to don the uniforms of dictators temporarily, due to the regrettable backwardness of the population.

I could see now why all the young Chinese talked so much about the poverty of their country. It was the rhetorical whip with which they had been beaten into submission by leaders who would rather advertise the failure of the communist model than go one step further and assent to democracy. This was the partial concession the student rebellion had wrung from the leadership in the midst of defeat: the old men of Beijing had no choice but to speak the language of realism and forgo their usual rose-coloured rhetoric. Yes, the country was poor. That sentence had become public property.

But the regime had also responded in another, far more effective fashion: the growth in consumption, which carries with it the irrefutable argument of the increase in consumer goods, of economic reforms that worked.

At that moment in history China was experimenting with a burgeoning market economy, but not with democracy. On the contrary, the country was one grandiose experiment as to how long the move to democracy could be postponed and delayed. Is it possible to buy off democracy? That was the latest question that the warders grappled with in their waiting room, while they were turning the hourglass and still keeping their fingers on the trigger of their machine-guns.

One place the new era had not yet conquered was the riverboat on the Yangtse River. As the evening drew on and hunger made itself felt, so too did a gap in my vocabulary. What was I to call the bare room in the stern that contained so few stools and so little elbow room around the vinyl-covered tables that most people were reduced to eating standing up or taking their plates out into the cold winter air? More than anything else it put one in mind of a canteen in a barracks or a prison. In this place designated for the purpose of eating the democracy of moderation and necessity prevailed. Here there was no such thing as second, third, or fourth class. At one end of the room was a hatch at which meal vouchers could be bought. At the other, cooks in grubby white jackets stood over trays of chicken and vat-size pots brimming with rice.

Everyone was squashed up against one another, urgently shovelling food into their mouths. The cold, stark fluorescent bulbs accentuated the bare, scantily painted metal bulkheads and the hunched figures of the diners, whose skin seemed grey and dead in the livid light. This was feeding stripped of the illusion of comfort which so often surrounds boat trips in the West. Here, travel was transport.

The people eating had the same exposed look about them that I was to encounter again and again all over China. This was life at its most basic. And yet the food was well-cooked and tasty. Somewhere in all of this lay the mystery of China and the art of living in an ancient culture.

I ate standing up, out on deck. The sun went down like a perfect, blushing golden globe, so huge and tangible that it seemed impossible that it would eventually be engulfed by the dusty-blue shadows of the distant mountains. If anything, I was expecting it to drop down into the river like a weighty jewel fallen from a celestial hand.

There was snow on the rooftops of the houses on the bank closest to us, yet the bleeding sky possessed all the drama of a tropical night.

I shared my cabin with a rat. The previous evening I had caught a glimpse of it out of the corner of my eye, no more than a swift, darting shadow over by the wash-basin. Now it came ambling down one of the pipes which ran through floor and ceiling in the poky cabin. It had a long brown body and it was in no hurry. Halfway down the pipe it stopped and regarded me curiously. I hurled one of my shoes at it. It was gone in a flash and it did not show its face again, a discreet, polite Chinese rat that knew when it was not welcome.

I woke up next morning to the strains of "Edelweiss" sung by hesitant voices wavering in and out of the song. It was the family in the cabin next door, singing in unison.

I had had the standard Chinese/foreigner conversation with the father of the family up on deck.

"What do you think of China?"

"I like China very much."

"Ah yes, but China is a very poor country."

He was dressed in the uniform of the new middle class: a jacket over a V-neck pullover with a neatly knotted tie peeping out from between the points of a white shirt collar, a garb every bit as symbolic as the work jackets and Mao caps of the Red Guards but which would not have been possible were it not for the new economic boom in the country.

I was puzzled as to why he and all the other representatives of the middle class whom I ran into spoke so much of poverty. Was it merely government propaganda? Or was it because poverty was a stain on their newly acquired status, one that in some way dragged them down – in consequence of which they were prone to worry about it constantly?

It seemed to me, as he was speaking, that I saw signs of sincere sympathy and concern in his face. The thought of China's innumerable poor certainly troubled him. Perhaps this was the other aspect of middle-class thinking: concern for others, altruism and the desire to make a better world.

While we were talking his three-year-old son had been standing silently beside us, brandishing a plastic six-shooter.

"Why is he so quiet?"

"He's angry because I won't play with him."

I looked at the boy who was impassively staring down his father. There was something majestic about his self-control; the assurance of an emperor who is well aware that even his silence will be apprehended and interpreted.

One of China's countless only children, one sensed that he knew already the future of the country belonged to him.

The countryside bounding the Yangtse had changed. The banks had drawn closer. For the first time it was obvious that we were sailing on a river. When I came out on deck around nine o'clock we were passing hillsides of red clay which rose and fell in great waves parallel with the river. Each wave was like a staircase. It was the peasants' terraces.

This was truly a landform – a piece of land that had been formed – hewn, hacked, chiselled, hammered into shape; the quintessence of China: mountains and earth enhanced. Both man and nature had set their limits, then come to a compromise. There was only one way in which the mountains and steep slopes could be cultivated: in terraces. Which is to say, intensively as opposed to extensively. There was no room here for large-scale farming, for the long straight furrows of tractor-drawn ploughs or the armoured battalions of combine harvesters. And so the conservatism of nature was matched by that of culture. It could hardly have been otherwise in this pact between two ageing spouses locked together for thousands of years who, in the midst of all the wear and tear, had come up with their own graceful brand of give and take.

I thought of the figure of Buddha at Leshan which lay in store for me further ahead. It was the largest piece of sculpture in the world, a seated Buddha over 70 metres high, carved out of the cliff face. The Grand Buddha epitomised the Chinese's relationship with the landscape and was the pinnacle of their life together. For here the mountain had finally become the embodiment of what the Chinese were always striving towards: half a mountain had quite simply taken on human form; had acquired legs and arms, body, head and eyes.

A Fight in Chinese

IN A SHOP IN WUHAN I WATCHED AS A YOUNG WOMAN
went berserk. Yelling at the top of her voice she snatched small pottery
jars from a shelf and hurled them to the floor where they burst with
a loud crash, releasing clouds of a paprika-red powder that slowly rose
up around her legs until only her jacket-clad torso was visible, as if
she had just materialized in a puff of smoke, like an aggressive genie or
a Fury.

The customers and staff in the shop stood and watched, their faces
impassive, making no move towards her, in a state of paralysis or
perhaps acquiescence, as if the irate woman were really not of this
world.

There was something disturbing about the whole situation. The
screaming woman did not appear to be in the grip of any one particular
neurosis. It was more as if she raged with a collective tension. Her fit of
anger stemmed from the inner pressure that builds up wherever too many
people live cooped up too close together. Her screams were the inward
screams of everyone; her uncontrolled behaviour the product of too much
control. She had been possessed by the devil of overpopulation. That was
why they left her to scream and smash things. She was screaming and
smashing for them, too.

I spent two nights and one day in Wuhan while waiting for the next boat
to sail up the Yangtse. It was a stark and brutal town, humming with
suppressed tension; overpopulated, also by demons.

Scores of shoeblacks lined the pavements. One man stood with his
hands on his hips, having his trainers buffed – shoe-shining as a show of
power. There were blind people selling lottery tickets – impotence prevail-
ing on both sides, in seller and buyer alike. Grubby children begged in

the streets. The shelves in the newspaper kiosks carried magazines with pictures of naked women. There was a cinema calling itself "The Paradise of the Masses". The entire length of Wuhan's tall television tower was taken up by a gigantic advertisement for *Kent* cigarettes. Wuhan was a bare town.

In the Guiyuan Temple the faithful let off compact bundles of fire-crackers and incense at the bottom of large iron pots. I wandered around, ears ringing, in a cloud of cordite and drifting ashes.

In the temple yard a mother yanked her small daughter off her feet by the arm to leave her dangling some way above the ground, then proceeded to kick at her legs. The grandmother, who was standing alongside, also started laying into the girl with her feet. Then hand in hand the three generations resumed their walk, the child still sobbing.

Outside the entrance to the temple ran a narrow lane populated by palm-readers. I hurried past, afraid that someone might grab me and pass judgement over my outspread palm. I did not dare to have my fortune told in this town.

At Wuhan there is a bridge across the Yangtse that is the object of much pride: Wuhan Chang Jiang, named after the town itself coupled with the river's Chinese name. Work on the bridge was begun with support from the Soviet Union, but then, in the early 1950s, had come the rift between the two great Communist powers and the Chinese had had to complete it single-handedly, hence their pride. The bridge was built on two levels, with the railway line below and buses, trucks and cyclists on top.

I was walking across the bridge when a storm suddenly blew up. Pedestrians walked crabwise and dust and dirt filled the air, stinging the exposed skin of the face. Courting couples wrapped their coats around one another; for them the storm was an opportunity for a little public fondling. Bicycles piled high with cardboard boxes listed precariously in the wind. The riders had to jump off and push, shoulders braced against the swaying, lurching mountains of cardboard.

Far below, streaks of foam sprang up on the yellow waves of the river and whirlpools raced down into the depths. So compelling was the pull from the river that dizziness spun its own whirlpools inside my head;

a dizziness that was nothing other than a trial of strength between the instinct for self-preservation and the urge to jump.

Then the bridge was over dry land and I found myself gazing down upon narrow streets and a park containing old men sitting in bamboo deckchairs and a little bandstand where a group of musicians were packing up rather than having to play in the face of the storm. On a nearby cabbage patch, cabbage heads in earthenware pots tossed in the wind. It was an indication of how high up I was, and the length of the drop to the bottom of a cabbage patch.

I was on the other side of the river when a fight broke out in front of me. A man was walking along beside a woman when all at once he lashed out and punched her in the mouth. There was such disdain in the blow, for he did not so much as glance at her when he hit out, but calmly walked on. The satisfaction derived from hitting her was obviously so slight that he could not even be bothered to observe its effect. One would not even crush a mosquito with such indifference.

Howling with pain she flew at the man in a manner that seemed to imply it was not the first time this had happened, punching him in the face and then, as he tried to duck, in the neck. For a moment he was caught off guard, but then he launched a counterattack and took to hitting her in the face with some well-placed punches. Both were shabbily dressed, the man much taller than the woman.

A passer-by, a slightly built man in a light-coloured windcheater, threw himself into the fray, siding with the woman. With a succession of quick jabs to the face and chest he fought off her assailant. The whole thing lasted only a few seconds.

Up to this point I had had some idea of what was going on, purely because things were following a familiar and universal pattern: man attacks woman, another man comes to her aid. But the shock one feels when unexpectedly confronted by physical violence quickly turned to consternation: I no longer understood what I was seeing.

A circle of onlookers had formed around the combatants. All of a sudden three or four of them joined in the fight, not to help the woman, but taking her attacker's part. They set upon the woman's skinny little champion, kicking him in the stomach and groin, making him curl up, and pummelling at his kidneys and the back of his head until they had him pushed up against a fence, bent double and trying to protect his face and nether regions. They were trampling all over a street trader's rug, little wooden figurines lay smashed beneath their feet.

The woman had given up trying to defend herself. She was hit by yet another punch and fell to her knees with a high-pitched wail, covering her face with her hands. Blood ran from her battered lips.

At long last the crowd intervened and a wall of bodies cut off any further contact between the bruised woman and the man, whose fists were once more clenched. On the fringes of the crowd I caught sight of the woman's defender, now standing on tiptoe trying to catch a last glimpse of the drama. His face was swollen and puce-coloured from the beating he had taken.

Physical violence has always scared and unnerved me. Here an assault had been made on the simplest of all human ideals, the concept of justice and the instinctive defence of those who cannot defend themselves. I was left with the impression of having witnessed a collective punishment ritual prompted by violent, murderous forces of a nature unknown to me. I was being presented with another, darker China in which a restless multitude sought scapegoats who would have to pay the price for outrages so fundamental that they may even have been nameless, springing as they did from the fight for survival itself.

The Temple of the Yellow Crane lay only a few hundred metres away from the scene of the fight. The incident was still working on me, which may have been why the temple made such a vivid impression. At the sight of this building my scalp tingled and I all but wept with awe; it made my heart swell inside me, as if some great force were trying to escape in one enormous sigh.

A vast stairway built out of a pure, pale-grey stone led up to the temple. From there the building rose on massive reddish-brown tiers; five storeys high, each punctuated by a roof of sunshine-yellow glazed tile. The upswept rooftops reached out towards the sky in one wide soaring embrace and my poor, simplistic metaphor for the colossal and indeed indescribable effect which the temple had on me was that it resembled a flock of huge cranes taking to the air in a body; not in a gentle glide, but as mighty birds ascending by virtue of the power of their wing-beats, so majestic in its authority was the temple.

And I was lifted up and borne along with them, inexplicably, but unmistakably upwards, with no defence, in one great act of surrender.

I walked backwards down the stairway, inwardly bowing, feeling strangely honoured.

Nature's Stop Sign

THE JOURNEY UPRIVER WENT TO MY HEAD. THE NEXT STAGE, from Wuhan to Chongqing would take four days. I derived a quiet, peaceful happiness from this leisurely, uneventful mode of travel.

Traffic on the river began to tail off. On the crests of low slopes, children and adults stood and stared. The ferry did not often pass this way.

Now and again, along the riverbanks, solitary walkers came into view, far from all human habitation and society; alone; truly alone, providing as they did in their physical isolation a yardstick for the staggering scale of the landscape and the distances.

Not only were they alone, the thought also occurred to me that they had deliberately cut themselves off. So quickly did one grow used to the fact that people invariably came in large numbers, as if crowds were some sort of natural condition, that it seemed as though these people had taken themselves off, in the ancient sense of that term, like old animals leaving the herd to die. They were brooding, intense figures, with an unworldly air about them, as if born of the landscape itself, to be its consciousness, its mirror. They stood in relation to something other than people.

With the onset of darkness that evening I grew melancholy. The dramatic red of the evening sky induced in me the feeling that the day was bleeding away, as if it had been knifed. Out of the dusk that had fallen over the river loomed an enormous tug-boat, pulling four or five black barges; a monstrous, outlandish shape which, even as it glided past and I saw the brightly-lit wheelhouse and the deck, did not assume any familiar, reassuring form. It was a sight which left me as shaken as if I had just come face to face with something grotesque: a slice of nothingness made manifest, a hard, tangible darkness making straight for me.

One morning there was ice on the deck. The water in the red fire buckets was frozen solid, with cigarette butts and peanut shells encased in the ice.

We were approaching the three narrow gorges – Qutangxia, Wuxia and Xilangia – for which the Yangtse was so famous and which would in just a few years' time be engulfed by an immense dammed lake that would necessitate the relocation of a million people. The man-made lake would have a surface area of more than 600 square kilometres and contain more than 45 billion cubic metres of water. The dam would bring about a huge increase in China's electricity production and stop the river periodically flooding the surrounding countryside. But it would also obliterate some of the most beautiful scenery in China and lead to several of the country's ancient monuments being lost for ever, this area being one of the richest archaeological sites, yielding finds dating back as far as four or five thousand years BC. China still lived with the hubris of industrialization, which had already brought about the collapse of the former Soviet Union. Where ecological disasters were concerned, China was still a young nation and a textbook example of the optimism with which mankind always runs to meet its own self-made tragedies.

The dam across the Yangtse also contained that uniquely Chinese element of madness and unpredictability found only where a lone individual has gained power over many and has mistaken his own whims for human endeavour. Like the Great Wall of China, the result of one emperor's paranoia, the damming of the Yangtse had its inception in a mind possessed: that of Mao Tse Tung who had dreamt in a poem of seeing "the smooth surface of a lake rising up between narrow gorges". And as always in a society where the brakes of reason have been put out of commission, a poetic metaphor became a harsh reality for the masses.

Ba Dong Gang, which lay not far from the entrance to the gorges, represented just such a show of strength, built out of an urge to demonstrate the supremacy of the engineer and the builder over nature rather than any necessity. Constructed from rough, urine-coloured concrete it scaled a steep mountainside on massive piles, mesmerizing in all its ugliness and vain heroics; a huge and spiteful postulate on the superiority and inevitable triumph of Communism. People had never been meant to live here. And for that very reason, of course, they had to.

The cliffs on which the town was built were as steep as a ski jump. No streets led away from the harbour, only vast flights of steps constructed out of the same rough concrete as the buildings. Ba Dong Gang was a Marxist version of Benares, the great Hindu place of pilgrimage with its

49

ghats running down to the Ganges, where the faithful congregate and bathe. Here, instead, one had a place of pilgrimage and prayer to the economists of Communism, whose theories had been allowed to win a short-term Pyrrhic victory for, though new, the town had the makings of a ruin already. It had come into the world ravaged, as proof of its redundancy, and the abortiveness of mind that had determined its location. Its buildings resembled seven-storey chicken coops turned inside out, the floors were visible on the outside along with everything else. And what could there be inside? A master class of machinery and a servant class of workers? Or shelters, perhaps, for the soldiers of indomitable industrialism, here at the front line in the strategic war between man and nature?

Inside the gorges themselves the mountains had toppled over. Blue shadows lay like folds in a great cloth. There was not one spot here to which life might cling. There was just enough room for a scattering of earth and greenery growing in fine horizontal bands, as if someone had tried to create some order in those untamed rock formations with a comb. The riverboat worked its way upstream between cliff walls, in and out of indigo shadows and bands of dazzling light as the sun was ignited then dowsed somewhere high over our heads. Up above, the ravine opened out into a tumultuous, rocky world that turned everything upside-down. I noted with a shudder how close the gloomy rock faces had come to the vulnerable sides of the riverboat. Then it was a matter of head back and eyes up to a reeling firmament of pitching sandy-yellow, flame-coloured and blinding white peaks. I sailed through the Yangtse gorges, lying almost flat on my back, not wanting to miss one bit of this new, landsliding slant on things.

The passengers collected in the bow for the best view, laughing as they pointed out Nature's heady flights of fancy to one another. I had just time to think to myself that here life had little chance of gaining a foothold and Communism none whatsoever – but my triumphant conclusion proved premature. Closer inspection revealed that we were being followed all the way by pylons linked together by the loosely slung arcs of electric cables. High above, on ledges carved right out of vertical cliff faces, they hung poised like so many dauntless Chinese acrobats. A blade of grass could hardly have gained a purchase here, but the Chinese could; a missionary in the name of progress.

It had a festive feel to it, this stretch of the Yangtse. Here man celebrated his conquests not with crude brutality, but with artistry and daring, and so riotously fantastic was the countryside that its lack of order could only give rise to delight.

Only later did I give any thought to the fact that wonder at the sights in the gorge had excited laughter; not speechless rapture, awe or quiet reverie, but loud, high-spirited laughter. It was the Chinese on the foredeck who were laughing, but their laughter was so infectious that it carried me along with it. The Chinese's assumption of himself as being the centre of the universe ran up against an absolute and unyielding adversary. The cliff walls stood there like a stop sign and perhaps that was why the Chinese were laughing, out of sheer relief, out of a healthy humility because, when all was said and done they did not carry the world on their shoulders after all; because somewhere in the mirror there was a crack and something other than their own reflection was being thrown back at them. Even in the Middle Kingdom man was not always at the centre of things.

On my travels I had grown accustomed to viewing the Chinese countryside with other eyes, as a man-made landscape of refined mountains reconstructed into stairways and terraces; one that had grown out of a thousand-year-old compromise between nature and the peasants who, with deferentially bent backs and great fortitude had worked at the pace of a geological metamorphosis. The mountains had been like pebbles on the beach, ground down by the irresistible force not of water but hands. Here, however, in the gorges of the Yangtse, there could be no compromise, no symbiosis, and soon they would be filled with water in a flooding representative of another view of the relationship between man and nature, as a life or death struggle, bolder and bolder in its conquests, stupider and stupider, blind to nature's immense stop sign.

Around midday we made a two-hour stopover at one of the new ports on the Yangtse. Here, as almost everywhere else, we had to tie up at a pontoon-dock. The water level could fluctuate by as much as 20 metres. It being winter the river was quite low, and the towns along the Yangtse were encircled by vast black mud-flats which stretched from the pontoon-docks all the way to the monumental flights of steps that marked the entrances to all of these industrial towns so at odds with nature.

A barge was being unloaded. Sacks emerged from the hold on the backs of a long procession of dock workers and were then toted across to a steadily growing mound of others lying in the midst of a mud-flat. Farther off, a barge was being loaded with coal. Soot-blackened labourers in dark-blue overalls teetered along planks that ran onto the boat, yokes hung with brimming, swaying baskets see-sawing across their shoulders. In their hundreds they scuttled, ant-like, back and forth between the mountains of coal on the quayside at which they filled their baskets, and the hold, where a new mountain of coal was gradually rising above the hatch coaming. They moved at a little trot, every inch of their bodies loose and springy as they jogged on and on, as if attempting to outrun the burden on their shoulders.

Thousands of people swarmed over the mud-flats, bustling up and down the huge flights of steps or in and out of improvised stalls formed by an arrangement of straw mats roofed with sailcloth; all running at the same brisk trot, yokes on shoulders, seeming to fear that any minute the river might rise up once more and wash everything away: the mountains of coal, the sacks, even themselves and the future in whose name they were wearing themselves out.

Here the masses were the forces of production, as described by Karl Marx. He had been thinking of the pyramids of Egypt, whereas here the masses were building the pyramid of progress, but still using – as they had 5,000 years before – their bare hands.

Behind all of this towered the monochrome concrete town with its factories and smoking chimneys.

Several hundred people had pitched camp at the foot of the enormous flight of steps, where they huddled under large rugs, shivering in the bitterly cold, damp air. Whole groups had disappeared under their rugs, so that it looked as though a herd of odd, many-humped camels had lain down to rest. These people had to be waiting for something, but when we sailed by two hours later they were still there. They had taken on the listless, animal look which seems to come over those left to wait in extremely poor or extremely bureaucratic countries, or both, which was usually the case. For wherever it proved impossible to abolish poverty, the choice was made, instead, to administrate and browbeat it. Queues robbed poverty of its chaotic nature, thereby depriving it of one of its external features: the fight of all against all. But bureaucracy also deprived poverty of one of its few weapons: the possibility for the tough and the dynamic to stand on their own two feet. The law of the jungle was replaced by apathy and fossilization, and amid all the hustle and bustle of the mudflat, the people found themselves waiting in the grip of this apathy.

With their tremendous height, the steps constituted a world of their own and the multitude of people streaming incessantly up and down them seemed to belong there, as if this flight of steps were another society, with its own life and rituals. The celebrated stairway scene from Eisenstein's *Battleship Potemkin* could easily have been filmed here. At the top of the steps there was an opening in the breastwork formed by the blocks of houses overlooking the river. It was an industrial town, built along the lines of a medieval castle.

Inside, the streets were narrow, dirty and dark, hemmed in by walls that ran with dampness. The whole place was teeming with life; battered trucks sounded their horns as they nudged their way through a crowd of people in intricate motion, weaving this way and that around each other; there were market stalls and street traders at every turn – this was the eternal Asia, the Asia of bazaars, caravans, of overpowering sights and smells. The fouled paving stones and grimy, blackened walls rendered this Communist ghost town human; along with the noise, which was contained here as if inside a bottle.

All of the small shops and eating houses resembled caves hewn out of the industrial town's concrete terrain. The congested streets were full of stalls selling vegetables, fish, meat, tape cassettes and woven baskets. New deliveries kept arriving, dangling from yokes slung over the shoulders of small, wiry men moving at a smart, lightfooted trot.

Late in the day the river widened out again. We were out of the gorges, the banks receded. In the dusty heat haze of the late afternoon the industrial towns which continued to slip past on the steep banks gave the impression of already having been abandoned.

The Artistry of Violation

CHONGQING LAY IN THE MIDDLE OF THE YANGTSE RIVER ON an island shaped not unlike Manhattan, and like New York this town, too, had spread. The island as such held two and a half million people, Chongqing and its suburbs in the region of 13 million – another entire world which I had never heard of and which I came to not as an explorer but as a barbarian reaching civilization, a traveller gone astray on the vast continent of my own ignorance.

The time was 2 p.m. The riverboat had been due to dock at 9 a.m., but we had been held up by thick fog which had enfolded the craft in its clammy grip, making it impossible to see from stem to stern. Now here we were, tied up at one of the pontoon-docks. Between the boat and the town, which stood at the top of a mud-coloured slope, the riverbed lay exposed. From the jetty a makeshift road lined with waiting taxis and mini-buses wound its way up the slope.

The boat was invaded by an army of porters; little, lean men in blue work jackets clutching bamboo canes: the yokes from which, only moments later, suitcases and shapeless packages would be balancing precariously.

In the narrow corridors and companionways between decks, the crush of bodies was so bad that I spent half an hour trapped on a landing. The frightful pushing and shoving from all sides, the frantic eagerness of the passengers to get off the boat, had brought everything to a standstill and no one was making any headway. On the deck below, an entire corridor-full of people jostled desperately, slowly, blindly groping, like a stream of lava finding its way around rocks. The porters elbowed their way through, boring into the throng. From my vantage-point on the landing I compared these people with my fellow passengers from the top deck. They were not merely from two different levels of society, they seemed to belong to two different races, the difference between them far

54

greater than that between upper-class Chinese and a white man such as myself; stocky-built, sunken-cheeked and hollow-eyed – the contours of hunger and hardship, which it had taken centuries to distort so far from the anatomical norm – and yet still with a dogged look in their eyes, that remorseless vitality with which they clamoured for the heaviest load, in order to be brought groaning to their knees for a couple of *jiao*.

I watched one of them struggling down the companionway with some baskets full of oranges and a suitcase. His face was taut with pain and his body shook as he struggled to keep his balance. Then he was swallowed up in the stream of people at the foot of the companionway. The exit was still a long way off.

That evening I had dinner in the restaurant of the Hotel Chongqing, which had made a specialty of Cantonese food. I ate my chicken in lemon sauce to the accompaniment of a fashion show being held on a stage in the centre of the spacious dining room. The models were tall and slim with stylish hairdos and make-up that served to accentuate their white skin. They had picked up the fashion model's steely glare and that aura of untouchability and detachment which surrounds a body that has become a showpiece. They took the short catwalk at a march, shoulders working aggressively, as if contemptuously pushing their way through a crowd. But their expressions and gestures were not inspired solely by the militant style of the fashion model. They had also borrowed from the striptease artist's arsenal: the glance over the shoulder, the frozen pose with the back to the audience, before the fateful items of clothing are shed and the body thus exposed is offered up at the same time as it issues its challenge.

Anyone who has ever seen a strip-show knows that if it is done right it is not the libido that is teased and titillated. It is fear. Striptease is for the sexually timid. Female sexuality is threateningly displayed while being safely caged in by a carefully choreographed sequence of gestures. It is the shiver down the spine in front of the tiger's cage that the audience experiences, not arousal at the sight of an inviting body. Striptease is the typical male initiation rite of a puritanical society, where it takes courage to desire.

The mannequins paraded back and forth across the podium wearing black cycling shorts, matching tops which left the midriff bare, and citrus-yellow capes made of a transparent, synthetic material. First they posed with their backs turned and legs astride, like soldiers standing at ease. Then came the glance over the shoulder – warning, priming, tantalizing. Then they swivelled round and strutted, in true mannequin-style, down the catwalk. And, as they did so, the capes came apart, baring one shoulder. But above all, what was being stripped bare here was a puritan ideal of decency.

There was a self-conscious historical awareness about this fashion show. As with everything else staged in public in China it constituted an ideological statement: a neatly stage-managed great leap from communism to liberalism and into the fluid ethical concepts of the consumer society. This fashion show blended mannequin attitudes and striptease posturing, because in the eyes of a Communist there had to be something pornographic about the delight in being well dressed.

Every exposed shoulder was greeted with applause. From the crowded tables small boys were dispatched to the podium with bouquets of artificial flowers. Next to the stage sat a group of coarse-featured men in shell suits. One of them forced his female companion to drain a large glass of beer, his arm wrapped menacingly around her throat, before bellowing out a belligerent toast to the surrounding company. They were as arrogant as gangsters. Twenty or thirty years ago such hoodlums would no doubt have been counted among Mao's Red Guards. Now they had money to burn, these men with their thick, drooling lips and crude, complacent smiles.

A steady stream of bouquets passed from their table to the catwalk, while they yelled and raised their glasses. They were gift-givers whose generosity seemed primarily designed to humiliate the recipient. Their compliments had the ring of commands and an extreme malevolence was detectable in their drunken euphoria. They stood for more than simply the old and the new China: they are a familiar presence in every society.

With its overcrowded shopping thoroughfares Chongqing's town centre was not unlike Shanghai. But the neon signs had not yet reached this far. Instead, long banners hung everywhere, and even though I could not read them I was impressed by the aggressive dynamism of the market economy which had taken possession of the town. Around every corner lay crater-like building sites. With what furious energy the old neighbourhoods were being flattened to make way for the erection, only a few metres apart, of tower blocks of a greyish-yellow, mildewed concrete. The front of a low, pale-blue building still carried the legend "Chung King Sweet and Cake Trade Center", but through the windows one could see right up to the sky: the roof had been lopped off by blue-overalled workmen wielding hammers and iron spikes with which they were hacking away at the past, brick by brick. A brand-new tower block with a crane on its roof lay hidden behind scaffolding that had been draped with woven straw mats, like a present waiting to be unwrapped. China was shedding its skin.

A group of day labourers stood around a street corner: joiners with saws over their shoulders, painters with splashes of white on their clothes and paintbrushes fixed to long poles. The troops of progress holding themselves in readiness.

The streets of Chongqing were far too steep for cyclists. Where the slopes of the island ran down to the river, and in the hilly island's interior where the inclines were too severe for tower blocks to gain a foothold, the Chongqing of the past could still be found, in the form of enormous, densely built-up, flights of steps. Here the China of old still survived, a picturesque underworld of untouched life unfolding in small, closely-packed houses with dark-grey roofs and walls black with dampness. At the top of the steps old women sat reading palms. Here there was as much need to know your fate as before setting out on a perilous journey.

As in the slums of Shanghai, the houses here had turned themselves inside out, exposing the life within to the street. One could look straight into den-like rooms their black walls glistening with grease and wear. A large bed, a table surrounded by child-size stools and some benches was all the furniture there was. Old men puffed away on long slender pipes; a girl sat outside the house doing her homework, another brushed her teeth over the open gutter.

Here, too, were small eating houses where the fresh raw ingredients for the speciality of the town, *hyuogo* or hot pot, were set out on skewers around pots of seething, heavily spiced oil. Innumerable shoe-repair shops filled the steps with the pungent smell of glue. There were billiard tables, card games in progress and mahjong. Here the shoeblacks were not cowed, as they had been in Wuhan, but cheery and outgoing.

By the river the housing on the steps ran down almost vertically, like the steps in a hen-coop. Chaotic lean-tos cobbled together out of planks and roofed with straw mats or bamboo were suspended in mid-air. The steps themselves were green with slime. Brass taps, the step community's only source of water, were bearded with moss. The 10,000 water sellers who had once supplied the residents of Chongqing with water drawn straight from the Yangtse River were no more. Other than that, nothing had changed.

I had seen a picture of the water sellers in the Chongqing museum, along with photographs of the step communities as they had looked at the turn of the century, although I had not visited the museum in order to delve into the history of the town. The only real attraction were the four dinosaurs which had been unearthed in the Sichuan province in the mid-1970s. They were the most Chinese of dinosaurs, belonging to no species I had ever heard of, even if they did look rather familiar. There was a "Yangtsenanosaurus", named after the river, and an "Omeisaurus" which had taken its name from a mountain in the centre of Sichuan province sacred to Buddhists. So even during the Jurassic period China had been the Middle Kingdom. The long-necked reptiles were forced to stand with their heads bowed because the museum ceiling was not high enough. Lack of space, the perennial Chinese problem, which even a dinosaur had to bow before.

The first floor of the museum was given over to vases, old weapons, drinking vessels and examples of calligraphy. Aside from the most ancient objects, which bore clear signs of their age and of a civilization still in its infancy, the articles on diplay were pretty much what one would have found in any gift shop. One became strangely blind to the beauty of these porcelain vases, which have become commonplace as part of the decor in archetypal Chinese restaurants. Only those objects which had become so shapeless with age or so aesthetically anomalous that they had not been considered worth copying bore witness to the fact that art history in the making had indeed existed and not merely stagnation and endless copying.

On the fourth floor, through a series of photomontages, the museum presented the history of the town, and here the difference was staggeringly apparent. The buildings in the photographs had been constructed haphazardly out of wood or bamboo, materials on which the years had taken their toll. Old rusting Texaco and Shell signs testified to the days when the West had established a footing here. For many years they must have looked like the flotsam from passing UFOs. Now the wheel had turned full circle.

The transformation of Chonqing was irrevocable. The only areas that evinced any traces of the past were the slums, waiting their turn for redevelopment. While the art of China did not change, everyday life was doing so with increasing rapidity. And yet there was a time when it had been the ordinary people who had seemed to live outside of time, in the grey eternity of oppression, while art tended to grow dated according to the shifting tastes of succesive epochs. Now art had opted out. There were, it seemed, no witnesses to these accelerating times.

On a square near the river a tent had been put up behind a hoarding where a troupe of travelling players were performing. On the hoarding hung a colour photograph of a recumbent and generously endowed naked woman. An enormous boa constrictor slithered across her body, concealing her sex and breasts. A large poster depicted three figures standing side by side: two women and a grinning skeleton. It was mankind's oldest spine-chiller, the universal challenge of sex and death.

Behind the hoarding about 20 people squatted on long planks laid out on the ground. A piece of stretched sailcloth was both backdrop and stage. A boy of about ten or twelve positioned himself in front of it and proceeded to make conjuring movements with his arms, while music blared from a loudspeaker. At the other side of the stage a large electric table fan rattled away. The boy let out a ferocious war cry and thrust his hand into the whirling fan. The machine immediately stopped dead. With another roar he pulled his hand out and, as the fan resumed its spinning, held up his fingers. There was not a mark on them. Then he increased the speed and repeated the performance.

The audience looked on listlessly. They were waiting for the woman with the boa constrictor.

But she did not appear in the next act either. A middle-aged man stepped out from behind the sailcloth holding a small snake, possibly about 18 inches long. It was thin as a finger and, sluggish, almost half-dead to look at, a poor substitute for the promises made by the posters outside. Squinting slightly as he focussed his gaze on the bridge of his nose, the snake charmer began to stuff the snake up one nostril. This he did several times, but each time, having managed to get it halfway up, he pulled it out again and regarded it with a worried look. One had the feeling that someone was not pulling their weight. It may have been that the snake kept getting lost up there, or perhaps it had plans which did not coincide with those of the nose's owner.

The audience was clearly restless. One man had called a shoeblack over and appeared to be more interested in his toecaps than in the miracle being performed in front of the piece of sailcloth. Another leaned forwards, pinched his nose and trumpeted, to leave a long, green gobbet of snot streaming from one nostril, an action which provided near enough a mirror image of the snake charmer's futile efforts.

Eventually the snake charmer, or perhaps the snake, gave up. Its slender body dangled limply from his hand like overcooked spaghetti, as if it had expired for want of air.

The man ducked behind the sailcloth and emerged carrying a fresh snake. This time he was successful in his endeavour. The snake vanished up his nostril until only the tail was left dangling just in front of his lips. He opened his mouth wide in triumph. On his tongue lay the snake's tiny triangular head.

Gently he took hold of the head and tugged at the snake until the tail threatened to disappear up his nose. Then he began to dance around to some unheard melody while pulling the snake back and forth, now with his fingers right up his nose, now with his hand all the way inside his mouth, as if the snake was a violin bow that he was rubbing across invisible strings deep inside his head. Back and forth, back and forth, hypnotised by the tune which only he could hear.

The audience was not interested. They were still waiting for the woman from the colour photograph, that marvel of voluptuous charms.

At long last she was announced. The shoeblack was waved away and the man with the running nose stopped blowing to fix his eyes expectantly on the stage.

She stepped out before them, no more than ten years old, with chubby, frost-bitten cheeks and wearing a shapeless winter coat which made her figure look as round as a bowling ball. She stretched herself out on a small trestle table with the look of someone awaiting their fate in the dentist's chair.

The snake charmer reappeared carrying a plastic bucket. He emptied it over the prone girl and a tangled mass of slimy, glistening snakes fell onto her stomach, then wriggled off in all directions. Whenever one was about to slither over the edge of the table, the girl would grab hold of it and place it back in the middle of the winter coat that encased her round little body. She stared fixedly into space the whole time, with that same distant, resigned look in her eyes.

And that was it. That was the show, the dream, the miracle that promised to reveal itself here in the heart of Chongqing; the inflaming intimacy of sex stripped bare amid the mud of the market place.

I looked around at the audience. Poker-faced, they accepted the swindle and got to their feet without applauding.

I could not help comparing all this to the child acrobats I had seen in Shanghai. Not only had they had complete control over their bodies, they had also expanded the space around them, moving through it according to laws that they themselves had created. The Chongqing showmen did quite the opposite. Their artistry lay in delivering up the body to the repulsive, the unnatural, to pain. Rather than pushing their bodies to the limit, they demonstrated how small a space the body commanded. They left themselves open to invasion. It was an art of violation, designed for people who were faced every day with the fact that they had no rights, least of all over their own bodies.

Upwards, Ever Upwards

ONE OF CHINA'S SACRED BUDDHIST MOUNTAINS, EMEISHAN lies only a few hours' drive from Chengdu, the capital of Sichuan province. It was an old Chinese custom to make the pilgrimage to the top of the mountain, 3,000 metres above sea level. The modern world has provided both a tarmaced road and a cable car, with the result that the only people who still walk to the top are either extremely devout believers or tourists making the most of this opportunity to experience the Chinese landscape at close quarters.

It had nothing to do with mountaineering. For hundreds of years pilgrims of all ages had been taking this road and while the idea might well have been for them to prove their faith through their exertions, the walk was not so tough that they would be forced to abandon it. Steps ran all the way up the mountainside, in some places hewn from the rock, in others no more than large stones pressed into the loose earth and held in place by their own weight. But the mountain was steep and on one stretch I eventually found it necessary to resort to using my hands, clambering up rather than walking. I was soaked with sweat in the sunshine.

There were also other, more readily negotiable stretches where one could stroll comfortably along a wide, paved path. Newly renovated temples, their red-lacquered pillars reflecting the sunlight, marked the stages of the pilgrim way. Refreshments were available from stalls set up along the route, but there were few pilgrims to be seen. On the other hand there were plenty of porters lugging up building materials for the restoration of the mountain temples, all of which had been destroyed during the Cultural Revolution. Every single stone was borne on the back. This work was perhaps a sign that China was leaving Communism behind. The country could now afford a past as well as a future.

But the porters seemed to come from a place outside time. Shirts flapped aside to reveal spare, wiry bodies, the sweat glistening on sharply defined muscles. These were the Sisyphian labourers of history. They knew the strain involved in rolling the stone up to the mountain-top, but were spared the disappointment of seeing it roll down again; for no one had told them there was supposed to be a point to what they did. Yesterday the temples were destroyed. Today they are being rebuilt. And tomorrow? What we knew as "past" and "future", "progress" and "hope" were to them another load to bear.

They carried strange-looking, short sticks which were of use to them only on the steps. By digging their sticks in a couple of rises ahead the porters pulled themselves up, like old men interminably hauling themselves to their feet. Upwards, ever upwards, not to the top of the mountain but on the treadmill of toil.

Four hours on, late in the afternoon, I arrived at the Buddhist monastery where I planned to spend the night. It was situated halfway up the mountain and bore the poetic name of "The Elephants' Washbasin". It was an old tumbledown place built from red-lacquered panels and between its scuffed, grey and unpainted floorboards gaped cracks which the monks were fond of aiming at when they spat.

A service was held before supper in a small, smoke-filled temple. A monk struck a bell that resembled an inverted cooking pot. At long intervals another beat a large cymbal, though without producing more than a dull thud like that of a hammer blow. This provided the accompaniment to the reedy singing of a choir swathed in ankle-length saffron robes. Outside in the yard stood mounds of dirty, slushy snow. It all seemed rather depressing, an empty ritual ostentatiously observed, but lacking any sort of commitment. From somewhere inside the building came the sound of a television.

When it grew dark, the monastery novices gathered shivering in the kitchen around a brazier on which a pot of water was coming to the boil. They passed the time by playing cards and spitting at the cracks in the floor.

To my surprise a couple of young girls were also staying at the monastery. Whereas the male novices sported the traditional shaven heads and quilted coats, the girls wore jeans and baggy pullovers. One of them asked to borrow my phrase book and proceeded to copy out English words while trying out her pronunciation. China was on the move.

Even in a tumbledown monastery one sensed the restless air of expectancy.

The next morning the sun rose over a flat, fuzzy horizon of darkness; the far-off edge of the earth the only dividing line between night and day. A bank of fog came rolling up the mountain slopes. The mist broke like cloudy surf against the hillside before dropping back, vanquished, to a valley floor that was slowly filling with a dusty, reddish light, as if the earth had caught fire beneath the steadily brightening morning sky.

As I walked out through the monastery gateway, which had been bolted during the night, I noticed a young novice silhouetted against the sunrise, a scarf draped round his shoulders against the morning chill; engrossed perhaps in the sight of the new day, or maybe lost in longings whose object only he knew and which this monastery was either too small or too big to contain.

On the last, long stage of the climb the pilgrim way ran in the shadow of the mountain. The snow had frozen and thawed so often that the path had iced-over completely. Where before there had been steps, the climber was now faced with a sloping ice rink. It was impossible to gain a purchase anywhere. Metal studs for strapping to the soles of the shoes were being sold from a wayside stall and, equipped with a set of these, I continued my struggle against the mountain. Far in the distance I could see the cable car, but I soldiered on – a pilgrim not in spirit, but in the flesh; in the last challenge modern man allows himself: the battle against the limitations of the body. It was here, on the steep, snow-covered slope with the clouds far below that I was suddenly seized by an overwhelming tiredness, not in my limbs, but of my will. I progressed only in a kind of slow motion which could have been either internal or external. I could not have said which.

The mountain-top was occupied by a radio mast, antennas and a crowd of photographers. Subsequently on my travels I was to meet other Westerners who, like me, had walked this pilgrim way and had been furious and disappointed to encounter modern China at the summit of Emeishan. But we had no right to indulge in such nostalgia. None of us were true seekers. It was only our ignorant expectations that had been offended. Climbing Emeishan one was given the chance to take a short-cut through a reservation dedicated to the past. That was all. The real China lay in wait at the summit of Emeishan, a profane blend of past and present which is the mark of any country in the throes of rapid development: the radio mast pointed to heaven while the gleaming porcelain roof-tiles of a Buddhist temple reflected the sun in a great blaze of light. Emeishan was an island floating on a milk-white sea of cloud, not a holy place where one could drink in the sight of the Creation, but the top storey of a Tower of Babel that was still growing.

A Shameful Rebel

I TOOK THE BUS TO CHENGDU. THE FACES IN THE VILLAGES WE passed through were of a different character. They had a mute air about them. But even the villages were jammed with traffic and brimful of people. They might have come in answer to a summons and be waiting only for the order to march towards some great objective. They were holding a dress rehearsal for the big city, but still had the blank faces of peasants.

Chengdu had street upon street of low, one and two-storey wooden houses with tiled roofs. The pavements were planted with plane trees, their tops pruned and trained to form an archway over roads on which the bicycle had not yet abdicated in favour of the motor car. It was a town on a human scale where every single building housed its own little shop. In the town centre, however, enthusiasm for all things modern had run riot. It looked like a set for Superman or Batman, it was Metropolis or Gotham City, and just as these two superheroes were a product of the 1940s and 1950s, so, too, the centre of Chengdu resembled a dream of the future from a Western past.

Mao was still there, in the shape of a gigantic pure white statue, in baggy jacket and trousers and with the languid, inscrutable face whose expression one could interpret, either as patriarchal benevolence or as lofty indifference to the sufferings of others. A local joke went: "It's such a shame for Chairman Mao. He has to stand out there in the rain and the cold. Don't you think we ought to move him out of the way?"

Directly opposite the statue of Mao stood Chengdu's department stores, built along the same lines as those in the West, with a well in the centre and four or five floors, each displaying a wide range of different wares. They did not need to get rid of Mao. He had become a museum exhibit.

The alley that led from Renming Zhong Lu to the Wenshu monastery also had a wide range of goods for sale, but of a different kind. Here one could buy joss-sticks of every thickness and fake banknotes bearing pictures of people playing music on a cloud. The notes were for burning before the altar of one's ancestors. They were yellow and red with a face value of 100 million yuan. *Hell Banknote* the inscription read: a currency that was valid in Hell, a sort of life insurance for the hereafter. It was bad enough to land in Hell. It was even worse, the philosophy went, to arrive without money.

There was a great deal of clear-sightedness in such folklore, which was particularly prevalent among the poor and the uneducated. The Hell of Christianity was absolute, a place of damnation, where suffering and despair, by virtue of their very punitive nature, were non-negotiable. It was a place where sentence was served and mercy ran out. Here eternity held sway. This Chinese Hell, where the post was delivered regularly and the residents had the right to receive remittances from the outside, was relativist. The lord of this Hell, whoever he might be, was open to corruption. One could buy a bit of comfort. One could improve one's lot, if only slightly. It was a humane Hell, accommodating, amenable to negotiation and all in all quite unprincipled. Rather like earthly life, it was unpleasant, but in practical terms, one could get used to it.

Outside the entrance to the Wenshu monastery a beggar lay on a converted delivery bicycle, which he moved by pushing the wheels with his hands. His body was swollen and shapeless, hidden in layer upon layer of tattered quilted jackets, which protected them more from prying eyes than the cold. Only his head was visible, puce-coloured from frostbite. He watched me all the time, like an animal about to pounce, as he manoeuvred his odd vehicle into position.

Next to him another beggar pulled up his trouser leg to reveal a sore; an enormous brown scab that covered the whole of his shin and oozed fresh pus. A woman poked her moonface into mine. It was appallingly disfigured, the features running down over the cranium like dripping candlewax. Either she had been horribly burned or she was a leper. Then they were crawling at me from all sides, waving their crutches, with the agility of wolf spiders leaping from their lairs. They stretched out their hands. Were they intent only on begging, or were they about to grab me? The bundled-up body in the homemade wheelchair propelled itself furiously after my shadow. My skin crawled with an age-old terror.

All was quiet in the monastery garden and there was no one to be seen until a massive, darkly dressed figure appeared and fell into step beside me with a muttered "hello". Somehow he managed to utter this simple word, which even people with the poorest gift for languages can master, in such a bizarre manner that I almost had to guess what it meant.

His unruly hair was badly cut and lay in matted tangles, as though he had just got out of bed. The black jacket with its Mao collar was clean but the sweater showing underneath was frayed. His trousers were covered in stains and his shoes laced with twine. He was not wearing socks, although the temperature hovered around zero. In a moment I knew he would either ask me for money or offer to change some for me. I assumed a dismissive air, but he stuck doggedly by my side, morose and unforthcoming, as if his only goal in life was to make me party to his own clouded silence.

Eventually I asked him if he was a student.

"Maybe," he replied.

I tried again. "Do you have a job, then?"

"Maybe."

My mysterious companion nodded in the direction of the monastery. "I lived there for six months."

"You were a novice at the monastery?" Despite his haggard and neglected appearance I could see that he was still young.

He nodded without meeting my eye.

"Why did you give it up?"

Looking down at his battered shoes, he said, "An injustice was perpetrated against me."

The sentence fell with a dreadful weight, as though it had been waiting to be spoken for a long time and he could no longer contain it. I had the impression of a person caught up in a confrontation with destiny. Then he spread his arms wide, in true man-of-the-world fashion, as though wishing to detract attention from what he had just said.

"May I invite you for a cup of tea?"

The Wenshu monastery had its own open-air tea garden, furnished with bamboo chairs arranged around low, stone tables. Shaven-headed boys in grey tunics moved among the tables pouring boiling water from copper kettles into white porcelain cups in which green tea leaves lay waiting.

My host nodded to one of the boys. "I used to serve tea here myself."

I asked him his name. He introduced himself as Shu. Later I was to discover that the name had been taken from a poem by his favourite poet, Tu Fu, the greatest poet of the Tang dynasty, who had spent some years in Chengdu during his wide-ranging travels across China.

The Chinese are hardy. They can eat outside in sub-zero temperatures. Only rarely does winter drive them indoors and the seasons make little difference to their love of the open air. I made myself comfortable in what here, a little to the north of Emeishan, was not yet spring, and warmed my hands on my brimming cup of tea.

I asked Shu the nature of the injustice that had been perpetrated against him.

His English was halting, his vocabulary extensive, but his knowledge of grammar minimal. We constructed every sentence, every piece of information, with constant detours and questions and much head-shaking, until suddenly his face would brighten and he would nod. Later, when I got to know him better, I realized that his life was like his English: a long series of stumbles over the rules of language and grammar. All the elements seemed to be there, inside him, but they could not find an outlet. He contained an incandescent inner core trapped within a shell of loneliness.

An injustice had been perpetrated against him, he repeated. The abbot of the monastery had punished him because complaints had been made about his behaviour. But the accusation was false, it had been a mis-understanding. No one would listen to him. So he left the monastery.

The accusation? What had he done? We never did find the right words. The explanation would have to lie there, in the murky area between my non-existent Chinese and his imperfect English. His name had been black-ened, certain things had been said. He was the victim of ill will. That much I understood. He had been left with a mute, gnawing sense of impotence. He radiated loneliness. How can one possibly share with others the injustices that are perpetrated against one? Look, already they are turning their heads away. As a victim of injustice one is condemned to powerless-ness, to complaint, to living alone. Even large crowds of people seem

69

lonely when they attempt to avenge an injustice committed against them. The alternative is to forget – but Shu did not look like someone inclined to forget.

He slumped moodily in his bamboo chair, blowing on his tea. He was heftily built, a hulking lad with the body of a hard-working peasant and a large, heavy head. There was a certain stubborn intransigence about him, something suppressed, as though he expected nothing but antagonism and, hence, unwittingly provoked it. He was his own worst enemy, wounded not only in his feelings, but also somewhere deep within him where the physical and the spiritual are neighbours, and from this wound he was slowly bleeding to death.

For three years he had struggled to adapt to monastery life, in several monasteries, but it was beyond him. Three years. It fell so heavily from his lips. Like a judgement, an inward accusation.

"Are you a Buddhist?" I asked.

"On a deeper level," he replied, "there is no difference between Marxism and Buddhism. Both say: 'Free yourself'. It is a doctrine with which I sympathize."

"But why the monastic life? Why not some other way?"

"I had no choice," he said.

Shu had been expelled from university after the student demonstrations in 1989. He had done something "irreparable" – his own word. He had put his name to a wall protest in which the students of Chengdu University had voiced their support for their fellows who had camped out in Tiananmen Square. He had done it in exactly the same way as he sat facing me, with all of his weight, the weight of his name, and he had brought the judgement on himself. Irreparable.

He brightened for a moment: "I was reading Chinese. But I was just as interested in the literature of the West." He started reeling off the names of the writers whose works he had read: Henrik Ibsen, Eugene O'Neill, James Joyce, Ernest Hemingway, Stendhal, Walt Whitman, his favourite poet. He knew whole poems by heart and proceeded to recite them in his faltering English:

> I have heard what the talkers were talking, the talk of
> the beginning and the end;
> But I do not talk of the beginning or the end.

There was never any more inception than there is now,
Nor any more youth or age than there is now;
And will never be any more perfection than there is now,
Nor any more heaven or hell than there is now.

Shu's expression softened. Then he resumed his story. Coming from a small village in Sichuan province, he had been the bright country school-boy, the first in his family to make it to the city and the university. His father's wrath, when he was expelled, had been terrible. No worse disaster could have befallen them. It was an act of treachery, not against the State, but against his ancestors. He had entered the monastery in order to placate his father, and because he had no choice. The jobs he found he couldn't keep for long. When word got around, as it always did, that he was an expelled student, he was promptly dismissed.

"I have no future, and no hope of getting into university," he said gloomily. "That world is closed to me now."

His shabby clothes, his bad teeth and greasy hair attested to the truth of his words. In the three years since his expulsion from university he had sunk to the lowest level of Chinese society. He produced his identity card from the inside pocket of his black jacket and handed it to me. His hands were rough and covered in sores. The photograph had been taken a year before and showed him with the shorn head of a novice, but the difference between his face then and now revealed how drastic his decline had been and how tough it was at the bottom. He was 29.

His last job had been with a privately owned electronics factory. A few days before I met him he had been called in by the manager and told not to come back. He had been working there for a month and a half and had even slept there, having nowhere else to go. No explanation was given for his dismissal, but Shu knew the reason.

I was beginning to see that with the mysterious "Maybe" which had opened our conversation, Shu had actually been expressing the truth about his existence. His whole life had been put into limbo.

"But there is always a place one can turn to," he said, as if pursuing an earlier train of thought. "I was standing on the street one day when some gangsters came up to me and said: 'Join us. You would fit in here,' but I said no, because, as Buddha says: one has to find the true path."

He broke off, then bent forward and regarded me intently. "Am I not right?"

This question was blurted out with an intensity which suggested that he desperately needed to hear someone else endorse his dogged commitment to what he called the true path.

That evening I was taking a stroll along Nanlu Renmin, the broad pavements of which were completely taken up by exhibitions of Chinese painting, when I caught sight of Shu's dark, stocky figure at a pedestrian crossing. He was plodding along with his hands behind his back and his head bent forwards, ruminating, completely engrossed in his own thoughts.

"Where are you going?" I shouted.

He stopped. "Nowhere. I'm just killing time."

He had turned up the narrow collar of his Mao jacket against the growing chill of the night air and buried his hands deep in his trouser pockets. The tops of three ballpoint pens stuck out of his breast pocket: all that remained of the peasant boy's dream of becoming an intellectual.

He suggested that we walk a little way together. We turned off the main street and began to walk by the river. I could sense that he had need of my company to help keep solitude at bay and put off the moment when he would be left alone in the cold night air. He had told me about the homeless people who slept on the bank of the Jin Jiang river behind the Wenshu monastery, but only now did it occur to me that he was one of them and that he would have to get through this cold night dressed only in his threadbare clothes.

"Do you have somewhere to sleep?"

"It's good for me to walk. I think better that way. I need to have a clear head. I have decisions to make. I have to work out what to do about my future."

I asked again, choosing my words carefully, as I did not want to hurt his pride.

"Maybe," he replied after a prolonged pause. "It was colder six weeks ago. Now it's not so bad."

I took his reply to mean no and offered him a bed at the hotel where I was staying. At first he refused, then relented.

"I have nothing to give in return."

His statement was neither an objection nor a warning. It seemed rather a way of describing himself. Here spoke a man who had been banished from human society, denied a chance to participate in any act of exchange.

The staff at the hotel reception desk were hostile. They eyed Shu up and down. No, there were no rooms. When we took our leave of one another I gave him 50 yuan. It was more than enough to tide him through one night and we said goodbye, having made a date to meet the next day.

The following morning he looked tired. I asked how he had slept. "I'll explain later," he said, as mysterious as ever.

He had not spent the night in any hotel or hostel. He had sat down on a bench to think and had stayed there until sunrise.

He put his head in his hands: "I need to think."

By late afternoon he was numb with exhaustion. As I cycled away he stood staring straight ahead, as if he had simply ground to a halt.

A young student had taken to joining us. He was the antithesis of Shu, but they knew one another and occasionally took tea together in one of Chengdu's many tea houses.

Xiao's English was almost perfect, spoken with a slight American drawl. He was well-groomed and smartly dressed and he wore a pair of gold-rimmed glasses topped with a narrow band of horn. His skin was white, his features soft and he had the plump, Cupid's-bow upper lip of a baby. Beneath a burgundy-coloured, V-neck sweater he wore a white shirt and a neatly knotted tie on which, if you looked closely, you could just make out the words "Bank of China" forming an almost invisible pattern.

Like Shu, Xiao had taken part in the student demonstrations of 1989. Several of his friends had been killed by the police, others arrested. He told the story I had heard before of how, when term began again, the students had been forced to write down their "innermost thoughts" and to denounce themselves as traitorous. Prior to this they had always been hailed as the flower of society. Now they had to add their own voices to the chorus that accused them of being criminals.

The clashes with the police had obviously made a deep impression

73

on him. "I've never seen a war," he said, "but this was a war. A curfew had been declared, but no one told us. The police were waiting. It was a brutal attack."

"Change is necessary," he went on, "and there is only one direction it can take: towards more capitalism. And democracy will follow. But the future of China is impossible to predict."

While I was listening to Xiao's well-formulated reflections it occurred to me why he took such a great interest in his country's future. It was because he, too, had a future. He was reading physics at university and his studies would soon be completed. His participation in the riots of 1989 had had no repercussions for him. Unlike Shu, he had not signed anything and had avoided being dragged under when the student dream of a more democratic China was ended. He had faith in his own career, in change within the Communist Party, in democracy and more capitalism. He was on the right side. Young, gifted and adaptable people like him would have the job of building the country's future. It was Xiao who had told me about the banknotes in Hell and their symbolic meaning. Like Shu, he had believed briefly in the possibility of paradise, but not long enough for that belief to prove fateful. Now he was saving up for a future in Hell.

I looked from one to the other. If anyone doubted that, even after 40 years of Communism, the class barriers were being more rigorously maintained than ever, they only had to study these two young men. Xiao's parents were both intellectuals. His father had fallen out of favour during the Cultural Revolution, but he had long since been rehabilitated and was currently writing a history of the Communist Party. His mother was an academic and a scientist. Xiao was slightly built and fine-featured. He might have been descended from a long line of mandarins who had never been exposed to the trials of life. If he had had to survive on the street like Shu, he would have succumbed long ago.

In Shu's body I perceived the countryside. He embodied all the stoutness that is called for when people take it into their heads to move mountains, and it was the constitution of the landscape-builder that kept him going, even now in his abasement. His grubby, swollen hands covered in cuts and old scars said it all. He could hold out for a while yet, but he was gradually being worn down and brutalized. The dignity normally associated with the destruction of the political prisoner had been denied him. Here a harsh society was doing the work normally left to prison guards. He had not been locked away. Nonetheless, he lived under circumstances that offered no way out.

I was the first foreigner to talk to Shu. Everyone else had turned away when he tried to start up a conversation. He was convinced that his poor English was to blame for this. Incapable as he was of seeing himself objectively, he did not realize that it was his appearance. He looked like someone who lived on the streets; and to outsiders, unable to tell the difference, he exhibited none of the pathos with which, in the eyes of socially conscious Westerners, the homeless are associated. His scruffiness was not that of the political martyr, but that of the down-and-out; his air of tragedy came over as surliness, his diffidence could be read as menace. He already seemed to belong to the underworld which he so steadfastly shunned.

"I must improve my English," he said over and again. "It is my only hope."

Xiao's English was fluent. He had been helped by his parents. Shu had had to make the giant leap from the country to the town, from village life to university. He might as well have been trying to learn Martian.

"You'll never guess what the first English sentence I learned to say in school was," Xiao laughed.

"'How do you do?'"

"No, no. 'Long live Chairman Mao!' And by then he was already dead. He died when I was eight. We were forced to weep in public. Anyone who did not weep was considered politically suspect. Some people were arrested because they did not cry when Chairman Mao died. China is a strange country."

The three of us had met up at the Tu Fu Pavilion on the western side of Chengdu, a 40-minute cycle ride from the city centre. The poet Tu Fu had lived in the eighth century and during his restless wanderings around a turbulent and war-torn China he had spent four peaceful years in Chengdu, which had considered itself his home town ever since.

We sat down in an open-air tea garden with tables set round a large, decorative rock. I had bought a volume of Tu Fu's poems translated into English. The Chinese text printed alongside the English with exactly five signs to each line, had the appearance of tall, graceful pillars. I could tell that Tu Fu was a poet who meant more to both these young men than just a compulsory part of the school syllabus, and I invited them to read me their favourite poems.

When Shu announced the title of the poem he had chosen I realized where he had got his name. It had been taken from the poem entitled "The Prime Minister of Shu".

"I'm particularly fond of the last two verses," he said.

The poem depicted the Prime Minister, who had become advisor to the lord Loi Bei and later to his son, but all his wisdom was to no avail, because death overtook him before he could finish his life's work.

Shu reached the last two verses:

> Alas, death befell ere victory was achieved,
> Which makes the heroes shed tears of deep regret.

"There you have my life," he said. "I, who was expelled from university before I could take my degree." Brooding, he retreated into himself.

Xiao chose one of Tu Fu's early poems and with perfect enunciation he read "Gazing at Mount Tai", which described the young poet's fascination with nature and the exaltation he derived from the sight of the mountain's graceful heights.

It closed with the lines:

> Some day I must ascend the summit
> And see how small other mountains are.

Xiao, too, had selected his poem with great care. Tu Fu's lines expressed his youthful hopes for his life and the future for which China was preparing and in which he would quite naturally take his place.

It was while staying in Chengdu that Tu Fu had written two of his most famous poems, both of them concerning his "thatched cottage". The first was an idyll. After years of roving fraught with hardship and want he had settled on the bank of the Jin Jiang river, where the trees hung thick with blossom and a passing shower had lured the fish to the surface. Then came the second poem, remorselessly revealing. An autumn storm had ripped the roof off his cottage, exposing more than just its furnishings to the falling rain. Mankind's true nature had also been revealed in all its wretched nakedness. Boys from the neigbouring villages had taken advantage of his helplessness and looted the cottage before his very eyes. He had been too tired and weak to put up a fight. His clothes were in tatters, his cotton robe was stiff with age and cold as iron. There was not a dry spot to be found anywhere.

This poem was displayed in a pavilion, mounted on a large panel of dark, lacquered wood. Xiao and Shu pointed it out to me and took turns at reading it aloud. It was the last lines which had secured Tu Fu his fame, even in Communist China, where Mao admired him.

> Would that there were thousands
> Of spacious houses
> To shelter all
> The poor scholars and ensure their safety
> Even in the most furious storms!
> Oh, when such buildings appear
> Before my eyes
> I would not mind dying of cold
> Alone in this damaged cottage;
> No, I would die content.

To Shu, the outcast scholar, whose life had come tumbling down about his ears just as Tu Fu's cottage had around his, every aspect of this writer's life must have invited identification. As we strolled around the park surrounding Tu Fu's pavilion, famed for its collection of more than 120 different species of bamboo, he quizzed me about one writer after another.

"Sappho," he said. "*One Hundred Years of Solitude*." Distant stars he stared at from the bottom of his well.

"You must have heard of Susanne Long." His voice had taken on an undertone of desperate insistence.

I shook my head.

"*Aestheticism and Symbols . . . Feeling and Form.* You're not familiar with them?"

I searched my memory. Could he be thinking of Susanne K. Langer? But I had never read anything by her. Again I shook my head.

"What about Erich Fromm, then? You must have read *The Art of Loving*. He has some good theories about social order."

Erich Fromm. Yes, I had read Erich Fromm. When I was 17 or 18 years old, over 20 years ago. I no longer recalled any of it and felt embarrassed by my own privileged forgetfulness.

"I burned that book," said Shu with unexpected fury.

I stared at him, shocked at the vehemence in his voice. "You burned it?"

"I burned so many books at that time." His tone had altered. "I wanted to put an end to my life."

"You wanted to commit suicide?"

"No, I mean my earthly life. I wanted to put an end to my earthly life. I intended to start a new life as a Buddhist monk. That is why I burned my books. But I was wrong. I was fooling myself."

"And now you regret burning your books?"

"Yes, 'regret' is the right word."

I began to see that Shu's mind remained a battlefield in which the conflict that had begun in the streets of Chengdu between police and students was still being waged. His expulsion from university had been a disaster so terrible that the concept of justice on which his protest rested had not been strong enough to keep him afloat.

Instead his defeat had been turned inwards, and become personal. He now regarded himself as someone who had failed to attain his goal in life and his self-loathing was even greater than his loathing for the system that had ostracized him.

Instinctively he sensed that if he was to survive he would have to wipe out everything in himself that had moved him to put his name on that fatal wall. It was to this end that he had used Buddhism, with its doctrine of the extinction of the self and the need to sever all of the ties that bind one to life. He had not looked upon this as religious instruction, but as punishment for failure. It was also a strategy for survival, since only without hope could he survive.

He had reduced the books to ashes, but he could not do the same with his appetite for life and in this lay his drama and his dilemma. He was too strong and knew that his lust for life would drive him even further down. Paradoxically, he distrusted all that was best about himself and yet gave in to it, as if it were some forbidden and fearsome desire. He was this paradox: a shameful rebel.

Xiao and I said goodbye to Shu in the late afternoon in order to take a bicycle ride through the city. Xiao wanted to accompany me to the Temple of Wuhau to show me a flower garden. Sprays of flowers had been strung from the gnarled branches of the ancient trees in a small temple courtyard. The flowers were so beautiful and so delicate that I had to stroke them gently in order to convince myself they were not artificial.

We had come out of the temple and were walking toward our bicycles when Xiao asked me an astonishing question. "How much do you think I should be paid?" He cringed obsequiously and his voice was low. He was clearly appealing to my authority and I was struck that at that moment he presented the classic picture of a young Chinese, true to the spirit of Confucianism, asking the advice of those older and wiser than himself.

"Paid?" I asked.

"Yes, paid." His voice was still oily, but an insistent note had crept into it. "We've spent two days together now. Naturally I expect to be paid. This is my first job as a guide. If you pay me I will never forget you."

I was speechless, first with disappointment, then with anger. I told him I had no intention of paying him even one yuan. He had not said in advance that he was a guide, besides which I was under the impression that we had both profited from our conversations, since he had questioned me at length on all aspects of life in the West.

He persisted, obsequious but insistent. He had invested time in me. He wanted his money.

"Now listen," I told him, "I forgot to tell you that I also consider the hours I spend with inquisitive Chinese students as work. I'm a sort of teacher, you see. And my rates are high. I'm sure you can well understand why I didn't mention this before."

Xiao gaped at me.

"Now let's see. You charge 50 yuan per day, is that right?"

He nodded sheepishly.

"I'm a bit more expensive, but then I'm older and more experienced. I charge 100 yuan per day. We've spent two days in one another's company, so you owe me 100 yuan."

I held out my hand imperiously. "I want it now."

Xiao stared at the ground while the blood flooded into his pale face. Now he was the young man on the receiving end of a scolding. "Forgive me," he stammered, "I have made a big mistake. It is because I am so young. I am still inexperienced. I did not think you would be offended. You have taught me an important lesson today." He paused, then looked up: "Is my English good enough? Do you think I would make a good guide?"

Every Tuesday evening a little park beside the Jin Jiang river was the venue for a meeting of the "English Corner". All over the park, small groups formed and huddled together conspiratorially, an animated hum of voices rising up into the tree tops as they practised their English.

I was soon encircled by a dozen or so people who proceeded to bombard me with questions.

"Which English writer do you consider to be the best? Evelyn Waugh, Graham Greene or E. M. Forster?"

"Do you believe that family planning in China constitutes a violation of human rights?"

"Is it true that the German government rewards large families, with a view to the advancement of the Aryan race?"

There were also those who were plainly hankering after a good argument. The Chinese presence in Tibet was one topic that was on everyone's mind.

"We're trying to help the Tibetans," said one, "they are a great financial burden to us."

"China has no business in Tibet," I broke in, undiplomatically.

"Yes, but don't you think the Dalai Lama would be a totalitarian leader?" objected another, giving me to understand that China had invaded Tibet in the name of democracy.

"But don't you realize that the whole world regards you as a totalitarian country? Besides which you have almost totally destroyed the Tibetan culture."

"Ah, but that was the Cultural Revolution. It was just as hard on us. China suffered just as much damage as Tibet."

At this point a short, fat, bespectacled man dressed in a dark-blue coat and sporting a narrow, carefully tended moustache interrupted with a question he had obviously been preparing to ask ever since I had revealed I was a writer: "Dare I ask, whether you, being a writer, have had any romantic encounters with the other sex during your visit to China?"

"Oh, come on!" a young woman interrupted. "He's a serious person. Can't you ask him something worthwhile?"

A young man who introduced himself as a doctor spoke of the poverty that was rife in Sichuan. "There are some people," he said, "who are so poor that even though there are two daughters in the family they only have one pair of trousers between them and when one goes out the other has to stay at home."

His lecture petered out into a defence of family planning. Only the one child per family policy could save the country from the impending overpopulation.

"That's right," someone else agreed. "If we don't have family planning it will be a disaster for China."

People nodded emphatically. "Disaster," they echoed. And they all opened their eyes wide in horror as if the disaster had appeared right between their feet.

I went for a last walk with Shu, under the trees along the Jin Jiang river at twilight. I would take the train to Kunming the next day. Shu walked for a long time in silence, then he stopped abruptly in the middle of the path.

"This is very important," he said, as though speaking to himself. "I must get the words right." He looked me in the eye. "I cannot keep the money you gave me yesterday."

Trying to persuade him was a rather tricky balancing act in which I had to take care not to offend him. After all he had already told me that he was a person who had nothing to give in return.

In my coat pocket I had an envelope containing 800 yuan which I had exchanged a couple of hours earlier through a black marketeer on the street outside my hotel. The envelope also contained a letter in which I told Shu that I thought his treatment unjust and undeserved, and that I was sorry to see his considerable gifts being squandered. I went on to say that I realized that money was not the answer to his problem, but that it might at least make life more bearable while he gave some thought to his future.

For someone like Shu 800 yuan, the equivalent of $100, would be enough to survive on for four or five months – or he might use it to start up some kind of small private business. I was even rash enough to hope – although I did not say so in my letter – that this money might enable him to break the vicious circle of rejection and self-loathing from which he seemed unable to escape. A little freedom from Fate, that was all I was offering him. Or possibly this: the chance for a while of being a person who could give something in return.

I pulled the envelope out of my coat pocket and handed it to him. He took it without protest and slipped it, unopened, inside his jacket. It was time to say goodbye. I quoted the lines:

> There was never any more inception than there is now,
> Nor any more youth or age than there is now.

Shu continued:

> And will never be any more perfection than there is now,
> Nor any more heaven and hell than there is now.

Then we hugged one another and I watched him walk off towards the river, where the homeless hung out; uncompromising, proud and full of shame.

In the Heart of Civilization

THE RAILWAY LINE FROM CHENGDU TO KUNMING RUNS THROUGH some of the roughest terrain in the world. On average, about 50 minutes of every hour is spent in the thundering darkness of a tunnel. In between, a blinding light assaulted my gaze. It was hard on the eyes, yet I gratefully laid myself open to such an onslaught for a precious glimpse of the hidden countryside.

It was so overwhelmingly beautiful, whenever the train broke free of the mountains. A turquoise-green lake smouldered, its surface as smooth as polished stone, its shore dotted with unpainted boats, their grey wood looking as old as the landscape, a tableau forsaken by man. The mountains soared in massive escarpments the colour of old iron, criss-crossed by an arterial network of shining tracks. Figures with baskets on their backs worked their way up the slopes, on the point of disappearing into that vast landscape. Farmers swung their hoes heavenwards in great arcs on a tiny, square scrap of field; before them lay red dusty earth, behind it was rich, moist and black, freshly dug. Even at that distance I could see the power in their swing as they raised their hoes. I could not see the pearls of sweat on their upper lips, but they were there just the same, like the steady invisible drip that hollows out rock.

On a little bridge stood a soldier ready for combat: legs akimbo, bayonet fixed to his rifle, as stiff and theatrical as a tin soldier, his sole enemies in that deserted scene were the mountains themselves.

I saw the graceful terraces, their surfaces like blood-red, polished marble; the water over the red earth of the rice paddies reflected the evening sky.

Faces flashed by, closed off in a bruised way and I thought to myself: *We are far from civilization.*

Then I realised the perseverance it had taken to reshape these mountains and I thought to myself: *We are at the heart of civilization.*

The landscape magnified everything. The people looked as though they were the last human beings in a depopulated world, or the first in a world still waiting to be populated. A lone figure walking became the epitome of solitude; a child gathering plants in a field, an image of isolation; a grubby, ragged boy with an appallingly adult face which lit up as he waved to the passing train, an assurance of the capacity for joy; peasants lying side by side around a fire in the twilight, the embodiment of human fellowship. There was a timelessness about these people, more than in the mountains that surrounded them and which they were forever grinding away and down.

I awoke the next morning filled with elation. I had not slept in the darkness. All night I had drunk of that landscape and its ruddy glow.

Partisans of Love

THE BUS JOURNEY FROM KUNMING TO LIJIANG TOOK 18 HOURS, from noon to seven o'clock the following morning. I was unprepared for the rigours of such a journey, my uncommunicative fellow passengers, and the small and uncomfortable seats. I felt somehow displaced, jolted out of the mental rhythm of my journey. In Kunming I had taken it easy reading, writing letters and watching MTV Asia on the satellite television in my hotel room. A balance of some kind had been tipped. I had become too absorbed in myself and was no longer taking things in. The Chinese man on the seat next to me kept slumping against me in his sleep. I pushed him away – then caught myself waking from a doze to find my head on his shoulder. After that I was more tolerant.

I had not realized that we would not be arriving in Lijiang until 7 a.m. and I kept waiting for release from the cramped seats and the cold. The stars ran in sparkling waves across the clear night sky and far down on the horizon I spotted Orion and held him as my fixed point all through the night, until he keeled over and sank behind a mountain range. I keeled over with him and sank into my own gloom, brimful of self-accusation and reproach over real and imagined betrayals, until the voices in my head fell wearily silent. You are at the mercy of your past when travelling. It is all you have. You journey forwards in space, but backwards in time. Alien sights and sounds roll over you like a millstone, crushing your personality, the acquired habits, your so-called character, revealing it to be a fiction that can only be reinforced by familiar surroundings. But there was one thing left intact: a concentrated core of things left undone, suppressed, never spoken of to anyone else, but which, in the manner of a chain reaction, made you who you were. Time was when I believed that the only continuity to be found in my life lay in the mistakes I had made, and this I now saw confirmed. As a traveller you are nobody in the eyes of others. And in your own eyes: the accused. Hence the necessity of

85

travelling when young, with less history behind you. Then the journey may become a formative experience. Perhaps I was making this journey to store up future memories; in order, later, to yearn for the peacefulness of all these foreign landscapes which I was far too anxious and breathless to take in while actually looking at them, and which only became real once they had receded into the distance.

I may have been travelling in the hope that the dark core would be crushed along with everything else, for the voices inside my head would not leave me in peace. You learn to value company when travelling. Solitude is a grand idea, but also something to be on your guard against. The ability to be alone with yourself should not be learned, since no one should be left alone with their executioner. But this was the very situation in which I had put myself. And then there was just one dream left: the dream of disappearing. You had to have the will to let yourself be crushed. Completely. But who was strong enough for that?

Eventually I fell into a deep sleep which nonetheless seemed to last only seconds before being broken by our arrival in Lijiang. The air was thin and keen and the cold chafed at my face and fingers.

It was an hour before daybreak and there was a faint blue cast to the darkness. A fire blazed in the middle of the street. Around it hovered black silhouettes, the murmur of voices. A woman emerged from the dense gloom between some buildings and passed through the light cast by the fire. In her long skirt and fabulous headdress like a medieval burgher's wife, she appeared to glide rather than walk over the ground. A triangle of stretched fabric framed her sharply defined features, to which the flickering light of the fire lent an appearance of unfathomable mystery. Then she vanished into the dark like some creature of the night as it senses the approaching dawn.

I was awoken by hunger at noon. The wood panelling in my room was yellow with age, the ceiling decorated with plaster curlicues and dragons. The mosquito net, a canopy of dove-grey muslin, was suspended over the bed, ready for the summer invasion. The little window offered me a view of upswept rooftops and, beyond, the jagged, snow-covered peaks of the 5,000-metre high Yolungxue Shan, Jade Dragon Snow Mountain, towering above the valley in which Lijiang lay.

I could have done with more sleep and was in no condition to sift through my impressions of the place as I walked along a broad boulevard flanked by ugly, new concrete buildings, in search of somewhere to eat. Everything had the washed-out look of the morning after the night before. Was my mood colouring my surroundings?

I had not spoken to anyone for days as I made my way around the little cafés in Lijiang. All of them catered for Western tourists, with menus that represented a primitive decline from the refinements of Chinese cooking; a peculiar form of gastronomic regress in which the forbidden favourites of early childhood became the chosen travelling companions of adulthood: milkshakes, banana splits, yoghurt with heaps of fruit, half-cooked pancakes which were far too thick and drowned in layers of chocolate or honey. It was the culinary Internationale of an infantile age; a language with all the universal appeal of Coca Cola or McDonalds.

The old town of Lijiang was a maze of grey stone houses and whitewashed walls. Its cobbled streets were narrow, but did not seem either poky or gloomy. Reflected sunlight played across the white walls. The sound of running water issued from the innumerable canals and gutters, down which it rushed through the steep streets. Women squatted on their haunches, washing or rinsing vegetables. Men, too, were busy washing clothes. The sound of bicycle tyres on cobblestones, a quacking duck, footsteps, small, intimate sounds, which carried with perfect clarity on the still mountain air, pervaded the town. As did the smell of dust and the acrid odour of woodsmoke. A solitary puff of wind brought with it the scent of a joss stick from an altar behind the whitewashed walls.

The very shadows seemed to give off light, reflecting the seething blue sky that arched over the whole scene, as only the sky over mountain regions can. The light streamed down over the town and made you feel as if the universe were close at hand; not the dark, star-studded canopy of night, but a universe in which bright and endless day prevailed. And the Naxi women's thick aprons and blouses took their colour from that cerulean universe, as if they had stood, on tiptoe, on the mountaintop and gathered it.

The trees had just come into leaf, their branches decked with tender, bright-green foliage. A soft breeze set the long branches of the weeping willow swishing across the sparkling, fast-flowing water in the canals and if you followed the canal you soon found yourself out in the open countryside, where everything was green and Jade Dragon Snow Mountain leapt up towards the heavens.

There were about 250,000 Naxi people, and of these the majority lived in the Lijiang area, although they had originally entered the country from Tibet. Theirs had once been a matriarchal culture, but things changed when the Chinese invaded the area in the eighteenth century and ground the Naxis under their heel. Prior to this a man would spend his nights with his intended, but his days working in his mother's house. No great effort was made to establish paternity, since the succession passed through the female line. Some matriarchal features were said to have been preserved, and I took the large number of men washing clothes along the canal banks to be a vestige of days gone by. The female influence also manifested itself in the language. A feminine suffix to a word increased its value, a masculine one had the opposite effect. Add a feminine suffix to "stones" and you had "boulders". Add a masculine suffix and you had "pebbles".

The Naxis possessed a unique written language, the only one in the world to consist of pictograms, in which – as with the hieroglyphics of Ancient Egypt – signs take the place of letters. The signs were simple and easily recognisable. More often than not a sentence resembled a rebus or a cartoon strip. Only cultural differences prevented you from getting the gist of the message straight away. Their pencil strokes and characters bore a certain resemblance to the works of Miró. Their coloured inscriptions, on the other hand, called to mind Paul Klee's quest for an archetypal primeval symbolism. The human body cropped up everywhere in the pictograms. As did the ox, the plough and the rain, which always fell in three parallel drops. The lake, not the sea (which they had never seen), was depicted as a rolling wave; snow by three tumbling snowflakes. The firmament was like a pagoda roof; spring: melting ice flowing past a pagoda; summer: rain falling from the sky; autumn: a bird taking to the air. The massive Jade Dragon Snow Mountain at whose foot the lives of all Naxis were played out was ever present in their pictograms. The rising and setting of the sun was represented according to its position relative to the snow-capped mountain, likewise to the phases of the moon.

I bought a scroll inscribed with a little epigrammatic legend. I recognized a full-length human figure, then a lily-like flower, a face, another flower, eyes, another flower and finally a sign I could not decipher.

The position of the flower kept changing. It began by tilting to the left, then it was standing upright, and finally it was leaning to the right. The translation read: "The beauty of the body is no greater than that of the face, the beauty of the face is no greater than that of the eyes, the beauty of the eyes is no greater than that of the heart."

The Naxi sign for happiness showed a man and a woman hand in hand, riding on the back of a flying crane.

In some strange way I could not help feeling that the picture of the mighty crane carrying off the lovers was also a reminder of death; a happiness which could know no place on earth, because the lovers were ultimately united only in death's all-embracing arms.

I do not know whether I was interpreting this correctly, but the pictographic Naxi sign language was closely related to the so-called Dongba culture in which love and death go hand in hand. The Dongba were peasants, doubling as part-time shamans, whose secret wisdom had been handed down from generation to generation. The influence of the Dongba became particularly marked after the Chinese quelled the Naxis and abolished the matriarchal order. Many Naxis protested against the introduction by the Chinese of compulsory marriages, and young lovers, who were forbidden to be together, chose to commit suicide. These double suicides were cloaked in religious ritual and as many as ten couples might commit mass suicide at an appointed spot in the mountains.

Unlike most other cultures, the Naxis did not take a negative view of suicide. On the contrary, ancestors who had committed "love suicide" were honoured and idolized. If the Dongba had supervised the suicide and seen that it was carried out according to the proper religious guidelines, then the lovers' deaths were in the nature of a divine wedding with the tomb as altar, in which the vow of fidelity was taken with a knife. In a paradise of the hereafter the loving couple would attain the happiness denied them on earth.

Love suicides became an institution in the Naxi society, and the influence and prosperity of the Dongba increased at the same rate. The pictograms evolved as a means of keeping track of the complex and increasingly lengthy rituals. So perhaps my intuitive interpretation of the sign for happiness was not so wide of the mark after all. It was death which carried the lovers off with great, lazy beats of its wings.

*   *   *

In his celebrated work *L'amour et l'occident* Denis Rougement asserts that love, or at least the word for love, did not exist in China. He cites various authorities in support of this, one of which states: "Chinese civilization has its roots in the family, and the family is founded on the absence of love. Chinese tradition insists on this point. Every and any show of tenderness between husband and wife is regarded as improper." Another source adds: "The concept of love does not exist in China. The verb 'to love' is only used to define the relationship between mothers and sons. A husband does not love his wife. He may entertain a greater or lesser affection for her."

Rougemont goes on to say: "The Chinese are married off by their parents at a very early age, but even so love does not present itself as a problem to them. They do not need to spend their whole life chasing love's elusive shadow which, while it is the most vague and indefinable of all our emotions, nevertheless is the one in which we seek comfort."

And the young Naxis? Were they partisans for love, rebelling against the lovelessness of the Chinese? Knife to the breast, were they martyrs to not one but two affairs of the heart, both patriotic and romantic, for having been unfortunate enough to have been invaded by a nation that knew nothing of love? Here, far from Europe, in a remote valley on Tibet's eastern frontier, in the shadow of the Jade Dragon, had there once existed a liberation movement composed of Romeos and Juliets, and had an obscure national epic been written, not with warriors as its main protagonists, but lovers; not with victories proclaimed on the battlefield, but tender words whispered in the heat of an embrace? Had such a thing really existed, a patriotism built on whispered pillow-talk, with the bedsheet as its banner?

The wave of suicides among the Naxis continued until the beginning of this century, at which time the newly proclaimed Chinese Republic, which had assumed control on the collapse of the empire in 1911, forbade the Dongba's activities in an effort to end the suicides. As far back as the 1940s, Joseph Rock, an American botanist who lived for over 20 years in Lijiang – using it as a base for expeditions – was able to report that there were very few Dongba left and, consequently, not many guides to assist the young lovers on their perilous voyage to romantic bliss in the hereafter. (It was the quest for traces of Joseph Rock's world that drew the English writer Bruce Chatwin to Lijiang in 1986 and, behind Rock, was another figure whom Chatwin was pursuing: Ezra Pound, who had acquired a copy of Rock's eccentric book on the Naxi culture, *The Ancient Na-Khi Kingdom of South West China*, in the 1950s. This book was a source of inspiration for Pound. He created a kind of spiritual home for himself in the Lijiang that he would only ever experience through Rock's craggy prose, but which he resurrected in his *Cantos*).

The Cultural Revolution did what it could to eradicate the last remnants of the Dongba culture. Then the backlash came. It dawned on the Chinese authorities that a unique culture was about to be lost for ever and the world's last symbolic language was in danger of becoming lost to the world just as hieroglyphics had been until the discovery of the Rosetta stone.

In the park that runs down to the Black Dragon Pool stands the Dongba Research Institute. A small pavilion acts as a repository for Dongba manuscripts. Outside the pavilion a group of old men sit warming themselves in the spring sunshine. They may be the only ones left able to read the contents of those pages saved from destruction. The guardians of Tristan and Isolde in all their senile desiccation, national archivists of the most romantic rebellion in the history of the world.

The Music of Old Men

ONE OF THE ATTRACTIONS OF LIJIANG WAS NAXI MUSIC, PLAYED on instruments that were centuries old. The orchestra gave concerts twice a week, led by an 87-year-old wearing a leather cap with ear-flaps to protect his ancient skull in all weathers. There were 15 musicians in the orchestra, all of them sporting wispy goatees and dressed in threadbare, blue work jackets which gave them the look of Maoist sages who, in contemplative deference, had turned their back on earthly matters in order to dedicate the last vestiges of their attention to the worn-out instruments which they tenderly cradled in their wrinkled hands. A tripod censer stood on a table in their midst, alongside flutes, string instruments and cymbals.

As a rule these concerts were preceded by a short talk from Mr Xuan Ke, proprietor of Lijiang's folk museum. But he was away from home and in his absence a young girl made the introduction in hesitant English.

As she searched for her words, I caught the beauty of the melody contained in the Chinese language when, as here, it was compelled to falter and feel its way. The girl's diction and rhythm were pure Chinese, with a softness to the melody that seldom came through in the raucous everyday conversation of the Chinese.

Her English sentences were infiltrated by stray words that cropped up at random. The word "not" was one of her favourites. "This music is very, very not interesting," she said with a smile.

She pointed to the audience. "Where are you not from?" she asked two podgy young men in the front row.

"Israel," one of them replied.

"Ah, Iraq," she nodded knowingly. "Yours is the country which likes war."

The two Israelis protested. It was only a couple of years since Iraq had fired Scud missiles over Tel Aviv.

She nodded eagerly. "Yes, yes, not Iraq." For the rest of the proceedings she referred to the two young Israelis as "our visitors from Iraq". I was convinced that she was doing it on purpose, just as her wanton treatment of the English language was simply an excuse for sabotaging the whole show. She was a closet Red Guard born 20 years too late to wreck the concert with a hammer and so she had resorted to words.

I became quite sure of this when she explained that the traditionally minded Naxi music, its harmonic style unaltered for hundreds of years, had actually sprung from oppression. It was religious music, and so great was the power of religion that no one dared to alter a single note. "It is very sad," she said in her naïve English, for once forgetting her haphazard negatives, determined not to be misunderstood on this point, "when people lack the courage to change things." And her lovely red lips executed another sweet smile.

Unaware of the accusation of cowardice that had just been levelled at him, the second oldest member of the orchestra, an 82-year-old with a gaunt face and heavy black glasses in sharp contrast to his snow-white hair, made a little speech about the significance of the music and the spirit in which it had been created. "We Naxis are honest and pure," he said, "we do not change. Our music is played with the soul and the heart. So we must listen with the heart."

I observed the old men, few of whom were under 70. They seemed both monumental and frail, their parchment-like skin stretched taut over high cheekbones and sunken cheeks; hardy survivors to a man. No doubt they would also survive the young lady's anger.

The music struck up. It pulsated with a heavy beat that forged ahead with measured, stately strides. It was not the sort of rhythm that carried you away, but it was insistent. It spoke of power and destiny, in sweeping, ceremonial circles. It was religious inasmuch as it had been ritualized.

The old men did not abandon themselves to the music; on the contrary, they seemed to be numbed by the majesty of it all. They closed their eyes like sleepwalkers. They were instruments playing other instruments, utterly devoid of any individual life.

Between each piece of music, a flautist would come to life and say a few words. The others sat perfectly still, their eyes closed, listening intently. "We wish to express our wonder of God," he said. "Our

93

orchestra's leader is very old, but his eyesight is keen and his hearing perfect. He has the music to thank for all of this."

Quite a few of the pieces had titles that pertained to water, "A Man on the Bank of a River" or "The Wind over the Water". And the music did indeed remind one of water, falling from above and sweeping downwards in great cascades, like rivers in springtime, swelled by melted snow. But even the eddies in the heavy surge of the music were part of a ritual, and every droplet of water thrown up to hang in a cloud of mist above the sudden plunge had its own appointed place. This was the music of old men, not because it lacked vigour, but because it spoke of life as fate, something that only the old can understand.

The young woman with the lovely lips had been right to challenge them. There was a sound instinct in the teasing, verbal guerrilla war she waged against this impregnable fortress of inviolable and intransigent music.

I later learned that Naxi music had no origin whatsoever in the ethnic Naxi culture. It was in fact temple music from ancient China where it had been performed at the Imperial court during the Han, Song and Tang dynasties. This was a process one observed again and again. The culture of the overlords lived on among the people long after the lords themselves had gone, and gradually the people came to adopt it as their own. Finding a fragment of their oppressor's soul on the road, they hid it in their own breasts, unwittingly becoming the custodians of a culture that had long ago been spurned by its originators.

The Biggest Tiger in the World

OVER BREAKFAST IN MAMA FU'S CAFÉ IN LIJIANG I FELL INTO conversation with a Scottish girl called Sandra, a town planner from Glasgow who had set out to cycle round the world in 18 months. She had cycled through Malaysia, but had given up China as a bad job: there were too many bureaucratic restrictions placed on foreigners – or foreign cyclists at any rate. Australia and Canada posed her greatest challenges. A raw-boned girl with a long face, milk-white skin, freckles and a mop of strawberry-blond hair, she sent me a warning glance when she happened to mention her "boyfriend". Baffled, I asked how any relationship could withstand an 18-month separation. She replied that they had celebrated New Year together in Hong Kong six weeks earlier and that in any case usually she only saw her boyfriend every three or four months. I could see why she had a passion for cycling around the world.

At Mama Fu's everyone was waxing lyrical about the famous Tiger Leap Gorge, a section of the Yangtse, roughly 100 kilometres away from Lijiang. The cliff walls shoot up 3,700 metres over the river at this point, not far from its source in eastern Tibet where it has gouged its way deep into the mountains. My travel guide mentioned in cautionary and yet tantalizing terms "the somewhat dangerous trek that attracts daredevil trekkers from around the world" and added that it was not recommended to anyone "susceptible to vertigo". Having read this passage several times I concluded that Tiger Leap Gorge was one of those things in life I would never attempt, like skydiving or becoming a black belt in karate. But then I surveyed the visitors to Mama Fu's café. If they could do it, so could I.

We left for Tiger Leap Gorge mid-morning in a rented mini-bus. As well as Sandra and three young Englishmen we were joined by an Italian girl and three Hungarians who were all studying Chinese in Shanghai, and a Dutch couple whose attire – red, turquoise and purple jackets and overtrousers – and excessive baggage, which seemed to include the stock of half a sports shop, made them look as alien as Martians. Lastly, there was Francisco, a mild-mannered, introspective Spaniard who had studied classical guitar in Barcelona for eight years, but had always been so dissatisfied with his own abilities that he was eventually persuaded to take over the family farm. Now he grew cherries and olives while his dreams faded away and his fingers lost their suppleness.

In blizzard conditions we ascended a ridge in order to reach the mouth of Tiger Leap Gorge, passing sloping meadows in drab, wintry hues, with an occasional house that could have been mistaken for a pile of timber. Cowherds draped in voluminous, sodden hides resembled walking stacks of mouldy hay. Long-haired cows, dripping wet and gaunt and as light-footed as goats, clambered rather than walked up the precipitous mountainside.

The snow lay thick as we climbed higher. Monumental pine trees, long strands of moss hanging from their branches, were shrouded in white. In many places the steep dirt road was partially blocked by fallen rocks. On the other side of the ridge a valley afforded us a magnificent view, bright with all the colours of the spectrum. At the very top were the white-peaked mountains; farther down, where the snow was less tightly packed, the mountainside showed through in a sharply contrasting mosaic of black and white. On the valley floor the rice paddies shone bright green, encircled by slopes covered in blue vitriol soil, and the iron-hued massif rearing up on the other side of the mountain was criss-crossed by a glittering web of streams that had worn their way down the rock face.

Way off to the west, at the farthermost end of the valley, shimmered the jade-green waters of the Yangtse and beyond them the steep sides of Tiger Leap Gorge faded into midnight-blue shadows. A storm was threatening, many kilometres away, clouds hanging low on the horizon, as if the daunting landscape had found its equal in the sky.

Palms grew at the bottom of the valley, and little gardens sheltered behind tall thickets of cacti. The houses were solidly constructed from undressed grey stone. Although many were new, they were built in the traditional style with tilted roofs and wood-carvings on their gable-ends. A broad and dusty main street ran between rows of low houses. This was the village of Daju.

When we reached the Yangtse River and a waiting ferry an epidemic of mistrust broke out. The propeller was being repaired, one of the ferry-men informed us. We would have to wait for tools and spare parts to be collected from the village. The Dutchman, a former mechanic, waded out into the water to inspect the propeller and declared there was nothing the matter with it. We looked at each other. "They're making it up," someone said. "Out of spite," said another. "Because they can't be bothered," added a third. "To annoy us." "To con us." Only through hostility towards those around us could we be certain that – in this alien environment – we were still ourselves. We sat in the sand, resigned to a pointless wait, the apathetic victims of an obvious conspiracy.

A shout came from the top of the slope and a man bounded down through the soft sand with a sack over his shoulder: tools and spare parts! Ten minutes later we were out in the middle of the river. It was a tribal ritual we were performing.

The ascent on the other side was tough and left us soaked with sweat and red-faced with exertion. Faint from the altitude and the physical strain one of the Hungarian girls threw up. Rain began to fall in great, heavy drops as we made our way across a grassy plain bounded by mountains on all sides. We climbed through terraced rice paddies and past a small village as close and humid as a stable, redolent with the pungent smell of animals and people, riddled with muddy rivulets coursing between the cobbles. The houses glistened black in the rain. We were to turn off when we came to three small windmills. Beyond these the terrain opened out again. The proportions were immense. On the one side lay the valley we had just left, on the other the entrance to the gorge. The predominant colour was a mellow rust-red, but the path we followed was turquoise. I deliberately lagged behind, wanting to be alone with the mountains. Far ahead the tiny figures gave me some idea of the scale. My head reeled, not so much from vertigo, as from an inner intoxication brought on by the combination of the thin air and the lavish landscape.

Then I saw the tiger. On the other side of the gorge the massive cliffs reared up in a strange and splendid alternating pattern of black and faded yellow: the tiger's flank. Only now and then, when the layer of cloud broke above, did I catch sight of the snowy peaks. Everything here was too gigantic for the words "ravine" or "gorge" to have any meaning. The mountains seemed to have been used in the manner of building blocks, set one on top of another. They served as foothills, forerunners, to the tiger's flank that rose up behind them, precipitous and never-ending, like a dress rehearsal for the end of the world; a curtain of stone that one day would come crashing down with awful finality on the universe.

Late in the afternoon the wind rose and the rain intensified. The mountains before me disappeared in the drizzle. The cloud had closed in; far below the green and iridescent Yangtse river could be glimpsed through the storm. The umbrella I had brought with me was useless against the fierce wind.

Around half-past seven, just as the last of the light was fading, we came to another small village situated halfway down the gorge. A very hard bed at the Hotel North Face cost two yuan. The hotel had a balcony built from unpainted, weathered wood, with an elaborately carved balustrade, and it was here, seated at small, round tables that we ate a supper of rice and fried eggs.

Most of our party were on the last stage of their visit to China. Claudia still had six months left of her course at Shanghai University, but she had already made up her mind about the Chinese. If a Chinese man tried to befriend you, she said, you could be sure he was prompted by one of the following three motives: he needed to practise his English, he wanted you to do him a favour, or he hoped to form a relationship with a girl from the West.

The others nodded. They had all had bad experiences of the Chinese. The incident at the ferry was, in that sense, symbolic. They only remembered their own frustration and not that it had no real cause. The two Englishmen were the most defensive. Everyone else had to speak a language that was not their own and had thereby surrendered a little of their identity. The Englishmen, however, had not even had to take this small step into the unknown, which learning a foreign language always is, and had instead invested all their energy in establishing themselves as the majority and the norm in a country where they were in the minority and far from the norm. To them the English language was a means of domination. They wanted to discover the diversity of other cultures, but not the relative aspect of their own. Perhaps travel only really begins when one is compelled to speak another language.

Francisco and I were the only ones with a good word to say for the Chinese. It was not hard to see why his experience of China should have been different to that of the others. He was not that different from the

Chinese themselves in colouring and build – slim, dark, glossy haired, brown eyed and olive skinned – and he shared their somewhat reticent, yet smiling and receptive disposition. The Chinese with whom he had come into contact had simply behaved in the same attentive and discreet manner towards him as he had towards them.

The following morning I found that the village was full of cherry trees in blossom. The rain had ceased and the gorge was revealed in all its colourful splendour. Large and small mountains stood out in every shade of red, yellow, orange, spring-green and brown and beyond them the vast black and yellow-striped mountainside disappeared into the clouds. Sometimes women in blue would cross the path, descending from the upper slopes laden with high bundles of withered bracken. Seen from behind, only their feet were visible. In the wide-open spaces of the mountains they looked like strangely animated plants.

Along the last stretch the path was no more than an increasingly narrow ledge jutting out from a white marble rock face. On one side was a sheer drop to the sparkling jade-green ribbon of the river. I heard the distant sound of rushing water as an irresistible, untameable song. It had a joyous note to it that made me laugh out loud with delight at the landscape.

In the distance, great chunks of marble dislodged themselves from the path and launched into an endless, lingering plunge towards the bottom. It was the end of our trek through Tiger Leap Gorge: a marble quarry full of men no bigger than ants, swarming over the white stone, intent upon detaching a handful of dust with which to continue building civilization. The path widened out into a road. A yellow bulldozer appeared, then signs in English and Chinese warning of explosions and rock slides. We came to a marble mill with enormous saws that sliced through the stone while the blades were continually sprayed with water to prevent them overheating. The rain began to drum down on the corrugated iron roofs protecting the saws. On the road men in shabby jackets and baggy trousers stood in two rows, swaying back and forth restlessly, heads swivelling this way and that, while a hefty man in a straw hat made a speech. He stopped and uttered a short peal of laughter at his own joke. The men lined up in front of him responded with an echo, as if laughing to order. Then the lines dispersed and the men sauntered down to the marble mill, the icy rain plastering their thin clothes to their wiry bodies.

They were convicts.

A road ran up the slope and past the prison. From here I could look down into the yard where naked prisoners washed themselves at big stone basins. In the middle of the yard a pitch had been chalked out for some sort of ball game. The high walls around the buildings were topped with barbed wire. White insulator caps indicated that the fence was electrified. I saw no armed guards. Maybe in the Middle Kingdom there was nowhere left to run.

The rain let up for a moment and a rainbow arched over the prison. My journey in China was about to end.

As the Wall in Space,
So the Book Pyre in Time

IT WAS RAINING AGAIN. RED, YELLOW, BLUE AND PURPLE umbrellas were everywhere. The recent leaves on the trees had a delicate sheen and the water in the canals rushed along with renewed energy. In the shops people huddled round large pans filled with glowing charcoal that gave off a faint scent, a last reminder of winter.

I sat alone with my tea in Mama Fu's Café, a brazier at my feet. Outside huge puddles collected on the uneven cement surface of a public square in the centre of which a whitewashed statue of Mao raised a hand in salute. At the other end of the square, green baize tables had been set up in the shelter of a lean-to and while a placid Mao gazed out towards the far horizon, young men played snooker with easy professional movements and did not even glance in his direction.

I had bought a tape-cassette – *Picturesque Music of Tu Fu's Poems* – and after having inspected it thoroughly Mama Fu inserted it in the café's cassette recorder. The unfamiliar Chinese music seemed shrill and discordant to my ears, full of dramatic shifts in tempo that I found quite at odds with the serenity of Tu Fu's poetry. I had lived with these poems ever since saying goodbye to Shu in Chengdu and had come to know them well. They did have drama, but they were written as if hardship, grief and loss had never shaken the writer's sense of dignity. There was no screaming, no martyrdom, no heroism. Tu Fu had experienced warfare and had seen the dead lying on the battlefield. He portrayed the starving in the wartorn villages and the homeless in the cities, famished and freezing in the streets while "behind vermillion portals meat is left to rot". At the Imperial court he had been forced to kowtow to the men in power. He had known the occasionally desperate joys of alcohol. And always he had been alone, exposed to a chaotic world in which his roving existence seemed like an escape from the succession of disasters that constantly befell the Chinese people because of emperors as unpredictable as the vicious nature of the country.

Aside from a handful of optimistic poems from his youth, there is an ever-present note of longing and sadness in everything Tu Fu wrote; dearly bought insights into the fragility of life and his own powerlessness. This manifested itself most acutely in those poems in which he described his lengthy, often unforeseen separations from his family and belated reunions between people who had long since given one another up for dead. There was a feeling of vulnerability, not only with regard to his body as it succumbed to the effects of old age, but also his inability to protect those he loved. He had to watch several of his children die of hunger and had learned all about powerlessness from seeing those whom he loved more than life itself perish before his eyes, as if there could be no domestic bliss on this earth. Paradoxically, it was here, in his depiction of misfortune, that the serenity of his poems was to be found, in the assurance of his diction, the balance he creates between suffering and the poet's control of its expression in words.

Once again I read Tu Fu's poem "My Cottage, Alas! Damaged by the Autumn Wind" and the last lines, in which he dreamt of thousands of spacious houses offering shelter to homeless souls like himself and in which, according to Mao, Tu Fu demonstrated his altruism and his solidarity with those on the lowest rung of society. I had no doubt that he was indeed an altruist. But in the last lines of this celebrated poem Tu Fu does not dream of houses for everyone, only for scholars. For his own part, he could die happy, albeit cold and alone, if only this dream would come true. It was on behalf of his own kind, poets like himself, unheeded, unrecognized scholars that he dreamt it. It was respect for words and for learning that he spoke of when he saw a thousand buildings spring up in his mind's eye.

So the whitewashed man in the square had no right to appropriate Tu Fu. Mao preached hatred and distrust towards academics, and system-atized self-loathing and self-denial among intellectuals. The communist intellectual spent most of his time apologizing for the fact that he was an intellectual – a perpetual penance.

Nonetheless I could see the allure of the spiritual masochism inherent in voluntary submission to the authority of an illusory people. In this there lay release from loneliness and the responsibility that came with always being one's own worst critic. What intellectual had not been plagued by a nagging doubt as to their value in society? Now the question of responsibility and conscience had been resolved once and for all. The Party had taken that in hand. From now on a spiritual agency other than conscience came into play: the ability to believe and go on believing, to reject all the temptations of bourgeois thought – such as doubt, criticism and independence of mind. To be an intellectual and a member of a totalitarian Party was a contradiction in terms, since, having once acquired the Party's book, the intellectual laid aside all others. The Party Book was to him what the Koran was to the Mohammedan or the Bible to the Christian fundamentalist, and all the libraries in this world were, in essence, unnecessary as far as he was concerned. He had renounced reason as a tool for the testing of the truth and yielded instead to the most anti-intellectual of all things, regression into blind faith. It is easier to live with faith than with reason when reason falls short, and that is precisely the dilemma of the true intellectual. Reason invariably falls short.

The failed intellectual will always be a potential book-burner. Contempt for reason is as intellectual an invention as reason itself. Hatred of bespectacled individuals is generated not among the peasants or the workers, but among failed students. It may well be the mob who shovel the books onto the flames, but there is always an intellectual to deliver an inflammatory speech by the bonfire.

The Chinese invented the book pyre. The self-same emperor Qin Shi Huangdi who made China a united nation and built the Great Wall also commanded that all texts written before his rule be consigned to the flames. It was perhaps no coincidence that the same man should have erected walls and burned books: as the wall in space, so the book pyre is in time. The walls shut out the outside world, just as the book pyre cuts off the present from the past, whose thinking and testimony are reduced to ashes. And what arises out of ashes? The Phoenix, the symbol of every totalitarian regime: to erase history and begin again from scratch at the year zero. Emperor Qin Shi Huangdi himself must have realised that there was a connection between his desire to build a massive defensive wall and to burn the books of the past, because he sentenced anyone found in possession of these forbidden books to forced labour on the Great Wall, of which it has been said that every stone laid on it cost a life.

The Cultural Revolution was nothing but an enormous book pyre. "Remember first to possess his books," Caliban tells his confederates, instructing them in the murder of Prospero. That was how Mao spoke of his opponents. Tu Fu on the other hand had been on Prospero's side.

The tape of "the picturesque music" had come to an end and Mama Fu brought me my food. It had taken her an hour to prepare, because she never put the dough in the oven until a customer placed an order. This may have accounted for her lack of customers.

The helping I had been given was so big that I could not possibly eat it all. Papa Fu suggested I take the rest away in a doggy-bag. Mama Fu, who had a better head for business, proposed I should come back and eat the rest the next day.

"Tomorrow I'll be gone," I said.

Out of the Clay Pit

ONCE AGAIN I FOUND MYSELF STUCK IN THE MIDST OF THE migration that appeared to have taken over every small village in China in this time of change. There were vehicles of every description, lorries full to overflowing, pick-up trucks, buses and weird, home-made contraptions that looked like a cross between a tractor and a lawnmower, with labouring engines and drive-belts exposed; all loaded with humanity, the seemingly inexhaustible raw material of China. Where were they heading? Into the future!

Young girls with ponytails and the straps of their tight ski-pants hooked under the soles of their shoes minced their way self-consciously between men and women carrying on their backs chip baskets full of cauliflowers or large rocks or children. All of them were inching forward, crowded together, as though the streets were a narrow gateway, forcing them up against each other. Most of them had the rudimentary features of peasants, like the teenage boy in the seat next to mine, whose face was comprised of nothing more than a snub nose, a downy upper-lip and a gaping mouth which stubbornly remained set in the same position for the whole of the eight hours we spent sitting side by side. The Creator seemed not to have devoted too much attention to these faces, whose souls were not yet fully awake.

I saw two blindfolded water buffalo working in a circular pit. They were kneading the clay with their huge hooves, rendering it soft enough for making tiles. Strips of mud-coloured cloth had been bound round their eyes, for only their blinded state prevented them from going mad from the monotony of walking around in circles. This was the eternal slumber of poverty, the blind round of toil, from which the masses occasionally roused themselves, wakening to hopes and victories, fresh disappointments and defeats. Right now the press of people around about me was in the process of climbing out of the clay pit, in a gradual awakening, with open mouths and unfinished faces, all of them, for an instant, equally youthful, even the old people to whose faces a life of drudgery had otherwise lent character. Where were they bound? For the most uncertain and indefinable of all things – the future.

Halfway up a winding mountain road we came upon a large, black saloon car with tinted windows slewed across our path. The front end was completely smashed in; the driver's seat was empty. There was a man sitting to one side of the steering wheel, his head fallen back against the headrest, as though he were sleeping.

Further round the bend a lorry was drawn up at an angle. In the front seat two men sat still as statues, staring into space. Their faces were blank and unfathomable, they might have been in a trance, or perhaps the crash had called down a curse upon them.

The traffic swerved slowly round and past them. No one stopped to help. It was as if the passing motorists were afraid of being struck down by the paralysis that is always brought on by the presence of sudden death.

A Blessing for the Traveller

AN AVENUE OF FLOWERING MIMOSA. IT WAS SPRING AGAIN! An overpowering scent had pervaded the countryside and driven winter back up the mountain slopes. Then: a rosy peak. The blue leaves of the eucalyptus trees.

Three pagodas. I counted 14 storeys, each lower than the one before, with the result that even from a distance I had the impression of standing at their feet, head tilted back, and seeing them tower, foreshortened, above me. I would never have the chance to take a closer look at them. Already they were falling behind. That is how I will always remember them. From the perspective of the departing traveller, mysterious in their remoteness and rich in their mystery.

Such is the blessing we may grant ourselves: not to see everything.

CAMBODIA

Hour of the Tiger

I wish to leave a scar on the landscape here.
ANDRÉ MALRAUX, *La Voie Royale*

But see that you make no level spot of ground
that is not trampled over with blood.

LEONARDO DA VINCI
(*from a guide to painters on
the depiction of battlefields*)

Invention of a Nation

WHERE THE SHADOW OF OUR PLANE FELL ACROSS THE CLOUDS
a circle formed; an aureole of light that tracked our course like a gun-sight,
gliding over the impenetrable clouds in search of a target. A gap opened
up in the cloud and the aircraft's shadow dropped and dwindled as it flew
over jungles and sun-baked plains far below. Then the clouds gathered
again and the dark crucifix of the aeroplane's shadow leapt up at us,
spectacularly magnified, while the refraction of the sunbeams in the dense
mist reignited the rainbow aureole.

There was a crowd outside the little airport. Taxi drivers were asking
up to $25 for the short run into town. A gang of youths with Honda
scooters were hanging about a little further off and one of these, a tall,
well-built man with wavy hair, offered to take me in for just $5. I
wondered whether he might have French blood in his veins, even though
he had the dark skin and hair of the Cambodian. It was from him that
I was later to hear the most scathing assessment of the country, said with
the annihilating yet resigned fury that drives people into exile or disaster:
"Cambodia no good!"

Angkor Wat lies about five kilometres from the village of Siem Reap. The
broad, tree-fringed thoroughfares of Siem Reap were peopled with lean
matchstick men, their faces contorted as they lurched along on wooden
crutches, their empty trouser legs dangling lifelessly. Some of them had
pinned up their trouser leg, or cut it off, as if they could no longer be
bothered to pretend they had two legs like everyone else. Their sunken
torsoes heavier than their remaining leg, they resembled swaying dashes,
stray notes blown off the music score by the war. The only thing keeping
them going was hunger.

They were the victims of war, but also of peace; everywhere they met
with rejection and contempt. The missing leg – in all probability shattered

III

by a mine – had cut them off from society; unable to work, they had become non-men. They begged, but there was something menacing in their desperation. They were powder kegs without fuses, not even capable of turning to crime.

It was the French who gave Angkor Wat to the Cambodians and with it the notion that they constituted a nation.

By saying that it was a Frenchman, in the middle of the last century, who discovered the immense, abandoned temple complex and the remains of what had once been a great city and the hub of an empire, buried deep in the heart of the Cambodian jungle, one immediately raises the question of what the colonialist actually does when he "discovers" something in the midst of an already inhabited country with its own ancient culture and history.

The story of the finding of Angkor Wat is a curious one, since the ruined city boasts quite a few discoverers. History, however, has chosen to nominate just one man. Diogo do Couto, a Portuguese, came upon the place as early as 1614, but the account of his journey was not published until 1958. A French missionary, Charles-Èmile Bouilleveaux found his way there in the middle of the last century and was overwhelmed by sadness at this scene of bygone grandeur, which had been deserted for centuries. At about the same time that Bouilleveaux published his heartfelt sigh at the relentless march of time, in the form of a little travel journal, Angkor was officially "discovered" by another Frenchman, the botanist Henri Mouhot, who entertained no notion of being the first Westerner to visit the place. Mouhot modestly stated that his sole purpose had been to "contribute to the expansion of our scientific knowledge" and, in fact, he died a year after making his discovery, in 1861, in the neighbouring country of Laos.

Why is a botanist and not a missionary remembered as the discoverer of Angkor? Possibly because the nineteenth century was more inclined towards science than towards the Church, and also because French colonisers saw it as their mission to spread the word of progress rather than that of the gospel. Modest Mouhot, who wished to expand the boundaries of our knowledge, was very different to the melancholy Bouilleveaux, whose ambition it was to increase the number of the baptised. It was not progress's mission to fill heaven with new converts;

it was to increase the number of subjects under French colonial rule. Progress cared nothing for the souls of the thousands of Buddhist pilgrims who travelled to the derelict temples in the Cambodian mountain jungle. It was more concerned about their hands, which for centuries had done little more than turn a clay pot, construct a grass hut or assume the intricate poses of ritual dances. The jungle ruins of Angkor Wat testified to the fact that these hands had once accomplished great things and it was progress's mission to set them to work as part of the French empire. That was the difference between the frail and unassuming Henri Mouhot and Father Bouilleveaux, who outlived him by several years and never ceased bemoaning the fact that he had been robbed of the credit for discovering Angkor Wat. Both were pawns in a game, but Bouilleveaux turned out to be a redundant pawn.

But for the French, Angkor Wat would never have re-emerged from the jungle. Strictly speaking, they did not discover it, but they did re-invent it. Angkor Wat came to have the same associations for Cambodians as the Louvre, Notre Dame or the new Opéra had for a nineteenth-century Parisian: not as a symbol of Church or Crown or of the more spiritual power of art, but the focus for a sense of national unity. The French gave the Cambodians the metaphysics of nationalism, embodied in the mighty towers that now came to light, liberated from the mountain undergrowth, and which would be depicted on the banners to which each of the opposing sides in the forthcoming civil war would swear allegiance.

The colonists gave the subjugated people an idea of history; a coherent sequence of events for which the nation provided the framework. Archaeology is like an acid bath. It strips buildings of the verdigris of piety, mystique and timelessness, and hands them back to history.

While the celebrated research institute, the École Française d'Extreme Orient was deciphering the ancient Khmer inscriptions and charting the line of the empire's rulers, they were also unwittingly compiling the manifesto for a nascent nationalism. Previously, the Cambodians had had no sense of their own past. Only those living nearby had known of Angkor's existence, and they believed that the colossal piles of stone had been put there by the gods. Now they realized it was their ancestors who had built them and that for six centuries they had been masters of the greater part of south-east Asia under a glorious succession of kings who appeared to have had no equals when it came to intelligence and vision.

And it was that single word "nation" that enabled them to go back about a thousand years in time and to identify with the people of a bygone age. It was their own talents and potential that they rediscovered in the towers of Angkor.

No one had stolen their history from them. They had never been aware that they had one. When the French presented them with a past they began to dream of a future. They entered the twentieth century, rudely awoken by an oppressor on whom they would soon be turning his own weapons, marching under a banner bearing a device drawn from his archaeological tracings, uttering slogans learned from his philosophers and political theorists, with an assurance that mirrored his own.

For Cambodia the result was not liberation but disaster. The revolution which was intended to give birth to a new society produced the opposite, a non-society, a nation that was to be the first of many more in the late twentieth century to embark on a suicide mission and which, even now, does not resemble anything like a humane society.

The immense ruined city of Angkor Thom itself provides some evidence of this suicide mission. It is not visible to the untrained eye, but if one has reference to photographs it is plain to see. Here is a photograph of a jaunty, beaming Prince Sihanouk, taken in 1973. He is shown a few kilometres from Angkor Thom, in the little temple of Banteay Srei, wearing a Khmer scarf, a Mao cap and the uniform of a guerrilla. He is making a propaganda tour on behalf of the Communist partisan groups within the Khmer Rouge with whom, for tactical reasons, he had sided against the Americans after being overthrown in a coup. Based in Beijing, he has been travelling about the jungle with the guerrillas for a fortnight, having been smuggled into the country along the Ho Chi Minh trail. Banteay Srei, also known as "The Citadel of Women", is so far away from Siem Reap that Sihanouk can move freely without risk of any immediate danger. I was advised not to visit the temple in the afternoon, as there were Khmer Rouge posts only a few kilometres away. (When I asked why it was safer in the morning, I was told that the guerillas slept late.) But why does Prince Sihanouk have his picture taken here, outside Angkor Thom and so close to the enemy? Because he is the nation's son and its ruler – and the temples of Angkor are a symbol of the nation.

In the background are some sculptures, human figures with the heads of monkeys, guardians of the minor temples. Those same pedestals are now bare, the sculptures gone. The anarchy that has engulfed Cambodia has swept the temple ruins along in its wake. If Prince Sihanouk had posed for his photograph on the same spot on the day I was there he would have found himself in an empty clearing.

For almost a thousand years the jungle, the relentless passage of time, battling armies and guerrillas had respected these fragile stone symbols. Today, when the guerrillas have nothing left to fight for, no one respects their symbolism. They were not sold to museums, for gone are the days when the West, as the inventor of History, used museums to promote its own view of evolution and progress, employing extinct or suppressed civilizations as examples. These missing sculptures simply circulate in the global market, prey to private international art collectors, owned by the few and invisible to the many.

I crossed a wide moat with cows grazing in its dried-up bed, then stepped out onto the huge square in front of Angkor Wat's stone mounds two to three hundred metres away. At that moment a cloud passed over the sun and the colours flared up in this world of stone as the harsh noonday light was blanked out. Pale sand, smouldering red, iron-grey and brown combined to give an impression of indomitable age.

A silence reigned here unlike any I had ever experienced, and there was not a soul to be seen. It was like finding oneself on St Peter's Square or Trafalgar Square knowing that Rome and London have been evacuated and that their greatest buildings are now no more than monuments to forsaken, forgotten civilizations.

I was surrounded by the sounds of the jungle: the unremitting rasp of cicadas and the screeching of birds, testifying to man's absence. The vast empty space in front of the temple seemed to gather to itself another, even greater silence that wrapped itself around you with an almost smothering urgency. It was the silence left by history at the point where it runs out and man has vanished, having left his mark all over the world. Only the great lost cities of Asia have the power to induce in me this feeling of the cessation of history, a sensation with which Asians are quite familiar, and which Europeans fear.

Only thirty or forty years before these buildings served still as the symbols of a nation's rebirth. After all the bombing and massacres, the archaeologists seemed simply to have laid bare the silence of history, as if having dissected a once vital body. I shuddered as another cloud hid the sun, but I knew the cloud was not the cause: I was shuddering at the sight of universal death, which the European is so unprepared for and can never accept, representing as it does a disavowal of the syntax of our way of thinking; the incessant, confidently optimistic manner in which we at all times keep our minds fixed on the future.

Angkor Wat was a petrified world. In the labyrinth surrounding the five vast temple towers – the middle one more than 70 metres high – it was not, in fact, life which was reflected in the innumerable bas-reliefs and sculptures. The contours of the flesh, reproduced in the voluptuous curves of the heavenly dancing girls, the apsaras; the delicate petals and stamens of the flowers, reflected in the soar of the columns; the balustrades, which looked as if they had been modelled on the work of the wood turner – all these gave the impression of a physical incarnation of silence, a petrification of time. This was a building that prophesied the end of all things, and it seemed quite fitting that the only people I eventually encountered there were ancient women with shaven heads, dressed in robes as white as shrouds and offering joss sticks and fruit to be sacrificed before blackened Buddhas bedecked with mouldering rags.

Running all the way round the main temple building of Angkor Wat was a frieze 800 metres long, a series of stone bas-reliefs depicting episodes from the Hindu epic poem the *Ramayana*. The predominant motif was that of war; murderers and victims, human beings and panic-stricken animals entangled in a huge mass of bodies, no longer capable of break-ing free of one another in the eternally re-enacted ecstasy of the scream, the killing, the extermination.

In the evening, just after sunset, I watched the full moon rising in the east, behind the temple towers of Angkor. A narrow sliver appeared behind the central tower. Then slowly the moon broke free and drifted off across the deep-blue evening sky, its fiery blush fading until eventually all that remained was a flat, cold, shimmering disc. Angkor's massive stone towers were left looming densely in the darkness, as if it were they and not the moon's fading disc that would live on for evermore.

* * *

Above each of the five gates leading into Angkor Thom – the fortified royal city once the heart of a megalopolis – a colossal face stared down. That same face reappeared all over another of Angkor Thom's famous temples, the Bayon, from whose 55 towers it gazed out to the four corners of the earth, 220 faces in all. No longer a decorative feature, the face had become the formative element of the architecture. It was not like the stupas of Nepal – where the nethermost section of the tower is painted with the features of Buddha – eyes and nose, like an upside-down question mark. Here, architecture had become physiognomy. On every side one was met by the aloof gaze of the towers, the same Buddhist smile, the wide, sensuous lips seeming to embrace both sublime wisdom and sublime pleasure, merging into an awareness of life which could easily be confused with cruelty and which may perhaps have been just that.

From a distance the Bayon resembled a ruin, a chaotic mound of rubble. The stones were overgrown with mosses, turquoise, white and black, which gave them a phosphorescent, emerald-green patina and made it look as though the jungle had grown back to envelop the Bayon in its gloom, the shadows of branches, creepers and leaping animals playing across its towers. When approached, the faces emerged from the moss and crumbling stone, time and decay having transformed them from dictates into enigmas.

King Jayavarman VII, who reigned during the late twelfth century, was the great builder and general of the Khmer kingdom, Kambuya, and regarded himself as the reincarnation of the Buddha.

The story goes that he was the rightful heir to the Khmer throne, but when his brother attempted to usurp him he abdicated voluntarily – true to his pious Buddhist beliefs – to save bloodshed and fratricide. He lived in exile for five years and did not return until he heard of his brother's death. He then discovered that another, equally shameless, brother had already usurped the throne, his predecessor's blood still warm on his hands. Again Jayavarman relented and not until the corruption and debauchery of his brother's incompetent rule led to the kingdom of Kambuya being overrun by its neighbours, the Chams, and its capital left in ruins, did Jayavarman assume the throne that was rightfully his. He repelled the enemy armies and also conquered Champa, which lay in what is now south Vietnam. He went on to extend his realm in all directions, invading Thailand and part of Burma, and shifting the northern boundary of his country as far north as China's Yunnan province.

Jayavarman was 50 by the time he took the throne, but he reigned for almost 40 years. He possessed unheard of energy and strength and he could do no wrong. Combining overweening worldly ambition and spiritual asceticism he ordered that the city he had rebuilt should take his face as its most salient architectural feature.

It is said that the Kambuya Empire reached its peak with Jayavarman VII and that he also brought about the downfall of the Khmer civilization. Seduced by his megalomania, it had exhausted at a stroke the resources on which it should have been able to draw for centuries to come. Angkor Thom survived for another 200 years, until the beginning of the fifteenth century, when the city was forced to surrender to an invading Thai army and the moss began to spread over the face of the reincarnated Buddha and world emperor.

Perhaps Jayavarman's conceited belief in his own divinity is the key to why he was forgotten, and with him the empire he encouraged to excess. The gulf between Jayavarman and his subjects had grown so vast that the people felt no pride in his temples. The work of their hands had not ennobled them, it had brought degradation and suffering. In the end, so estranged were they from what they themselves had created, it seemed natural for their descendants to assume that gods had built these buildings, which, with their menacing faces and labyrinthine colonnades, appeared to be part of a conversation which the gods were carrying on among themselves.

What was there for them to identify with once the great empire had collapsed? These stone temples into which they had never been invited, a kingdom which they had borne on their aching backs and which had never, in any true sense, looked upon them as its citizens. Thus Angkor Thom and the 220 faces of Jayavarman were left to the mercy of the jungle.

Unlike Jayavarman VII, the Khmers found true eternal life in the transience of all things: their own brief life span, the flimsy structures of their huts, the mirror-like surfaces of the rice paddies (shattered twice yearly by fresh green shoots heralding another harvest), the lumbering ox-carts which would remain unchanged for the next thousand years. And so life continued, generation after generation, in an eternal present in which wood outlasts stone and flesh and blood outlive the names of kings. While Jayavarman was never to live on, not even in memory, the ox-cart – depicted on the crumbling, weathered stone of his temple – continued undisturbed along the same dusty tracks.

Behind a door in the most central of the Bayon's 55 towers, dim corridors led to a series of small chambers where figures crouched before stone altars lit by oil lamps. The tiny flames dazzled the eye, increasing the darkness all around. A woman materialized in front of me surrounded by a cluster of half-naked children who scurried into the gloom like a litter of cubs. Back outside in the daylight, under the watchful eye of Jayavarman, I saw one of the children crawling on her knees over the verdigrised stones of the temple. From her ragged dress dangled one short arm without a hand. The other arm terminated in a lobster-like claw, the thumb folded over the other four fingers, which had fused into a stump. One of her legs was shorter than the other and furnished with a similar claw instead of a foot. She moved on her knees instead of her feet, but was so agile, cheerful, and playful, it was as though she were a perfect specimen of a unique species that felt just as at home in Jayavarman's jungle temple as any other creature.

The hundred or so temples in and around Angkor Thom were scattered over an area so large it was impossible to visit them all on foot. The young man who had driven me from the airport to my guest-house took me on his Honda round the temples, along roads that had once been tarmacked but on which no maintenance had been carried out for the past 25 years, so that they were now pitted with spectacular craters and watercourses. There were no monkeys in the jungle, its fauna having been enriched by another species: soldiers. The soldiers were to blame for the disappearance of the monkeys. They had hunted them, regarding their brains as a delicacy. We drove past Khmer Rouge posts no more than five kilometres away and there were numerous government army posts, although the soldiers themselves were not much in evidence. Either the posts had been abandoned or the soldiers were taking an afternoon nap, to escape the intense heat that made drinking up to five litres of water a day a necessity.

A few well-heeled tourists were looking at the temples accompanied by a uniformed guard with a Kalashnikov slung over his shoulder. This seemed an extravagant precaution, more likely to provoke violence were one to run into Khmer Rouge guerrillas.

According to the professional Asia experts, the journalists and photographers filling the newly opened guest-houses in Siem Reap, now was the time to see Angkor Wat, which had been cut off since 1970 when the Lon Nol overthrew Prince Sihanouk in an American-backed *coup d'état*. None of them had any faith in the idea that the UN-monitored election would bring new stability to the country and they all shared the same excited sense of catching Angkor during a rare hiatus in the permanent and bloody chaos of Cambodia.

I read the Frenchman Pierre Loti's book on his visit to Angkor in 1901, *Un pelerin d'Angkor*. Loti, a member of the French Academy, had travelled the world over and was already an elderly man when he spent a day at Angkor, having sailed up the Mekong river by steamer in the company of his French valet, his Chinese boy and a Cambodian interpreter. King Norodom of Cambodia had placed four elephants at his disposal for such expeditions, but Loti sat outside the temple which he had dreamt of seeing as a young boy and found it colourless and flat in the fierce midday sun: "It is not as I expected. It has undoubtedly come too late in my life and I have already seen too many of all these fragments of past grandeur, too many temples, too many ruins." What Pierre Loti saw was the impenetrable jungle, the ripped tree trunks on which tigers had sharpened their claws, the metallic glint of mosquitoes in the sun, foretelling of fever; the fragility of civilization. Fifteen hundred years the Khmer empire had lasted, he thought (in fact it was only 600), no more than a twinkling of an eye compared to the enduring life of the jungle vegetation.

What had been brought home to him was the tragic self-awareness of the nineteenth century; the European, who dreamt of becoming lord over nature and the earth and yet suspected rather than recognized his own isolation and vulnerablility, something which no conquest of new territory or new knowledge can remedy, since nature can never be brought totally under control and death never be postponed long enough. Such were the fearful phantasms by which the European must constantly have been haunted at his crowning moment as conqueror: that the entire world could not become one enormous Europe; that he, this restless Faust, could not stay awake 24 hours a day; that the night, the darkness, the jungle remained unconquered – also within himself.

The natives told Loti about the Hour of the Tiger. It was the hour when the tiger went on the prowl and claimed the deserted royal city for his own. Today the tiger is gone. Vanished, wiped out, vanquished. The elephants are gone, even the monkeys have been shot, the jungle is on the retreat, Angkor's uncovered ruins are surrounded by emptiness. From an ever-more distant forest fringe the tiger watches us, the tiger of memory, while timber-dealers all over the world take the vegetation hostage.

Not all temples were as well-preserved or as well-restored as Angkor Wat or the Bayon. There were headless Buddhas everywhere, and there was no way of telling whether time, bandits or roving guerrillas had been responsible for their decapitation. Whole passageways were blocked by gigantic chunks of fallen masonry. But this was not the result of some recent bombardment. The jungle, the rain and the wind had taken upwards of half a millenium to create a scenario reminiscent of an item from a television news broadcast.

In many places, banyan trees some 20 to 30 metres high had taken root on the roof of buildings and slowly forced the massive stone edifices to give way and collapse. Every stage of this process could be seen and often it appeared that at a certain point wood and stone had entered into a strange symbiotic relationship. Like a long arm ending down below in the vice-like grip of the huge roots, the tree seemed to be all that now supported the building, preventing it from tumbling down. Its walls had been completely encased in the steely corset of the roots and, conversely, the stability of the temple building – upright still, but riddled with cracks and partially caved-in – seemed to be a prerequisite for the continued existence of the tree. When the temple fell, so would the tree.

The roots, which ran above ground, measured as much as 10 to 15 metres in length, and often a metre thick, their bark pale and wrinkled as the trunk of an albino elephant. In tortuous, snaking coils they crept over stones and walls. It had taken them hundreds of years to cover a distance that an animal would have crossed in seconds, but the sequence of movements was the same. Here a root had insinuated its way over a wall, there along the ridge of a roof, here a pillar had been locked in an embrace, there a crevice unearthed. In one place a root had shot out into mid-air in a vain attempt to gain a purchase. Other roots that had not yet reached their destinations looked like hands trying to touch solid ground. It was as if nature itself had been inspired by the Khmers' elaborate architecture to experiment with new and daring forms. The temples dictated the movements of the trees. The trees dictated the ultimate collapse of the temples.

The archaeologists had left the Ta Prohm temple as they had found it. On this site they had not interceded on behalf of the buildings, hacking away at the trees. Faced with this surfeit of temples they had deemed that they could afford to leave one to rot and let the romantics have their way. In Ta Prohm the process of decay and the relentlessness of nature's assault on mankind's creations was quite plain to see, magnificent and beautiful. Here nature at its most splendid came face to face with a splendidly conceived work of man. The temple had stood here for more than 800 years. No tropical tree lives that long, not even the giant banyan trees which formed the front line in the war against the temples. But for every tree that fell, nature sent in fresh, new troops. Again they thrust against the stone, with trunks which were themselves hard as stone and yet running with sap. These colossal trees lived one or two hundred years before they came crashing down to make way for new growth. And bit by bit the stone yielded, first one crack, then another. It might hold out for another thousand years, before Ta Prohm at long last capitulated.

Among the tumble of stones in one of the smallest of Angkor's temples I came upon an empty pedestal. Its statue was gone, only a pair of feet no bigger than a child's still stood amid this petrified chaos. For the first time it crossed my mind that people had once lived here.

A Scar on the Landscape

NOT FAR FROM ANGKOR, AND EASILY REACHED BY WAY OF the dusty highway from Siem Reap, lies Tonle Sap, a vast freshwater lake abounding in fish. I had heard of the poverty to be seen along this route. As far as most visitors were concerned, this short stretch of sandy track represented their only encounter with rural Cambodia.

There was nothing here bearing any resemblance either to the West or this century. But was this poverty? A stream meandered along the side of the road, with spindly, lazily turning windmills lining its banks and little bridges spanning the green water. Colours were muted, ranging from dark-green vegetation and grey earth to sun-bleached cottages and the olive skin of the local people. I can reel off all the things that were not there: electricity, sanitation, tarmac. But why did none of this strike me as poverty? Had my reserves of pity been exhausted? Or was it this landscape's absence of history, a merciful relief after the stony realms of Angkor and the calamitous history of the Khmer Rouge? I knew that all sorts of diseases were rife here and that the average male life expectancy was 39 years, even lower for women. But I saw none of this. Did I not want to see it?

One enormous white UN truck after another drove past on the narrow, sandy track. The dust clouds they threw up had already covered the surrounding palms and houses. They reminded me of a herd of stampeding elephants, trumpeting the advent of a new age, grotesque in their intrusiveness, as if they arrived not with aid, but to flatten the place yet again.

On the lake shore stood a cluster of grass huts whose proprietors were all selling the same selection of beer and soft drinks. They did get tourists here, but not enough to justify the range on offer. Coca Cola and 7 Up seemed more like a lifeline to the world outside an isolated Cambodia; a hope rather than an opportunity to quench one's thirst.

The fishing village of Chong Rea ran out for several hundred metres over the muddy yellow waters of the Tonle Sap lake. There were hundreds of houses and houseboats, occupied by thousands of people. Some of the houses were built on stilts, most bobbed about on rafts that were kept afloat with the aid of empty oil drums. Chong Rea was a tiny, full-fledged world, complete with a red-painted wooden hut which served as the police station. Women sat, repairing nets, on a platform of bamboo suspended a metre above the lake waters. There were floating gardens with trees planted in oil drums, and a pig with black bristles lazed under an awning in its own small floating pigsty.

Being near water always seems to lift the spirits, holding as it does the promise of infinite freedom, of travel and adventure, and one could have been forgiven for thinking that all of the inhabitants of the village had actually embarked on a ship that had carried them away from Cambodia and into another, happier world. People popped up everywhere, smiling and waving at strangers, and the children's glistening, wet bodies reflected the sunlight as if they had been anointed with oil.

Farther out on the lake, where horizon and shore had faded from view in the glowing blue and white pastel tones of the noonday heat, yet another bamboo platform reared up out of the water, crowned by a tall, slender watch-tower from the top of which protruded the nose of a machine-gun. There was no one up there. Maybe the war really was over and no enemy was going to run out of the heat haze to challenge the machine-gun. Just as all that was left of Angkor Wat was the stone, so perhaps redundant steel was all that remained of the sufferings of past decades. Over at last, I thought, inspired by the solitude of being in the middle of the lake and seduced by the wavering heat of midday, which hid the shore from my eyes.

Eight hours later, long after I had returned to Siem Reap, a troop of Khmer Rouge guerrillas came along in a boat and set about massacring the defenceless residents of Chong Rea. The attack lasted half an hour. The guerrillas pulled back after killing 35 people, including a family of nine. No one came to the aid of the villagers. The Khmer Rouge had chosen its victims with care. They were all *yuon*, a derogatory Cambodian term for the Vietnamese. Even though these people had not come to Cambodia in the wake of the invading Vietnamese army in 1979, but had been living on the Tonle Sap lake for centuries in their floating homes, they, too, were victims of the wave of anti-Vietnam feeling rife among the Cambodians, who had barely recovered from the terrible trauma of genocide before they started looking for new targets for their hate. It was as if national unity amounted solely to being united against someone else. Not one Cambodian politician voiced any condemnation of the killings. Prince Sihanouk alone sent word – from Beijing where he was taking one of his innumerable cures – that he had some sympathy with the victims of the massacre – immediately adding, however, that the only sensible solution to the problem that he could think of was for the Vietnamese to leave the country without further ado.

Some weeks later in one of the international current affairs magazines, which I occasionally managed to track down on my travels, I came across a photograph of a flotilla of boats and floating houses making its way down the Mekong River. The villagers from the Tonle Sap lake had joined the world's great and ever-swelling stream of refugees and were heading back to the native land they had left three or four hundred years earlier and to which they were now strangers.

An unmanned rapid-fire machine-gun pointed straight up at the sky from the crest of a hill not far from the banks of the Tonle Sap lake. A cartridge belt laden with heavy ammunition sagged to the ground, as if the gun had stopped short in the middle of a salvo. The earth was littered with empty shell cases, but there were no soldiers to be seen. Not for the first time, Cambodia left me feeling as if I had stepped on board a ship that had suddenly been abandoned at sea, leaving only the smouldering cigarettes in the ash trays and dinner cooking on a stove in the galley. Only here it was the machine-gun barrels that were still warm; and the earth, red with blood, was a battlefield that had been deserted abruptly as if both sides had fled in horror from the evidence the blood-stained soil presented of their deeds.

A path ran into a sun-dried patch of scrub. Across the path hung a sign showing a white skull on a red ground. A warning: the area was mined.

Some way off stood the remains of a temple. The building had been new, not reduced to a ruin by time, but blown to bits by a bomb which had left only the outer walls and part of the roof intact, the latter held up by some primitive wooden scaffolding. Tufts of yellow grass sprouted from the tops of the walls. A half-naked Buddhist monk melted into the shadows of a lean-to. A cigarette drooped over the dark lower half of his face like a white plumb-line, the shaven crown rendered the line of his head clean and classical, giving him the look of a statue which had escaped the destruction.

The bombed temple was encircled by a collonade of blossoming frangipani trees. The frangipani tree has almost no leaves, and bears a huge and opulent snow-white flower. With its pale bark and sprinkling of flowers the tree conveys an impression of coolness rather than of luxuriance. Beneath a sun so fierce that it can make the sky burn white-hot, it husbands its resources in the midst of a flowering otherwise notable for its exultant abundance and extravagance of form. It was a tree that had elected to make a pretence of forever being on the point of extinction and, in what might have been its swansong, of having invested all of its energy and sap in these flowers, finery and mourning combined.

I could not help but feel that if there is one patch of earth in which one tree grows with some justification and with a greater right to be there than anywhere else, then it had to be the frangipani in Cambodia. Nature had endowed the country with this tree as a way of showing its sympathy for humanity, and its huge blossoms lay scattered over the earth at the foot of the ruined temple like a wreath laid on a grave.

Banteay Srei is about 20 kilometres from Angkor and it took some hard bargaining and more money up front to persuade my guide to drive out there along churned-up roads, long stretches of which bore no traces of asphalt or gravel, only sand. The scooter wobbled unsteadily on the sandy surface, slewing along between jungle and flooded rice paddies.

Five kilometres away from the nearest Khmer Rouge positions I saw a gang of soldiers dozing in the shade while children fiddled with their discarded Kalashnikovs, In the stillness and the heat, where everything seemed as inert as the stones themselves, the threat of violence seemed unreal. Six weeks later I read that this unit had been attacked and wiped out by guerrillas who had also advanced on Siem Reap and occupied the airport on the outskirts of the town for some hours.

Banteay Srei, a little temple built to a human scale, was originally thought to date from the late Khmer period, and its gracefulness mistakenly seen as a sign of decadence. The opposite was the case: Banteay Srei marked the beginning of the Khmer period, and its gracefulness is evidence not of degeneration, but of confidence and boundless energy, while the profusion of stones piled one on top of the other in monstrous shapes speaks of a power falling into decay. There was still a lightness about the working of the stone in the bas reliefs, in its tiny sculptures of people with animal heads and the lacy filigree of its doors – and, above all: no air of mortal dread hung over Banteay Srei.

This temple had not been built to evade time. Stone – the material of choice for those who believe they are defying eternity by reproducing the living, breathing world in the imperishable fabric of rock – had presented a different challenge to the hand of the artist. He had set out to impart a touch of transitoriness to the rock and endow the red sandstone with a delicacy it did not possess, by making everything so small and fine that it acquired a certain fragility: the dancers, warriors, horses and fabulous creatures no bigger than a hand. The feeling the temple excited was not simply one of admiration at the sight of a well-wrought work of art, but also the protective instinct aroused by a delicate flower made of porcelain.

In this lay the miracle. It seemed that the jungle, the wind and rain and remorseless sunshine had answered this prayer and by mutual consent had let time stand still. Here, in the heart of the jungle, alone and unprotected as a Chinese porcelain tea set stood child-size statues, human figures with the heads of monkeys and parrots, guarding their little temple, and time had bowed to them and left them untouched.

Nor had man laid hands on them, until recently. In 1923 the French writer André Malraux won notoriety for sawing off a chunk of the temple and transporting it to Phnom Penh where he was arrested and released only after appeals from a group of French intellectuals who evidently cared more about the fate of French literature than about the art of the Khmers. Malraux's experiences at Banteay Srei informed the novel *La Voie Royale*. Cambodia forms the setting for a drama dealing with the male death-wish, fear of lost youth and impotence, in which death, voluntarily sought, becomes the last, rebellious swipe at "man's fate", at time – "this monstrous thing" – the tumour that is spreading throughout the body and sapping it of strength.

In his game with death Perken, the central male character, feels the urge to leave "a scar on the landscape", on gentle, compliant colonial Cambodia which becomes no more than a tool and a victim in his own private existential conflict. This may also have been Malraux's dream when he left a scar on Banteay Srei, this temple which, unlike a body, seemed to have entered into a pact with time not to age.

This was before Malraux became involved in politics. He would later support the Chinese communists in their struggle against colonialism, but even when he was acting the part of something as despicable as a temple-robber his actions already had a symbolic dimension. At Banteay Srei he picked a flower, he deflowered a land, and it may be that Banteay Srei is one of the many places where the twentieth century prepares for its future atrocities.

An old man was showing people round the temple. He pointed out things that had once been statues, untouched for a thousand years. Now the pedestals stood empty, torsoes had been decapitated or heads halved, split down the middle, so that the face with its features was gone and only the anonymous back of the head remained.

"Stolen," he said, pointing. "Vietnam" or "Khmer Rouge".

The different temple desecrators appeared to have had their own particular methods. The Vietnamese had opted to slice off the head and leave the rest, the Khmer Rouge carried off the whole figure.

The old man spread his hands resignedly. "There have even been thefts from Conservation d'Angkor. The museum curator is in league with a ring of professional art thieves. The police have been bribed and don't lift a finger. It's a watertight system. Everyone knows about it, even UNESCO, who sponsored the restoration of Angkor. But it doesn't seem as if anyone can or will do anything about it. The man was on good terms with Pol Pot. He even managed to get on the right side of the Vietnamese. These days he's declaring himself to be neutral."

We had stopped in front of a fenced-off area. Beyond the stone wall the grass grew lush and wild. Two branches nailed crosswise barred the entrance. I pointed to the other side.

"What's in there?"

The old man struck one of his legs. "Boom!" he said.

I needed no translation.

Behind me my young guide hissed: "Cambodia no good!"

In the March 12th issue of the English-language *Phnom Penh Post* I read that a statue of a woman had been stolen some days earlier from the courtyard of Prince Sihanouk's summer palace just a few kilometres outside Angkor. Although the police station was 200 metres away and police guards had been posted 30 metres from the spot where the statue stood, no one had seen or heard anything.

Around the same time five heads were sawn off and removed from the gigantic statues ranged along the bridge that runs across the moat to the northern gate of Angkor Thom.

A month earlier about 50 armed men on motorbikes attacked Conservation d'Angkor with rockets and machine-guns and carried off eleven works of art from the museum's unique collection. Three people were killed and eight wounded.

The bandits behaved like an army – and the army like bandits.

Several times I heard young men in Cambodia say "Cambodia no good". In Phnom Penh I heard it from a young man who, like my guide in Angkor, had got hold of a Honda and was making a living out of tourism. I knew him well enough to know that his condemnation was not really absolute. He had been thinking of his youth, of his lost years, of his hopes for the future, which had been given a sudden boost by the arrival of the UN troops and all the promises of prosperity they brought with them. He felt Cambodia was holding him back and he longed to get away. But it was not frustration that had found a voice in my guide to Angkor when he uttered those same three damning words about the wretched country of Cambodia. That had been a more deeply ingrained and more comprehensive anger, which not only condemned the vandalism at Angkor, the Khmer Rouge's insane urge to kill, and the mines hidden in the lush, green grass, but which also seemed to equate the vandalism, the killing and the mines with Cambodia itself, in such a way that the soul of the country became indistinguishable from the darkness in which dreams of annihilation are born.

I could not blame him for such drastic equations when I thought of how as a boy he had grown up in the shadow of Angkor Wat's world of stone with its kilometre-long bas-reliefs depicting nothing other than the orgiastic delights of fighting and killing, and of how he had never lived anywhere but in a town dominated by the pathetic sight of one-legged men, victims of the same mines which lay in wait, indiscriminately and democratically, for everyone; not only for men-at-arms brandishing Kalashnikovs, but also for women, children and young men like himself. As a child he had probably experienced and seen things that were still capable of keeping him awake at night, perhaps even lost one or more members of his family, so systematic and sweeping had the slayings been that no family had been exempt, so why should he think any different?

The legacy of the Khmer Rouge had to be even more difficult for the Cambodians to live with than the legacy of the Nazis was for the Germans, because it was so much more baffling from a psychological viewpoint. There was no talk here of acts of violence perpetrated against people of another race, creed or colour, but of a kind of self-mutilation. Geno-suicide would be a more correct term than genocide. It was not the promotion of certain qualities or traits at the expense of others which had driven the Khmer Rouge to commit such wholesale slaughter. It had been the downright degradation of life.

My thoughts kept returning to the impression the scenes of life along the road to the Tonle Sap lake had made on me. Perhaps I had failed to see the poverty because the peaceful uneventfulness of the landscape made it seem as if history had taken a short break from inflicting violent turmoil.

In the West, poverty implies exclusion from so much that life has to offer: education, good health, social welfare – and on which the future depends. The poor have no time for anything but the immediate questions of naked survival. The first indication that poverty is lifting comes when people can start to plan for the future. It may, however, be no coincidence that the languages of south-east Asia (including Chinese) have no future form and, hence, no specific grammatical tense to use when speaking of what is to come.

Past and future always serve to provide a yardstick for the present time. They represent the optimistic and yet tragic conjugations of grammar. The concept of revolution represents the transfer of the future tense from grammar into everyday life, and in Asia the concept of revolution invariably arrived from the West, as an import from a foreign, but inflammatory grammar. "Loyalty to the future" is how the Australian historian David P. Chandler, in his book *The Tragedy of Cambodian History*, defines the sentiment by which the adherents of the Khmer Rouge were driven in the early 1970s and which to a great extent took the place of previous social ties. The concept of the future is also what eventually makes poverty intolerable, and indeed causes it to be felt as poverty at all, and not merely as a god-given state, a prime condition in which it is simply a question of endurance. Poverty means exclusion not just from wealth, but also, in the most fundamental way, from the potential for change, from the future. They have no future, we say of those in direst need, not because they are going to die tomorrow, but because their lives are static.

Perhaps that was what I had seen on the road to the Tonle Sap lake: a farewell to the future, the imperceptible healing of the wounds inflicted by a foreign grammatical system, a return to the pivotal points of the present – in other words, to that which we call poverty, which is also a kind of forgetting.

Propaganda with a Stammer

CHOUENG EK LIES SOME MILES OUTSIDE PHNOM PENH AND is better known by its English name, "The Killing Fields". Under the Khmer Rouge's Maoist inspired dictatorship Cambodia became one big killing field on which the regime committed murder as instinctively as its leaders drew breath. Indeed, the murders formed an integral part of the regime's respiratory system without which it could not have survived. Democratic Kampuchea, as the country was officially known, breathed through a mouth full of blood. Death was a part of this monstrous State's infrastructure in much the same way as road-building or the health service are in a normal society. Choueng Ek was the closest Cambodia came to a death camp, for although one and a half million people out of a population of seven million were killed (some sources put it at three million), placing the Cambodian people's bewildering bid to commit suicide on the same scale as the German production-line mass murder of the Jews, its implementation was not entrusted to mechanical efficiency but consisted of primitive, hand-to-hand killing.

Choueng Ek was not a camp, it was simply a bare, sun-parched field bounded by palms and rain-trees. Somewhere in the region of 20,000 people had been executed here, without a single shot being fired. All were prisoners from the notorious Security Prison 21, a converted high school in the centre of Phnom Penh, who had survived being tortured and now had an end put to their suffering, not with a bullet, but with axes, shovels, clubs, knives and old-fashioned swords.

The field was covered with hollow depressions in the bottom of which bits of bone could still be found. A number of signs provided terse details of the contents of the mass graves: 450 bodies here, 166 headless corpses there, 100 women and children, the majority naked.

In the middle of the field stood a tall, white-washed stupa in traditional Buddhist style. Windows ran all the way to the top of the tower and through the glass one could see yellowed skulls, 8,000 in all, placed on shelves and arranged by age and sex, but otherwise anonymous. There was nothing here, only the field and the graves. Death itself had had to supply the monument.

On the memorial to the dead hung a Red Cross poster: "Are you looking for your family? We can help you." Not everyone who came here was a tourist. The young man of 22 who had driven me to Choueng Ek had lost his father, his brother and his sister under Khmer Rouge rule.

At the entrance to Choueng Ek there was a plaque which, when one considered that its appearance had been supervised by the Vietnamese occupying forces, was remarkable for its choice of words. It began with a good helping of calculated political jargon. Then the propagandist seemed to have broken down under the weight of events that he was in fact only meant to describe in order to exploit them politically. Instead the sentences took on an oddly hesitant tone, religious images appeared, there was a halting quality to the wording as reason confronted horror. Here is man starting to stammer at the sight of himself:

> The method of massacre which Pol Pot clique was carried upon the innocent people of Kampuchea cannot be described fully and clearly in words because the invention of this killing was strangely cruel. So it is difficult for us to determine who they are, for they have the human form, but their hearts are demons' hearts. They have got the Khmer face, but their activities are purely reactionary. They wanted to transform Khmer people into a group of persons without reason or a group who knew and understood nothing; who always bent their heads to carry out Angkhar's orders blindly. They had educated and transformed young people and the adolescents whose hearts are pure and gentle and modest into odious executioners who dared to kill the innocent and even their own parents, relatives or friends. They had burnt the market place, abolished the monetary system, eliminated books of rules and principles of national culture, destroyed schools, hospitals, pagodas and beautiful monuments.

S-21: Where the World Vanishes

SECURITY PRISON 21 – S-21 – WAS ON A SIDE STREET IN PHNOM
Penh, where the unsurfaced road ran between concrete walls and trees
without any picture of a residential town emerging. The prison had been
set up in a former high school, a three-sided building of grey cement, built
on three storeys with external stairs and walkways. The lawn in front of
it was withered, and in the middle stood a dead palm tree.

The choice of a high school as prison and crime scene had a grisly
symbolism. The Khmer Rouge had plenty of buildings to choose from
in the evacuated city. Phnom Penh had been left practically deserted after
the great exodus of 17 April 1975, the day on which several millions
were forced to march out into the void and death reaped its first harvest
in what was dubbed, with gruesome irony, Democratic Kampuchea. A
high school is, of course, practical. The classrooms could be used as
cells and interrogation rooms. But a high school is also a place where a
society shapes its own élite, educating and grooming them for future
responsibility. It is a place where a young man or woman takes a crucial
step towards the wide world that waits outside – but with the Khmer
Rouge's entry into Phnom Penh this world no longer existed. The high
school, once a place designed for the building and moulding of the
character, became a setting for the obliteration of the character.

There is a logic to this, one which is classic and which in all modern
dictatorships is pursued in the executioner's choice of his instruments
of torture, that are rarely designed specifically for that purpose. Instead,
they are deliberately "improvised" or "primitive", everyday items
suddenly robbed of their normal function and turned into implements of
terror and pain; a bathtub filled with water, an electric cable, a bedstead –
all objects which, besides their safe, familiar function also stand as
symbols of civilization and comfort, part of a world in which we recognize ourselves and which tells us who we are. Now they became the

opposite, tools for the destruction not only of the body, but also of the world which that body had until now inhabited as such a matter of course: there is no bathtub, no electric cable, no bed, no civilization, no protection. Only horror.

In S-21, the tools of destruction were improvised from everyday objects – the bedstead, the cable, a hoe, a spade, barbed-wire whips, ropes – nothing sophisticated, all things that anyone could lay their hands on, a democratic DIY executioner kit.

The classrooms had been left as they had been found when the Vietnamese occupied Phnom Penh. There were fewer than ten interrogation rooms, but 20,000 people had passed through them. There were no dark cellars or dank, labyrinthine subterranean passageways. The windows were large. Detainees would have always been able to see the sunlight shining through them or hear the rain when the rainy season set in. But the deserted city itself had been silent, populated only by the executioners and their victims. The victims' screams were the only sound to ring through the empty streets and along the acacia-fringed boulevards.

The rooms had chequered tiled floors, yellow distempered walls, a silver enamelled bedstead, now half-eaten away by rust, to which an iron bar with two hooks was fixed. In this room children sitting at school desks had learned about the world. The bed was where this process was reversed, where, in the course of a few hours or days, the victim forgot everything he had ever learned; and what he was; forgot that he was a human being, finally becoming nothing but shrieking, bleeding, suffering, dying flesh.

In each room hung a picture. A photostat pinned to the wall, a photograph of the victim during the proceedings, taken by the torturers who, with bureaucratic zeal, kept a record in journals and photograph albums of everything, including the results of their own most monstrous acts. An electric current was passed through the bedstead. That was why it was so perfect for the job. Not that one could see that in the pictures. One saw something else. Large, black pools of blood beneath the bed; the victims themselves, their bodies twisted out of shape, soiled with their own blood. One face was an unrecognizable mask, a ghastly caricature in which the skin appeared to have been ripped off.

In the black and white photographs the marks of suffering showed up as flat grainy planes. There was so much black. Foolishly one hoped

135

this was due to poor reproduction, while knowing that the photographs mercifully disclosed little of the last journeys that 20,000 people had taken in these rooms.

The next room was larger and papered from floor to ceiling with photographs of the murdered; pictured, as in all classic recordings of criminals, face-on to the camera, chin slightly raised and the gaze rendered defiantly vacant, as if to shield itself from a groping hand, in precognition of the trial of strength to come. But these faces bore no resemblance to the standard pictures of terrorists and wanted criminals. The terrorists had been standing behind, not in front of, the camera; these were not photographs of criminals, but the documentation of crimes committed. These people were defeated, the trial of strength behind them, their resistance broken down. Their eyes told that story. One woman held a baby in her arms, doubly vulnerable with the life that she could not defend. There was a gaunt man with wide, staring, clearly insane eyes. An elderly, well-groomed man with white hair and a freshly trimmed beard suggesting that he had once been a refined and self-assured individual, but the stony expression on his face testified to the horrors from which he would never escape. The arms of the young men were twisted up their backs and their faces bore signs of violence, broken upper lips, cheeks smeared with blood.

There were children, a great many children. One of them looked about ten or twelve years old. His arms were twined behind his back, his skinny body contorted with pain. His mouth was small and soft, his eyes, dark with resignation, seemed to have been seized by some deep sorrow and despair, extending beyond himself; an expression usually only seen in old women who have lost all their close relatives in war; a spiritual refinement brought on by loss. In the throes of their loss, they will never escape from it, and yet in a sense they have already gone beyond it. That is how he looked, that boy. His eyes held no appeal for pity, mercy or understanding. Here was a child who knew he was to be murdered and who had already drained all the deepest wells of fear and mortal dread.

The walls of the last room were hung with photographs of those who had died under torture. Every stage of the torture and annihilation had been scrupulously recorded by the executioners. What did they think they were documenting with these pictures? Their own efficiency? The victorious revolution? Had they been unable to see the mirror they were holding up to themselves here, or that, in the end, it was they who were on trial, with all of these dead souls acting as judge and jury? All these dead, appallingly emaciated faces helplessly distorted in demoniacal grins, upper lips curled back and teeth bared. Around their heads, haloes of blood spreading across the floor on which they lay sprawled. I recognized the chequered design. It was the floor on which I was standing.

On the wall hung the "safety regulations" of this house of death, the prisoners' ten commandments and the formula for their extermination, brutal and direct in their curt wording, the closest one could get to an executioner's admission of his motives. I copied down the rather shaky English translation:

Rule no. 1: You must answer accordingly to my question. Don't turn them away.

Rule no. 2: Don't try to hide the facts by making pretexts this and that. You are strictly prohibited to contest me.

Rule no. 3: Don't be a fool, for you are a chap who dare to thwart the revolution.

Rule no. 4: You must immediately answer my questions without wasting time to reflect.

Rule no. 5: Don't tell me either about your immoralities or the essence of the revolution.

Rule no. 6: While getting lashes or electrification you must not cry at all.

Rule no. 7: Do nothing, sit still and wait for my orders. If there is no order, keep quiet. When I ask you to do something you must do it right away.

Rule no. 8: Don't make pretexts about Kampuchea Krom in order to hide your jaw of traitor.

Rule no. 9: If you don't follow all the above rules, you shall get many lashes of electrical wire.

Rule no. 10: If you disobey any of my orders you shall get either ten lashes or five electric shocks.

It was stark terror that spoke through these rules. There was no hope to be had there. The prisoner had already been found guilty. So what was it that he was supposed to confess? That he was nothing and that the executioner and what he stood for – the despotic power that had made itself lord over life and death – was all. The photographs showed what was left of the torturers' victims: bloody bodies, pain and silence. A tape recording was unnecessary. It would pick up nothing, the whole point of torture being to reduce the victim to silence, not to get him to talk. He was not even allowed to give utterance to his pain, according to these rules not even the inarticulate scream was permitted him, he was merely a body, while the executioner had the monopoly on the power of speech. The executioner asked the questions and with these he set the rhythm for the waves of pain that engulfed the victim's body. For the victim, the world no longer existed, there was only the pain. This was the admission the executioner wished to wring from his victim: that, as far as he was concerned, the world had vanished, leaving him free to divulge the names of friends or relatives, whoever; not in exchange for an end to the pain, but as a sign that the world no longer held any relevance for him, that, like a dying man, he had gone beyond it. The only thing he had to give away was this: not that the torture was a moral test of character which he failed by supplying the names of the guilty and the innocent, but that he was no longer the same person and that the torture had brought him to a point beyond humanity, where only pain existed. If ever the expression "to give up the ghost" has any meaning it was here, for the still living victim of torture. He confessed, not in the hope of surviving, but as an indication that here, on the brink of death, he was no longer the same man. Whether he was truly dying or not, that is how it must have seemed to him: the torture was like a long-drawn-out, simulated execution, a gradual departure from the world in which pain swamped all memories, feelings, ethics, care and thought.

The last words he speaks, his confession, his so-called betrayal, the denunciation that will leave the pain free to continue in an endless chain reaction as others are led into the interrogation room, is not even his own. He is merely saying what the executioner wants him to say. Just as his body has been drained of blood, so his words have lost all meaning and volition. He dies a ventriloquist's dummy.

The Children's Revolution

THE EXECUTIONERS AND EXAMINING OFFICERS IN S-21 kept records of their interrogations. The historian David P. Chandler has read these and in *The Tragedy of Cambodian History* he describes what he calls the examining officers' "utopia", the idea that all of these dossiers which had been compiled at the cost of so much human suffering would eventually constitute "a vast, complex and self-referential cycle of conspiracy, a full and final report on 'the great betrayal', of which the Party's leaders, many of whom were former teachers, could be proud."

Chandler continues: "The text is a marvel of neatness, single-mindedness and organisation, with sub-headings, parentheses and intricate cross-references to a multitude of dossiers ... the compulsion of the interrogators to cobble all the confessions into a series of master plots means that prisoners were often pushed to confess along lines that satisfied this obsessive sense of neatness: their confessions thus may not conform to anything they might have done. In fact, in many cases a prisoner's telling the truth about his or her activities might have derailed the interrogation."

It could hardly be stated more plainly: the torture was not by any means intended to bring secrets to light or get its victims to talk, but quite the reverse: to eradicate their personalities (as a prelude to the extinguishing of their physical lives) in such a way that their words and confessions became an echo of their interrogators'.

In some perverse way the reference to the relationship between teacher and pupil is almost touching: the executioners wanted to please their diabolical masters. They were the zealous pupils of bad teachers. Their reports were exercises written in blood.

Much has been made of the fact that Pol Pot and most of his inner circle were teachers of education – just as much was made of their having picked up their Marxist ideas while studying in Paris – this supposedly being the explanation for their dictatorial mania for order: they simply regarded Cambodia as one large classroom and themselves as idealistic teachers in the process of educating a crowd of unwilling children.

The comparison with the classroom is an apt one in the case of a regime which invokes a truth purportedly based on scientific fact, as the Communist States had done. If a truth is absolute then there can be no two ways about it and all communication becomes a one-way process, as in the old-style classroom, where all that was to be heard was the teacher's monologue, chorused by a score of voices. The teacher is not interested in the pupil's opinion, only in repetition. In the classroom only the teacher has opinions. All else is ignorance, and this calls for fresh effort, more learning by rote and possible chastisement, purely in the interests of education. Anything not coming under the heading of ignorance qualifies as defiance, sabotage or open resistance, which must be quashed. Culprits are sent to stand in the corridor as a symbolic underlining of the fact that dissent has no place in the classroom.

This model corresponds roughly to the Stalinism of the Soviet Union with its triangle of an omniscient Party in the role of schoolteacher, the ignorant masses in the pupils' place and a more or less numerous opposition playing the part of the class's naughty outsider, for whom the punishment is ultimate exile to the corridor of society: death. Historians have compared the mass-murders carried out under Pol Pot to the purges of Stalinism, in so far as they were determined not by ethnic or racial factors, but by politics; albeit a political line with its roots as much in the murky psychological realms of paranoia as in the history of ideas.

But if the Soviet Union could be compared to a classroom it was because the country's leaders did, in fact, have a programme: the vast expanses of Russia were to be electrified and its ignorant peasant masses trained to be citizens in a modern industrial society. This did not simply mean that they had to become literate; they also had to adopt a comprehensive, if one-way and predominantly technologically oriented culture. The Pol Pot regime also had a plan, but it was the opposite of Stalin's: as the first and only Marxist government in the world it closed down the schools, the universities and all other types of educational institution.

Democratic Kampuchea had no intention of enlightening its citizens. It was in a common state of ignorance that the democracy (to which the country's new name alluded with such vicious irony) was to be realized and total equality achieved: equality among those who had been stripped of everything, not only their property, but their cultivation and knowledge and, in the end, their personalities.

Kampuchea was not a classroom. The entire country was more akin to a gigantic interrogation room, since the methods used to bring about the new society were the same as those employed in S-21 to destroy the humanity of the detainees. Not only was the country totally isolated from the outside world, the abolition of the press and the postal service meant that all internal communication in the country was brought to a halt. The Communist Party had very little to say on the subject of the goals it had set for itself. It did not even term itself "communist", but simply "*angkhar*": the organisation. Of this organisation a terrorized population said that it was like a pineapple "with a thousand eyes": "Angkhar kills, but gives no reason."

Medicines and insecticides were no longer imported, and once again malaria became a major killer. The working day was increased to between 14 and 15 hours; this was known as "following the sun", in the same way as, in a parody of pre-revolutionary parlance, there was talk of "going on to further studies" when counter revolutionaries were taken away to be executed.

The control that was exercised over the people was not so much a censorship of opinions – the people were far too intimidated to express any – as an unscrupulous examination of the personality *per se*. Everything was interpreted: words, actions, attitudes; as if behind every human expression there lay a covert and thereby hostile cause which had to be delved into and exposed. Sadness or depression were looked upon as signs of mental confusion; happiness as an expression of pernicious individualism, while indecision suggested bourgeois intellectualism. Biographies were read over and over again, not in order to discover what their subjects could do for the revolution, but because one's past and social background were considered to hold the key to one's present actions. Spectacles belonged either to intellectuals or capitalists, as did pale skin or soft hands. Women were ordered to cut long hair, which was a sign of vanity. Play was forbidden. In other words, being a child was forbidden, just as families were forbidden to gather round the dinner table. Meals were reorganized on a collective basis and deprived of the aura of intimacy that makes them not only the heart of family life, but possibly one of the last sacred rites, even in a secular society. Here they were reduced to their merely animal elements, the basic consumption of the minimal nourishment necessary to survive. A new language was constructed; the language that light-skinned intellectuals with soft hands like Pol Pot imagined genuine peasants spoke.

The millions who only just survived in the rice paddies could be said to be the loneliest people on this earth: the borders of their country were the walls of a hermetically sealed prison; its soil, one enormous torturer's slab on which for three years they lay outstretched with no one to hear their screams; in the hands of their executioners the implements they had used to till the soil – hoes, trowels and shovels – were turned instead into murder weapons; the words with which they would have made their protest were permitted to pass their lips for one purpose only: to betray themselves and everyone else.

Fourteen years after the ousting of the Khmer Rouge, this silence of the lonely was still noticeable. I had been been struck by it in Phnom Penh's covered market place, where all of the stall-holders had the look of convalescents, sitting hunched listlessly over imported cotton sarongs and tin kitchen utensils, not even seeming to have the energy to extol the virtues of their wares.

When UN officials were investigating the state of the country's infrastructure as part of the build-up to the reinstatement of democracy, they went from house to house in Phnom Penh checking on the water supply and sanitation. In almost every home they found one dark figure, huddled alone in a corner of a room, refusing to communicate. When they asked the reason for this behaviour, they invariably received the same reply verbatim: aunt, uncle, sister or brother – only the name of the relative varied, never the reason for their conduct – is in mourning.

Cambodia had become a silent country. Cambodia was in mourning.

It seems wrong, almost, to accord the term "dictatorship" to the Khmer Rouge's reign of terror. "Tortureship" seems more appropriate, for, while people in Kampuchea may well have been reduced to becoming a means to an end, as in a traditional dictatorship, this was not done in order to build up or consolidate a power. They were simply the means of their own extermination and, ultimately, agents of the suicide of their nation as a recognizable or coherent society. Much to the surprise of the Vietnamese when they invaded Kampuchea, only three and a half years after the Khmer Rouge takeover, it took them less than a fortnight to overrun the country. Hardly anyone lifted a finger to defend what could no longer be regarded as a society; and Vietnam, which had for centuries been the arch-enemy, was instead hailed as a liberator.

The seeds of the Khmer Rouge's defeat were sown in the very hour of their victory. In ordering the evacuation of Phnom Penh and announcing that they intended to build a society without towns or institutions of any sort they were claiming that they could achieve in a day what the dogmatists of Marxism maintained would take decades, or possibly even centuries, to bring about: the classless society and the gradual demise of the State. When the inhabitants of Phnom Penh – whose number, due to the influx of war refugees, had expanded to several million – left Phnom Penh bound for the rice paddies, it was not a utopia they were marching into. It was a vast nihilistic void.

Hanging in one of the rooms in S-21 was a photograph taken on 17 April 1975, the day of the Khmer Rouge's entry into Phnom Penh. Here they come, the liberators in black, the peasants' traditional garb, with red-checked Khmer scarves around their necks and Mao caps on their heads. The people of the city crowd in on them from all sides, waving, but there is something not quite right about this scene which, in other respects, looks like so many other pictures of liberation armies making their triumphal entries. The soldiers do not invite the cheering, there is no hugging, no waving back. They march on, hung about with weapons, alone and unapproachable, in voluntary isolation. There is something forbidding about them, as if they have not yet accomplished their mission and are still in enemy territory, having come not to liberate but to exterminate. They seem wary, as if they are afraid that these rejoicing people with their arms outstretched might pass on some infection. The crowd seems to falter, they are not seeing what they expect either; even in the first hour of victory, a terrible doubt is beginning to grow: is this really a liberation that they are witnessing? Is that what makes them appear to respect a quarantine zone around each of the widely spaced, grim-looking soldiers on the march; just for a second they seem to sense what we, so many horrifying events and years later, know: that this photograph of the liberators' entering the city actually depicts an executioner entering a torture chamber and closing the door behind him.

They see something else which must surprise them. These soldiers are children, boys of between 12 and 15 years of age, seasoned war veterans, but children still. The witnesses to their arrival, who will go on believing for a couple of hours yet that they have been liberated, may have seen in the youth of their liberators some kind of judgement. We are adults, they may have thought, products of this city with its corruption, its compromises, its lies and blatant acquisitiveness. Life has taught us that nothing is black and white. But now here are the children, the innocent and pure, come to pass judgement on us.

That a large proportion of the soldiers responsible for the atrocities were children is an aspect of the Khmer revolution that has not been overlooked. David P. Chandler describes how in many parts of the country power lay in the hands of illiterate, heavily armed children who patrolled the villages at night, deciding, on the basis of their own crude concepts of morality, who had defied the demand for absolute obedience to the State, and summarily carrying out the punishment which, in almost every case, was death. Under such conditions no sort of order prevails, only despotism and chaos. Chandler also quotes from an interview with two young cadres, no more than children, who after the fall of the regime in 1979 stated that they had become Communists because "they did not have to work and could kill people".

This quote gives the impression that the Khmer Rouge cadres were made up primarily of callous youths and hooligans; misfits who in other societies were locked away in approved schools or remand homes, but who here became the prison guards of an entire society. Possibly not enough thought has been given to the fact that the Khmer Rouge not only staged the bloodiest, most arbitrary and openly destructive of all the bloody, arbitrary revolutions that have tried, in vain, to enforce the ideals of Communism, but that their revolution was also the first revolution in history to employ children as its driving force. Children ended up occupying the position usually filled by authority, as heirs to the State's traditional monopoly of violence, with the power of life and death. Between these two factors – the bloody and irrational nature of the revolution and the children's dominant role in it – there has to be a connection. Does all this horror, with its arbitrary mass executions carried out by means of any old tool that happened to come to hand (the official explanation for this being that bullets were too expensive), not seem, in some perverse way, rather like a game – in a country where more innocent games were banned? So much so that a journey through the Cambodian revolution is also a journey through the underworld of adolescence, not just another bloody chapter in the history of totalitarian thought, but also a plunge into the subconscious of the vulnerable, where childish innocence can be so easily perverted.

The obvious source of inspiration for the events in Kampuchea was, of course, Mao's Cultural Revolution, but where in the Chinese Cultural Revolution, the young people were no more than a pawn in a cynical power game which never really got out of hand or threatened those pulling the strings, the revolution in Kampuchea appears to have been a Cultural Revolution that went completely out of control – thanks to its leaders, who were at one and the same time extremists and political amateurs. Consequently, the destructive force that had been unleashed – in play, almost – was left to run unchecked. Kampuchea's revolutionaries were children playing at soldiers with real weapons and deadly consequences in a twilight zone between innocence and blood lust. They were given power over life and death before they even knew what life and death were, never mind guilt and responsibility. They were rendered omnipotent at a stage in the development of a child when it still thinks it stands alone in the world and its lack of empathy can lure it into committing atrocities because it cannot imagine that the hurt it inflicts on others could happen to itself.

Before the children in the black pyjamas had even encountered any real resistance from the world, they were given it without a fight. They had beaten one of the world's mightiest military powers, but, even so, the tough life of war in the jungle had tested their courage and physical prowess more like cubs at play than in any way conducive to the building of their character so that they might learn the meaning of compromise and humility. They were in no way qualified to wield the absolute power they were given. In a society which for a thousand years had been heavily patriarchal they had become the prosecutor, judge and executioner of their parents and elders. They could not even be described as teenage rebels; they became an armed power without ever having been in opposition; their own clouded childish mentality became law and order and its casual whim the only institution left standing in a society that had abolished all institutions. And, like 19-year-old rock stars suddenly overwhelmed by international fame, their overheated egos exploded. Except that these teenagers weren't addicted to money and sex – blood and revolution were their drugs.

During their exile in the jungle the Communist Party leaders had lived among the mountain tribes of north-east Cambodia and here they witnessed the practical application of a way of life which they saw as being identical to the ur-Communism of which they had read in Friedrich Engels's *The Origin of the Family, Private Property and the State*, a sort of political utopia before the fall from grace instigated by ownership and inequality. These tribes, who have never been colonized, live in scattered pockets all over South-East Asia, from Burma over northern Thailand and southern China to Vietnam and Laos, supporting themselves by means of hunting and primitive farming. Such mountain tribes, who know nothing of money or markets, served as models for the Khmer Rouge cadres, and in many cases the tribal warriors, who were famed for their survival skills, their obedience and their refined cruelties, were to form the regime's élite troops.

In praise of these warriors Pol Pot's lieutenant, Ieng Sary, said "they may be naked, but they have never been colonized" and went on to add, rather cryptically, that they possessed "class hate". Such statements demonstrate how superficial and curiously twisted Pol Pot's brand of Marxism was. The concept of development and growth constitutes the very heart of Marxism (as it does with its political arch-enemy, liberalism), but in Pol Pot this space was empty. Instead he was filled with a hatred of history and wanted to destroy it. Geographically and physically, the progress of history has always manifested itself as a shift from country to town. Pol Pot wished to go against the stream, clearing the towns in order to repopulate the rural districts. In saying of the mountain tribes that they were "blank pages" he was also giving away his true intent: He did not want to write history, but to erase it. And how better to do that than with the aid of a band of inexperienced, undisciplined children and some primitive mountain tribes still dwelling in the infancy of history?

Pol Pot was both an idealist and a destroyer. His socialism was the socialism of the tribe and in this there lay a solid bond between a man so convinced of the scientific truth of his own views that he had no qualms about ordering the deaths of his opponents and an ancient tribal society whose customs taught it that the members of the tribe alone were real people and that all others were not only enemies, but also non-people, to whom the instinctive inhibition against taking life, a precondition for civilization, need not apply.

Here lies the difference between Pol Pot's regime and the other totalitarian States of the twentieth century. In those, too, murder was committed, but the monopoly on killing remained at all times in the hands of a select group. At no time was it rescinded and democratically farmed out to everybody. In the case of both Hitler and Stalin, bureaucracy had been the preferred agent of genocide. It put some distance between the decision-makers and the victims and this made it easier to turn killing into an efficient routine. Pol Pot had no secret police, no Gestapo, no KGB, not even a visible uniformed police force. In this lay his radicalism: He put the killing back in the hands of the people, he cancelled out the distance between murderer and victim which bureaucracy had created, and brought them face to face once more.

Pol Pot's key weapon was the breaking down of man's natural inhibition against killing (when not in self-defence) and, hence, his advance guard was formed by those bodies in whom this inhibition is least developed: children and primitive tribesmen. His aim was to create a society bound by the premisses of the tribal community: isolated, permanently on the warpath, consisting solely of "real" people. Its enemies were not ethnically determined – apart, that is, from their neighbour and arch-enemy, Vietnam – but tribes in a metaphorical sense: the short-sighted, bespectacled tribe, the tribe of the doubters and confused, the tribe of the happy, the tribe of the downhearted, the tribe of the various social classes, the intellectual tribe – in short, all of the tribes which go to make up the great nation of mankind in all its diversity. Against them he set his own tribe: a black-clad, faceless, expressionless mass whose only passions were the inhuman grinding down and random slaughter of others.

This, too, can be seen in the photograph of the armed children making their entry into Phnom Penh on 17 April 1975. Do not be fooled by their modern weapons. What we have here is a tribe conquering a metropolis, proto-history invading the twentieth century, the end of the last war of anti-colonialism and the beginning of a new one; a tribal war which, for a while yet, is taking the trouble to disguise itself as revolution.

With Greetings from a Tree

I WAS STAYING AT THE HOTEL LE ROYAL, THE OLD FOREIGN correspondents' hotel, more or less in the centre of Phnom Penh; once a palace and hub of the capital's social whirl, now a battle-scarred, dilapidated monument to Prince Sihanouk's *belle époque*, built in the French colonial style with yellow-washed walls three storeys high, a red-tiled roof and green shutters.

The poorly lit corridors were wide enough for a tank to drive down. In the evenings, bats flitted about restlessly in the gloom under the high ceilings. The stairways formed vast wood-panelled wells, their unpainted treads blackened with age and wear.

No two rooms in the Hotel Le Royal were alike and only a few had the obligatory four corners of a standard hotel room. Although there was no difference in price some were as austere as a monk's cell, others opulently furnished with coffee tables and comfortable armchairs; some were claustrophobic cigar boxes, others more like ballrooms. The paint was peeling off everywhere, one room had walls of undressed cement, another had a coat of distemper. Only a handful of doors had handles on the inside, every one of them hung askew, and could only be held shut by means of rocks or heavy planks left on the floor for that purpose. The electric switches emitted a faint hum and delivered a friendly little shock when turned on. The light came and went in pulsating waves, first strong then weak, as if the tumbledown hotel were drawing its own laboured breath. Once or twice each night there would be a power failure. Then the corridors were lit by generator-driven emergency lamps not unlike car headlights, which were mounted high above the door lintels. The bats fled in terror to darker corners.

Street lamps were few and far between in Phnom Penh. The side streets lay in darkness, the sole source of light provided by those shops which remained open. An armed guard had appeared outside the hotel and the streets were dotted with checkpoints manned by police officers cradling rifles in their laps. The war in the outlying provinces seemed to close in with the darkness.

There were little stalls selling food by the glow of oil lamps, around which eating customers huddled in a circle. If they walked a couple of metres they were swallowed up by the tropical night. There was a faint scurrying of life, as if the people of the resurrected capital were still living in a house that had not as yet been vacated by its original resident: terror.

On the main street the bicycle rickshaws stood packed together in great clusters. Their owners had turned in for the night, sprawled in the seats which during the day were reserved for passengers. Others had slung hammocks from lamp posts and road signs. They slept as if drugged in the tropical night, mouths gaping and distorted, and I saw again the faces of the dead in S-21, with their curled lips and their bared teeth grinning demoniacally. Something appeared to be slowly working its way to the surface in the faces of the sleepers, under cover of night and slumber: the skull, ready and waiting beneath the skin; death, eager to get out and proclaim its victory over the still-living flesh.

A large, white hotel was under construction, the work continuing in the middle of the night. Spotlight beams pierced the night while shadowy silhouettes bustled about inside the pool of light. A nearby nightclub bathed the pavement and the surrounding asphalt in the glare of hundreds of coloured bulbs, all of this illuminated splendour seeming to defy the darkness and preserve some element of humanity; as if the hotels' and brothels' self-promotion were also part of a united front in defence of the continuance of life and in defiance of the children in black pyjamas somewhere out there in the jungle.

I caught a prostitute's whispered negotiations with a customer. "No, no – $20. No mother, no father. Pol Pot –" and then the gesture, evidently the same in every country, of a forefinger being drawn graphically across a windpipe; the sound of flesh being slit, of blood being shed, of the constancy of violence.

Andrew was an English computer engineer, working as a volunteer with the UN in Cambodia. "What do we do? We run this country. We're rebuilding it from the ground up, basically. The Khmer Rouge ripped the guts out of this country. Only a year ago there was nothing here, no cars, no telephones, no electricity. The Khmer Rouge – English hooligans equipped with machine-guns, that's all they were. I work with young Cambodian technicians trained in the Soviet Union. They know their stuff, they're professional, but they have no confidence in themselves. No one had ever told them they were good. The previous generation of technicians, older men who could give them recognition, from whom they could learn, whom they could measure themselves against and rebel against, they're just not there. They've been wiped out."

I hired a chauffeur-driven car to make the 40-kilometre journey to Udang, the old capital of the kingdom, abandoned centuries earlier. My driver was a timid middle-aged man who was devastated by shame every time he could not answer one of my innumerable questions. He shrank down in his seat, unable even to express his regret, his English too poor.

I asked him what he had been doing before 1979, when the Vietnamese ousted the Khmer Rouge from power. He had been in the countryside, he said and we both knew what that meant: He had been doing forced labour in the rice fields – like everyone else.

With this question I had unwittingly provided him with a key. From then on all of his answers were an echo of the last two words of my question: "Before '79." When I pointed to the remains of a bombed bridge over the Mekong River, he replied: "Before '79." The appalling roads, the ruined temples – always the same reply: Before '79, as if everything that had happened since then had been no more than a series of effects, all stemming from the same cause. It was like asking the inhabitants of Hiroshima about the atom bomb.

Cambodia left one feeling that the Khmer Rouge were simply taking a break from wreaking havoc and I was certain that my driver saw it in the same way: as if he were living within a parenthesis, where everything was merely temporary. The whole of Cambodia had the look of a monument to the Khmer Rouge's urge to destroy. This was their landscape. The landscape of liberation had not yet been shaped. The houses, the roads, the temples looked as though they remembered. The old folk, too, remembered, even if they were reluctant to talk. But they would only stand as witnesses for a little longer, the average age in Cambodia was now below 40. Nature was the great rebuilder in Cambodia. Soon all of those who remembered would be gone, despite the fact that the events in question lay only 12 to 15 years in the past. The new arrivals would gaze in wonder at the bombed bridges and wrecked roads, and perhaps, as with Angkor Wat, they would see the hand of the gods in all of this, and not realize that the true perpetrators had been their own inner demons. And the vicious circle of innocence could begin all over again.

Why on earth did I want to see the ruins of an ancient royal city? Everywhere I turned here there were fresh, new ruins, a whole country of them.

Udang sat on two sandy yellow hills overlooking a flat plain that shimmered in the heat. A red gravel track led up to the base of the hills; two Buddhist monks dressed in saffron robes were walking along the track, their shaven heads protected from the sun by buttercup-yellow parasols that cast their reflection over their golden skins. In a small temple at the foot of the twin hills a group of musicians laboured on xylophones, gongs and drums in honour of a group of Bulgarian UN troops who were filming them with video cameras. The music followed me on my walk up onto the ridge, with no dramatic leaps or bounds, no crescendos or pauses, a lazy flowing stream of sound.

A Cambodian in plain clothes with a Kalashnikov slung over his shoulder stood minding the car. Another armed man accompanied me up the steps to the temple. No words passed between us. They were simply there, like part of the landscape.

More crumbling masses of stone. Walls three feet thick, eight mighty columns standing in the midst of an overgrown courtyard; then a pillar that had toppled over a wall, suspended in mid-air with an odd kink in the middle; partially embedded in the wall, like a felled tree that had checked itself mid-way through its fall. An oval dais at the centre of the courtyard bore traces of some decorative motif: flowers in glazed porcelain. I looked it up in my guide book. No, I was not gazing upon the ravages of time, but those of the Khmer Rouge. The toppled pillar with the crook halfway along its length was the arm of a Buddha nine metres tall, whose crossed legs now caught my eye. The pillars in the courtyard were adorned with a pattern of great fan-shaped gashes: shrapnel, driven into the stone in a whirlwind of destruction.

The neighbouring temple was nothing but an untidy heap of rock, with fragments of Buddhas scattered about amid the rubble. Next to it sat a makeshift temple of straw and sailcloth and inside, in the gloom, bundles of joss sticks glowed. Buddhas cloven in two, shards of arms, legs and torsoes had been piled on top of one another to form an altar that served more to document the destruction than to heal it.

In Angkor I had seen the results of the greed of corrupt officials and disillusioned guerrillas, but here at Udang the sheer need to lay waste had prevailed. The temples had been lost for ever in the blasts and were beyond any hope of restoration.

On the hillside below the temples lay a grove of broad-leaved trees, all furnished with their own little blue tag bearing the name of their species in Latin, as in a botanic gardens. Someone had decided that attention to the little details could compensate for the massive despoliation.

Who could have come up with such an idea, here, in the midst of the sun-baked countryside, where no one would see it; in this country where the last of the scholars had been killed long ago?

Someone who had come back here on a journey of remembrance and had set his botanical names on the broad-leaved trees much as one lays flowers on a grave, in the hope that something might survive here?

In all of their prosaicness, the little blue tags inscribed with their Latin names seemed as intimate as letters, communications that could only be fully understood by one, but which, on reflection, were, nonetheless addressed to all.

Confession of a Fratricide

ALL DAY LONG THEY LOITERED OUTSIDE THE ENTRANCE TO THE Le Royal in gangs: men and half-grown boys, standing chatting in the shade of the plane trees, suddenly galvanized into action the minute a guest appeared on the wide front steps of the hotel and set out across the large, deserted car park: they completely blocked the entrance way, shouting, laughing, waving, ringing their bicycle bells or frantically revving up their Honda scooters: "Me, me, me, sir! – Where you go?"

No pleading here. Every one of them endeavoured to look like an old and dear friend celebrating an unexpected reunion after years of separation. So much warmth, so much charm, just to be allowed to transport a passenger through the tropical sun in one of Phnom Penh's monstrous bicycle rickshaws, all of which looked as if they had been built for a race of people much bigger than their drivers, who sat high up behind their customers, toes pointed like a ballet dancer in mid-leap, simply to reach the pedals.

Veassnar won the day. He was a young man of 25 who could have passed for 17. In Cambodia there seemed to be no transition period between the teenage phase and middle age. Cambodians went to bed one night when they were around 30, with wiry, boyish bodies and open, untried faces and woke up the next morning with prolapsed organs, stooped backs and contrary lines around their mouths. The last phase, old age, which manifested itself when they were in their mid-forties, resembled the outcome of some violent attack, with broken limbs and bones that never set properly again. But there were very few old people.

"I like your shirt, man!" said Veassnar with an American drawl while rolling chewing gum from one side of his mouth to the other.

His hair was nicely cut and he wore a Hawaiian shirt. His air of authority amid the crowd outside the Hotel Le Royal entranceway stemmed not only from his luck in landing the most customers, but more particularly from his superior command of English. For a couple of days I used the pillion of his Honda for getting around Phnom Penh, but I had to get to know him pretty well before I could ask him the one inescapable question. Before '79? A question that caused the majority of Cambodians either to clam up or to give one of those curious answers so typical of Asians, which seem to go full-circle, back to the original question, leaving one none the wiser. But Veassnar did answer, and his answer shocked me.

There was a great deal of insensitivity and a clinical ruthlessness in my curiosity. The Cambodians' silence, their refusal to tell a stranger about the life they had been forced to lead, revealed both great dignity and how much they had been oppressed. Later I was to read a book about the sufferings of Cambodia written by the French anthropologist, Marie-Alexandre Martin – *Le mal cambodgien* – in which she criticised the Vietnamese for having turned S-21 into a museum, "which they [the Cambodians] do not need", a viewpoint which I found alarming, since it seemed tantamount to maintaining that Europe did not need to remember Auschwitz. But her attitude echoes a sentiment that is widely felt among the Cambodians. Those individuals shut away in the protective gloom of the family home who "mourned", provided a dire warning to other Cambodians. Better not to remember. For the Cambodians, choosing forgetfulness meant choosing life.

Veassnar never volunteered any details about his past. The present, on the other hand, was the permanent butt of his bitter complaints. "Cambodia is a terrible place," he kept saying, the life which the UN troops had introduced to the city seeming to have provided him, not with hopes of the future, but merely with a yardstick against which to measure everything that he had missed out on in the years before; things that he would never be able to gain access to: the restaurants, with such enticing and romantic names as *Rose Blanche, Le Bon Rêve, Mont Rouge*; the nightclubs and gaudily lit brothels; the army of imported Toyotas and the UN's massive, white, four-wheel drive vehicles; the makeshift shops where UN personnel – or indeed anyone who had the money – could purchase Russian caviar, Norwegian salmon, French Camembert, *pâté de foie gras* and Swiss milk chocolate, not to mention Nutella, Heinz Mayonnaise and chilled cappuccino in cans, beers such as San Miguel and Miller's, French wine from such celebrated regions as Burgundy and Margaux, Campari and Pernod aperitifs and Moët & Chandon vintage champagne – none of which could inspire him or arouse any feeling in him other than the fiercest indignation, even though it was also his dearest wish to get his hands on all these things. Or perhaps for that very reason . . .

It was the arrival of these delights in Phnom Penh that had convinced him that he was doomed to be miserable. His excellent knowledge of English only served to reinforce this conviction. It was almost as if the self-same international language that enabled him to speak to all manner of foreigners acted on his imagination like a disease, leaving it feverish and distorted. It had opened up for him the door to a Paradise which he could never enter, but merely look at from the threshold, with the result that he now viewed everything through a veil of bitterness.

For four years he had driven a bicycle rickshaw, ten hours a day. In the evenings he had two hours of English lessons. It was his belief that the punishing work of peddling the bicycle had ruined his health. He had a bad cough, and woke up at five every morning unable to get back to sleep. Instead, he practised his English. His parents' house, where he was still living, had no electricity, only oil lamps. He stopped short in midstream, overwhelmed by all this waste, and began to reel off the years of his youth, one year at a time: '88, '89, '90, '91. Throughout this time a curfew had been in force. No one was allowed to be out after nine o'clock in the evening. And he was young. It was his youth that had been lost. He forced a cough to emphasize his words.

(Some years later I met a young man in Bucharest whom I asked about life under Ceauşescu, the notorious dictator whom everyone in the West took to hating and condemning around the time of his dramatic execution, and who – according to all official accounts – had transformed a land rich in potential into one huge labour camp. "There were two things which made life unbearable under Ceauşescu," replied the Rumanian, who earned a living as an interpreter, "one was that there was only two hours of television every evening, the other that all the bars in Bucharest closed at 9 p.m." Anyone who truly wishes to know how history is lived and experienced and how dictatorships are, or are not, borne, or how revolutions break out or fail to come to anything, ought to listen very carefully to such statements.)

"Cambodia is a terrible place," repeated Veassnar. "I would never marry a girl from Cambodia. I want to marry a Danish girl – or an Italian. They have big breasts. Cambodian girls have small, ugly breasts. If I were rich I could have anyone I wanted." He paused, then went on, as if reciting a litany: "If I had a car I could have anyone I wanted."

In that same bitter tone he explained the strict rules governing relations between the sexes before marriage. Veassnar had never had a girl-friend. Instead he patronized the Vietnamese prostitutes in a large shanty town ten kilometres north of Phnom Penh. You could have them just the way you liked them – tall, short, big-breasted or small.

I could tell from his voice that their accessibility and cheap rates rendered them of no interest to him. He strove to attain only those things he could not have. He flung out a hand in despair. "There's no point in getting drunk, if I don't have any money. Because I always get horny when I'm drunk."

Then his mood altered abruptly and he asked me, laughing: "How many bicycle rickshaws are there in Denmark? I'll bring my rickshaw to Denmark and become a rich man!"

At Veassnar's invitation I joined him on a Sunday outing to Tunle Bati lake, 35 kilometres south of Phnom Penh. This provided him with the opportunity to earn a full day's pay and gave me a chance to observe the nearest thing Cambodia has to normal, peaceful middle-class life, in the short cortège of cars laden with families out for a Sunday drive that rolled along the poorly maintained roads.

The roadside was lined by little wooden stalls where women with faces caked with white make-up lounged under straw lean-tos, hawking palm wine to the passing motorists. Now and again the cavalcade would be brought to a halt by one-legged war invalids who would lurch out into the middle of the road on their crutches, one trouser leg rolled up to expose an artifical leg, and demand a toll fee from the Sunday trippers. It was as if they imposed a levy on the happiness and freedom from care, that they could never experience. The smoked-glass window of a snow-white Toyota slid down. A soft, female arm dripping with gold bracelets appeared, a banknote held between the tips of two fingers. The one-legged man hopped aside and waved the car on. The levy on happiness had been paid.

In the waters of the lake, just out from the shore, stood hundreds of little straw and bamboo huts perched on stilts. They were reached by way of a bouncing gangway built out of split palm-tree trunks, which demanded all the balancing skills of a tightrope walker. Once out there you could sit in the shade, looking over to the palmy-green opposite bank, and be served baked fresh fish, together with rice, cold Anchor beer and coconut milk. Empty beer cans bobbed about in the muddy yellow water where swimming children collected them.

It was in the soporific heat of midday, after we had eaten, that I asked Veassnar what his life had been like prior to the year that had drawn such a crucial demarcation line in the lives of everyone in Cambodian: '79. He spoke of it so readily and in such a straightforward manner that one would have thought he did not attach that much importance to the events that had occurred during the Khmer Rouge regime. It was only when describing his present life that he seemed seized by the urge to strike poses and bemoan his fate. His experiences of the Khmer Rouge were, after all, no different from everyone else's. The atrocities had been accepted as being almost predestined and so unavoidable. Besides, he was only a child at the time, and children are always at the mercy of adults.

Veassnar was seven years old when the Khmer Rouge seized power. His mother and father had come through unscathed. He had nine brothers and sisters, only one of whom, an older brother, had lost his life under the Khmers. He had been caught stealing food and summarily executed. Not many families had got off as lightly as Veassnar's. He was lucky enough to have been brought up in a province where living conditions had been more tolerable than elsewhere in Kampuchea and there had not been so many killings. Like everyone else Veassnar had seen people executed. The condemned were made to stand in a long line. Just like in a school playground he added. Then one by one they were struck down; not shot, but killed with clubs, hoes and shovels. Veassnar mimed a blow to the back of the head. After that they were thrown into a mass grave, some of them still alive. He leaned forward and twitched his shoulders in imitation of the spasms that pass through a body in the throes of death.

His strongest memories were of boredom and interminable hunger. The schools had been closed – and did not reopen until over a year after the downfall of the Khmer Rouge. Between the ages of seven and eleven he received no schooling.

Hunger was still the prime topic after all these years; as if time had not affected his memory or transposed foreground and background. "My brother stole food for us children," he continued, "but I was so hungry that I never felt I got enough. I was always hungry. I wanted him to give it all to me. But he wouldn't. So I went to the Khmer Rouge and reported him for stealing. They came to fetch him."

He laughed abruptly and apologetically, as if at the memory of a boyish prank that had gone a little too far. Then he carried on: "I was thin as a rake, nothing but skin and bone." And it sounded as though his betrayal of his brother had been no more than an episode, a parenthesis, in the great epic of the hunger that gnawed at his vitals.

"Didn't you say that your brother was executed for stealing food?" The question escaped me, like a gasp.

"No, no," he said hastily, "not that time, that was later, that was nothing to do with me."

I felt certain he was lying. One accusation would have been enough for the Khmer Rouge, who were not known for their adherence to the due process of law. It seemed unlikely that his brother would have been set free after being reported by Veassnar. Whether Veassnar was only lying to me or to himself as well I could not be sure.

"It was nothing to do with me," he said without a hint of emotion. The question of guilt and innocence seemed never to have occurred to him, all he responded to was that screaming hunger which, I suddenly realized, had never loosened its grip, but still crouched there, inside him. His life since then had been like that of a fledgling in a nest with its yawning beak: a desperate cry for "more, more, more" that could never be sated.

It was his only protest, the defiant gluttony of the fledgling beak. That "more, more," in a country that gave nothing, but instead took and took from its inhabitants: their lives, their memories, their dignity, their innocence.

Black Spaces on the Globe

ANDREW WAS NO LONGER ON HIS OWN. HIS WOMAN FRIEND had arrived from Bangkok and moved into his room, which was one of the very largest at the Hotel Le Royal. She was a Swiss journalist, in her mid-forties, who had landed a job with one of Phnom Penh's newly established English language newspapers, the *Cambodian Times*. Franziska was a mature woman with a broad, open face which made a strong and reassuring impression. Andrew, on the other hand, had the look of one of those characters one encounters in novels set in British colonial days; gaunt-featured, with skin the same waxen hue as their unwashed, sweat-stained tropical "whites", lazing in the shade of the verandah while their morals dissolve along with the ice in their whisky. He was gaunt and often unshaven, with thin, unkempt shoulder-length hair. But the image of the tropical dissolute was purely superficial. He had a very idealistic side and I soon saw that his gentleness and his affability were not signs of weakness. He was a man who had lived his life in the way he wanted and had no need of affectation. I think this must have been what strong-minded Franziska had seen in him, and what she rewarded with untold signs of affection. She knew he could handle them and would never exploit them. She dared to mother him, because that was not what he was looking for. They were a delightful couple, two grown-ups who had decided to try their luck in troubled Phnom Penh for a couple of years.

It was Andrew who pointed out to me that the UN's presence in Cambodia gave me the chance to see parts of the country which had been inaccessible since the end of the 1960s, when the civil war instigated by American interference in Cambodian politics broke out. The UN had set up shop with its battalions in all of the country's provincial capitals, to make preparations for the election to be held in May, and all that was required was for me to register as a journalist and detail which places I wished to visit, and a UN helicopter would be placed at my disposal.

The only problem was, of course, that I had nothing to show that I was, in fact, a journalist. I decided to try presenting my membership card to the Association of Danish Writers of Fiction and Poetry and to my astonishment this small, nondescript, rather amateur-looking piece of cardboard was accepted. All that remained was for me to find out where I actually wanted to go.

Captain Rasneev of the Indian battalion was a tall man with a slight stoop and an impressive moustache. He circled the tip of a pointer briefly over a map of Cambodia. "What is it you really want to see?" he asked, as if he suspected that I did not really want to see anything, but was simply trying to get a free ride in a helicopter.

"I'd like to see the Khmer Rouge," I heard myself say. At that point the Khmer Rouge had pulled out of the preparations for the election, a move which was regarded as a major defeat for the UN, and possibly even as an omen that the mission would turn into a total fiasco. They had massacred the fishermen on the Tonle Sap lake and were stepping up their attacks against both civilians and UN troops. I had no idea why I said it. But somehow or other I felt this was the only logical way of justifying my presence at the UN headquarters, or perhaps it was the desire to look evil in the eye; an evil that is invariably pure and absolute; "that horrifying, irreducible purity" as Sartre called it in 1947 after Oradour, Dachau and Auschwitz.

Or perhaps that would be to credit myself with overly metaphysical motives. Maybe it was simply the peculiar mesmerizing lethargy that I felt throughout my time in Cambodia, coming to a head as Captain Rasneev put his question to me. I was like a rabbit transfixed by the mysterious power of a snake's eye – the snake's eye being the map of Cambodia hanging on the wall; and when I heard Captain Rasneev ask his question I surrendered to that eye.

"Kampong Thom is the biggest trouble spot in Cambodia. We have reports from there of almost daily breaches of the ceasefire," he said. "It's a good place for running into the Khmer Rouge. Then there's Stung Treng." He pointed to a spot high up in the north-east corner of Cambodia. "We have patrols on the Mekong River who report that they often have encounters with the Khmer Rouge at fixed checkpoints. If the Uruguayan battalion is willing to let you come along on their patrol boat then that might be a possibility."

He laid down his pointer. "Flying from Kampong Thom to Stung Treng is no problem. But unfortunately all the seats on the helicopter to Kampong Thom on Tuesday are taken. Which means you'll have to wait until the end of the week – unless, that is, you want to drive up."

"Is that possible?"

"There's no public transport, and our vehicles don't carry passengers. But you can hire a car. The road is open." He paused, in order to underline the significance of his words. "When I say that the road is open, what I mean is that it has been cleared of mines. I cannot say to what extent it is dangerous or not. Incidents can always occur. Many of the locals attempt to extort money from motorists."

Veassnar, who had become my trusty shadow in Phnom Penh, promised to get me a car. He himself would do the driving and we soon agreed on a price.

The evening before we were due to leave, Andrew schooled me in the basic rules for survival that applied when travelling outside of Phnom Penh; rules in which he, like everyone else who worked for the UN, had been carefully drilled. "Never set off early in the morning," he began, "all of the minor roads are mined at night. Every village has its cache of mines which the villagers haul out at night and remove again in the morning. Think of our Iron Age villages with their earthworks and palisades. The villages here are exactly the same, except that their palisades cannot be seen. We're talking the Dark Ages meets high-tech here. So wait – let the others drive out first. Never before 9.00 a.m., that way you can be sure that the peasants have taken in their mines. There are four million mines in Cambodia. In the UN they say that it will take a hundred years to get rid of them all. They claim three to four hundred victims a week, the majority of whom are left maimed. If you see an abandoned or uninhabited house never go inside it. You can be sure it's booby-trapped. The peasants have their own warning signs for the mines they have found. A piece of cloth bound round a branch, a Coca Cola can stuck on the end of a twig, two branches laid crosswise, an arrow made out of straw."

When we left Phnom Penh I could tell that Veassnar was feeling edgy. On the outskirts we drove past the ruins of a big bridge that had once spanned the Mekong, but which was now nothing but a concrete carriageway jutting out into mid-air, and we were both struck by a sense of leaving civilization behind and heading out into unknown territory. That is how much of a paradox this ravaged land was: one even got used to the ruins and, in the end, accepted them as proof of the presence of civilization.

The road was in fairly good condition. There were not that many cars, but a lot of cyclists, horse-drawn wagons and ox-carts, trundling slowly along. The flat landscape alternated between rice fields and jungle, interspersed with sun-bleached wooden shacks on stilts and red gravel paths running off into no-man's land.

On one stretch, where the tarmac was pitted with craters, a whole crowd of children had ranged themselves along the verge holding flat, woven baskets filled with sand. As we approached they raised the baskets pointedly aloft to show that they had just repaired the wrecked road and were now expecting payment for their labours. Their faces contorted with rage when Veassnar did not slacken his speed, and when they set off, yelling, in pursuit of us I had the feeling that this was deadly earnest and not merely child's play.

At every bridge there were manned machine-gun nests.

At Kampong Thom I reported to the commander of the Indonesian battalion, a youngish man whose white T-shirt strained over the chest of a wrestler, his dark face lit by a wide and winning smile. We fixed a time for me to be taken on to Stung Treng and he gave me directions to the town's only hotel, which he described as painted blue and standing on stilts in the middle of a lake.

It was not much of a town: wide, dusty roads with houses set well back, half-hidden behind bougainvillaea and green shrubs; in the centre was a great yellow rectangle of a building that served as market. It was Sunday and the stalls were closed. On one pitch, however, there was a tradesman selling pirate copies of music cassettes. A gang of Indonesian UN soldiers sat in front of the stall, handing tapes of Jimi Hendrix and the Police around for inspection.

The hotel was just as it had been described to me. The outside was painted blue, a shade darker than the lake, the surface of which reflected the white-hot noonday sky. A long wooden bridge led out to the hotel over an all but dried-up lake, its muddy bottom overgrown with water lilies and dock leaves.

*　*　*

On the opposite shore of the lake I found the UN observers installed in a similar house on stilts, the only difference being that this one was painted red and lay closer to the land. The rooms were large and airy, with walls, floors and ceilings of unpainted wood dark with wear. Two men were seated at a big table, one of them with his feet up.

I sat down across from them, filled with a strange sense of futility. What was I actually doing here? What was it I was so anxious to learn? I felt swamped by the heat, and the sight of the dead town had left me unsure of myself. I had said goodbye to Veassnar and I realized that even he had come to represent something of a lifeline for me.

"What goes on out here?" I asked.

"Everything!"

"What does that mean?"

"Lots of BCF."

"BCF?"

"Breaches of the ceasefire."

We carried on in this fashion for some time.

"It's a good day when no one dies – but an unusual day," said one of the UN observers, a tall, burly Englishman with a thick mane of hair and a cleft chin. "On a normal day a village will be blown to pieces and lives are lost." His tone was arrogant. He was trying to sound like an old hand, and to make the killings seem mundane. He acted like an initiate, a kind of compeer of death, conversant with its mysteries. He would not give his name. That was his way of finding something to hold on to in the midst of this wasteland.

As the conversation progressed, however, he thawed and confessed to me that there were two reasons for his being there: the English winter and boredom. He was an officer in the British army, stationed in London at Buckingham Palace, where there was absolutely nothing worthwhile to do. He thought that most of the people here just wanted to kill time – and to get back home alive. This last he added with a note of hearty conviction in his voice. His arrogance had suddenly vanished. It seemed that only now was he making himself known.

He knew very little about the people who he was here to help achieve a brighter future, except that they died. UN troops never ventured into the Khmer Rouge controlled areas. "We would either be taken hostage

164

or shot at," he said. "It's totally unknown territory. We know nothing about the people living under the control of the Khmer Rouge. We don't know how many of them there are, we don't know their names, we don't know what their lives are like, whether they are starving, or whether they are alive at all. All the roads leading in there are mined. It's not worth risking one's neck for."

The other UN observer, a red-headed and rather plump Irishman with milk-white skin who, up to this point, had not uttered a word, suddenly broke into the conversation. "The worst thing I've seen here," he said, "was a man having his leg amputated without any anaesthetic."

And he lapsed back into silence.

I went for a walk along the river that runs through Kampong Thom. On the one bank stood grand houses from the French colonial time, on the other wooden huts on stilts. At one point the river with its muddy yellow waters and steep banks was spanned by a snow-white bridge. It was a beautiful spot. I followed the road until it dwindled to a winding path. At the end of the path the rice paddies began. A clump of rain-trees cast their long shadows across the regimented squares of the fields. The sky was tinged with purple, a rosy flush radiating upwards from the horizon. The peace of late afternoon hung over this landscape, Sunday rest after the labours of the week and the promise that this would last for ever; a moment of unreality.

A little man had materialized alongside me, wearing a pair of shorts that left his sagging belly exposed. "Mathematics," he said, pointing at himself. "Teacher." His vocabulary was then exhausted, and we stood in silence smiling at each other. I felt like embracing him and telling him his country was beautiful. But I did not dare. I was afraid he would take it as an insult.

I strolled down to the lake and settled myself on the shore. Behind me a herd of water buffalo went past, with plodding gait and a moist, cud-chewing sound. I felt powerless and despondent. I was smitten with this country's inarticulacy, and as the colours above the lake soaked up the last of the light before the onset of a tropical darkness, I wrote in my notebook:

"You dare not allow yourself to be seduced by their gentleness, their smiles and their quiet charm, because you know that they had enough blood-lust among them to wipe out one in four of their own people; you dare not tell them that you find the sunset over the rice fields beautiful, because you know that they have defiled the same soil with blood; you dare not tell them that you like being in their country, because they would reply that it is a hell on earth; you do not even dare to think that there might be some values left in this country, because they have done away with all values and all the words that can give a society meaning – people, country, nation, history – have lost their significance for them. They have only themselves – for the brief time limit imposed by physical survival and they would consider you to be either stupid or cynical if you were to say that you cared for them. Every compliment represents a denial of reality, every hope on their behalf, a profanity. This is a sunlit land of the dead; a biblical Judgement Day has befallen this place, striking not at the good and the evil, but at the concepts of good and evil. And when the gates of Paradise were opened, it was only to reveal yet another graveyard. The last truly did become the first, the weak were given rifles, the illiterate became the lawgivers and the whims of children the ultimate authority. It was the humbled, the abased and the desperate who were raised on high, not to put an end to despair, but to extend it to everyone."

I went to bed early. "Whatever you do," the UN observer had said, "don't go out after eight o'clock. The government soldiers get drunk every night. Then they start shooting. Not at you. They just shoot."

There was no street lighting in Kampong Thom. I groped my way in deepest darkness along a churned-up cart track. Out on the lake I could see the glow of an oil lamp and guessed that this must be the hotel. Not even the bridge out to it was illuminated. An elderly woman appeared in a doorway and lit the last short step to my room. Then she handed me a candle and a box of matches. A pink mosquito net was draped over the bed.

A couple of hours later the full moon began its ascent and at roughly the same time the shooting started. First scattered shots. Then a couple of salvoes. Then scattered shots again. The soldiers fired their guns to save themselves from feeling lonely beneath the moon, or because their rifles had been doing the talking for so long that they no longer had any faith in the sound of their own voices. Or else they fired their guns in order to summon up Death, to keep them company.

I awoke after sleeping for several hours. The windows were shuttered and the room was pitch-dark. I had been woken by a faint rustling at the foot of the bed. All at once I found myself almost suffocated by a feeling of intense dread. I lay there, tense and numb, with the sheet pulled up under my chin. After a while I slid back into sleep once more, only for an echo of that same soft rustle to sound in my subconscious, unleashing a great wave of pent-up anxiety. I sat bolt upright in bed, gasping with fear. Outside, all was quiet, not with the stillness of the night, but an unnatural silence, as if the Earth had been evacuated, leaving no life behind except the unknown creature here in the room with me, biding its time in the darkness; not a rat (which it probably was), but all that creature symbolised: an incarnation of the murderous intentions of nature, concentrated hostility, contagion and whimpering death. I was naked and defenceless, as if there were no walls around me, no key in the door, no name to tell me who I was, nothing to hold on to. The dense gloom felt like a physical touch, already the creature was right up against me, I could feel it quivering, its panting intimacy. I was invisible, lost in the dark room and to myself. I had already been eradicated, nullified by the night, a cry of terror in the void.

With trembling hands I fumbled for the box of matches and lit the candle. Whatever had been there had gone.

A man was standing out in the middle of the lake on a little hummock. In his hand he held a long bamboo fishing pole and he was surrounded on all sides by marshy, half dried-up water-holes. With an easy action he cast out his line again and again, without ever catching anything. His torso was long, with a graceful curve to the spine, supple as the bamboo pole itself. After each cast, he reverted to the same position, still as a statue in a dried-up fountain.

For the next hour the fisherman's persistent and unsuccessful casts of his line provided the accompaniment to Seng Ti's account of his life. Seng Ti was one of the few, and in fact probably the only Cambodian I met, who had no hidden or apparent reluctance against talking about the past. He had once saved his own life by talking about it and it was this experience that had made him a willing informant, almost as if he were paying off a debt.

Seng Ti was 22 years of age and barely five feet tall, like so many other young Cambodians of his age whose diminutive size spoke of bodies that had not been given sufficient nourishment during the all-important years of adolescence, much the same years which in the West had seen a new generation grow taller than any generation before them. Seng Ti had a pale moon face, and a pair of round, steel-rimmed glasses that gave him the look of a child dressed up as an old man. Everything about him added to this impression of the meeting of two irreconcileable ages in one and the same person, making him seem both innocent and far too worldly-wise. Up until a certain point, his story was not unlike that of most other Cambodians, but from there on it deviated drastically from theirs.

Seng Ti was one of a family of eleven, only four of whom were still alive: himself, a brother and two sisters. The rest had been murdered by the Khmer Rouge. His oldest brother – who at the time of the revolution's victory in 1975, had been living in France, where he had trained as a doctor – had come home to Cambodia with the most idealistic of motives, ready to help with the rebuilding of the country. He disappeared without trace. Just a couple of years ago Seng Ti's only surviving brother had found his elder brother's name on the list of the detainees in S-21 in Phnom Penh. His photograph was not there, so they assumed that he had not died under torture in the prison, but had been taken out of town to be executed on Phnom Penh's Killing Fields at Choueng Ek.

After the death of Seng Ti's parents at the hands of the regime, he was sent to a labour camp for orphaned children. Here he worked in the fields from six in the morning until seven in the evening together with thousands of other orphans. When the moon was full they worked until midnight.

The Vietnamese invaded and the regime fell. Seng Ti ended up in a children's home in Phnom Penh, a situation he was not at all happy about. And so he did as millions of other Cambodians had done in the turbulent years following the country's collapse and took to wandering what was left of Cambodia's road system.

Three months later he came to the little town of Battambang, not far from the border with Thailand. Here he lived on the street and earned a living by doing all sorts of odd jobs. Then one night he had a dream: he dreamt that he lived in a country where there was peace. He woke up the next morning to find himself still in Cambodia, but now he knew that there was no future for him here.

So he took to the road once more, this time heading for Thailand. The land at the border was mined. But Seng Ti walked through it alone, a child who had experienced a strange and uplifting dream, without anyone to guide him.

He spent eight months in a refugee camp in Thailand and while there he was interviewed by an American journalist, Roger Rosenbaum, who told his story to *Time* magazine. Two months later Seng Ti was adopted by an American couple and at the age of 13 he arrived in Massachusetts, still a child, but with an old man's head on his shoulders.

At university he had majored in education; he was only in Cambodia on a flying visit, acting as interpreter for two young American politicians who were touring the country giving lectures on democracy. The things he had seen in Cambodia had not given him any cause for optimism. He was less concerned about the prospect of a renewed civil war the minute the UN left than the future if the peace lasted. "Foreign capital is starting to flow into the country," he said while we both watched the patient fisherman out there in the sun, still casting his line into the near-dry water-holes, "capital from Thailand in particular, but no one is taking time to worry about the interests of the Cambodians. There is no decent educational system – and the politicians could not care less. Parents are only interested in getting their children out to earn some money. The children are presented with no values other than those of survival. They are given no new role models or ideals that might provide them with an alternative to the life they have seen going on around them during 20 years of war. Unless something serious is done about their education and upbringing I'm afraid that the new generations are going to be even worse than their predecessors. There is no programme for the rebuilding of the country and the politicians find escape from the reality of Cambodia in high-flown rhetoric."

This tiny 22-year-old Cambodian, who had seen so much of life, was speaking out against the spirit of the times. Cambodia's executioners had been teachers and Marxists and in the eyes of later generations these two things had melded together to form a picture of the evil teacher and totalitarian educator who had led his pupils to disaster. Seng Ti was saying something else: that the evil schoolteacher had to be combated by good schoolteachers and that it was not enough, after the frenzy of collectivism, to purge the mind with the spontaneous impulses of selfishness.

* * *

In Phnom Penh I had bought a book written by Seanglim Bit, a Cambodian psychologist now living in the United States, in which he described the traits which had brought about the ruin of his country; traits such as compulsive submission to authority, social conformism and a generally fatalistic attitude towards life, inspired by the Buddhism which had rooted itself so deeply in the Cambodian psyche. Seanglim Bit had also endeavoured to present a counter-image, a personality type which he called "the upwardly mobile personality", resourceful, dynamic and extrovert, capable of setting goals and realizing them. Among Cambodian refugees in the USA he had come across numerous examples of this personality type, which he optimistically cited as ideal role models. These examples were all financial success stories. Annual income formed Seanglim Bit's measure of how far refugees from his own homeland had succeeded in overcoming the traumas of war and become whole human beings once more. And perhaps it is the case that for those who have lost everything – or never had anything to begin with – the dream of becoming rich is the only one they have. Money represents the ultimate dream of those who are disillusioned and bereft of ideals. And having cut all ties, the emigrant – provided he is not a political refugee – sets out with this one aim in mind: that of climbing the social ladder, of striking it rich. But to acknowledge wealth as an ideal is also to acknowledge disillusionment.

With his optimistic brand of psychology, a call to action, Seanglim Bit could only counter the individual fatalism of the Cambodian by outdoing it, with the even greater fatalism that comes into play when one ceases to ascribe any worth to a sense of community. In the end he substantiated the state of affairs he wanted to combat: that Cambodia was no longer a society in the original sense of the word, but merely a collection of individuals who happened to live side by side without drawing any strength from that closeness or discovering in it any hope for the future. He urged the Cambodians to look upon themselves as immigrants in their own land, with all ties broken, strangers everywhere, except within the four walls of their own home. In that respect his views were very much of their time, corresponding quite closely to the Western world's naïve reaction to the collapse of Communism when the only models it could offer to a world that had lost not only its tyrants, but also its inner cohesion, were profit and consumerism. This was what Seng Ti recognized when he said that Cambodia would never become a society again unless it could find itself standards other than the material values bound up with earning money.

As he spoke, I was reminded of Michel de Montaigne's essays where he draws attention to the similarity in French between the word for "value" and the word for "valour". In Seng Ti's small person this link was re-established. The values for which he stood were the "valorous" values, which were not merely confined to self-interest, while the value system recommended the whole world over as a remedy for the former Communist societies amounted to no more than the assertion of the practical dictates of the struggle for survival. The fact that civilization begins only at the point where the struggle for bare survival ends, was a lesson that had been ignored, but Seng Ti had learned that lesson, while caught up in a fight for life tougher than anything the majority of his contemporaries on this earth had ever had to face. He had had a dream, and he had followed that dream.

I ate dinner early, wanting to be back at the hotel on the lake before nightfall. While I was eating my noodle soup and surveying the wide, deserted street, I noticed an odd young man driving past on a Honda scooter. His huge, black horn-rimmed glasses, skinny arms and gaping over-sized white T-shirt conspired with his sickly pallor to give him the look of a patient newly discharged from hospital. As if aware of the impression he conveyed, he had tied a large, multicoloured silk scarf around his neck, but instead of detracting attention from his anaemic appearance this simply served to emphasize it. The end result was quirky, both eccentric and irresolute.

I would have thought no more about it, had it not been for the fact that a moment later he drove by again, going the opposite way. Some time elapsed. Then he came into view again, casting a sidelong glance in my direction as he passed and it dawned on me that he was plucking up the courage to stop and speak to me. On his fourth run past he at last succeeded in overcoming his shyness. He parked his scooter and walked over with his hand extended and a determined expression on his face, as if he were expecting to be rebuffed, but had made up his mind to make it as difficult for me as possible.

"Gerard," he said, seizing me by the hand. "I'm French, a priest."

"A priest?" I could not disguise my astonishment.

Gerard sat down without any invitation. "Yes, a priest." He sighed, and I could not decide whether this was prompted by the heat or by his choice of vocation.

"How long are you here for?" I asked.

"For life." He sighed again and this time I was in no doubt as to the cause. A couple of grey hairs sprouted from his side parting, although I guessed his age at about 35.

"It is many years since anyone did any work for the Catholic church in Cambodia. The Khmer Rouge killed all of the priests. But French bishops have now been ordained. There are six churches in the Kampong Thom area, with 800 parishioners. Unfortunately, four of the churches are within the danger zone. It's a big job. A difficult job." He mopped his brow with the gaudy scarf.

"How long have you been here?"

"Only a week. I don't know much about the place yet. I spent a year in Phnom Penh, working in a children's home, before deciding to come here. I didn't like the staff at the home. They weren't interested in the welfare of the children."

He took a swig of the Coca Cola he had just ordered. Then he turned to me and asked with surprising vehemence: "Are there any prostitutes here? Do you know anything about that?"

"No, I don't," I replied, taken aback by the force with which he had asked the question. Things were not easy for Gerard. Not only had he undertaken to stay in this devastated spot for the rest of his life in order to establish a Catholic community in a region where three out of four of his prospective parishioners were under the control of one of the world's most bloodthirsty guerrilla forces, he had evidently also decided to mount a crusade against the local prostitution racket. I could not help but wonder whether his interest in prostitution arose from motives that he fully understood. Bearing the cross both of his lust and of his Catholic vow of chastity I was not surprised that he looked so pale and gaunt. He aroused in me the same mixed feelings as Don Quixote: admiration – because he was indeed a man of valour – pity and the urge to laugh out loud.

"Do *you* know anything about prostitution in Cambodia?" I asked. The ambiguity of my question seemed lost on him.

Gerard nodded gravely and assumed the earnest expression of the preacher. "In Phnom Penh I sometimes ate at a restaurant just across from the Hotel Le Royal. Do you know the place? There's a young girl there who shows customers to their tables. There was this one time when I thanked her for attending to me and she promptly grabbed hold of my hand and nodded towards the hotel behind us. 'We go,' she said in English. She obviously thought I was a guest at the hotel. I pulled my hand away, but she kept on at me. 'Twenty dollars. No mother, no father.' A lost child. I gave her $10, out of pity, but I haven't eaten there since."

We were interrupted by an elderly Cambodian with a deeply furrowed face who came over to greet Gerard. "We met at a wedding in Phnom Penh," Gerard explained and nodded to the new arrival who took his acknowledgement as an invitation to join us. He worked as an interpreter for the UN troops and no sooner had he sat down than he started to hold forth on the situation in Cambodia.

"One must not forget," he said, "that Cambodia's problems have always been caused by external forces."

"Cambodia today is under pressure from Vietnam and Thailand, godless communism and soulless capitalism," added Gerard, who had clearly heard this argument before.

"You have a perfect grasp of our situation." Gerard was vouchsafed a nod of approval. Then the Cambodian continued: "Foreign powers were also behind the atrocities committed under the Khmer Rouge regime. They received weapons from the USA, from Vietnam, from the Soviet Union, Thailand, China, Belgium and Czechoslovakia." He came to the end of his list and looked at me, as if expecting me to contradict him.

"Yes, but it wasn't the arms manufacturers who ordered the Khmer Rouge to kill over a million people," I countered.

"No, it was the Chinese. The Cultural Revolution served as a model." This was the first time I had heard a well-educated and enlightened individual refer to the events prior to 1979 with the intention of providing an explanation, and his answer was a discouraging one, the eternal disavowal of responsibility: The evil came from the outside. The Cambodians themselves were innocent and had no need of any heart-searching.

I could see how countries in Eastern Europe that had lived under the sovereignty of the Soviet Union could respond to the repatriation of the Red Army by losing themselves for a while in spurious, nationalistic pipe dreams. But I could not understand how a land such as Cambodia which, in national terms, had come as close as any country has ever come to committing suicide, could do this. Nonetheless, during my time in Cambodia I came across it again and again. Hardly had this ravaged country begun to take on any semblance of nationhood, before it started looking around for someone to hate, as if hate could pull a country that bore only the faintest similarity to a society together again. There was only one thing on which the Khmer Rouge and their opponents in the Government agreed: the nomination of Vietnamese citizens living in Cambodia as the root cause of all ills, from the country's economic problems to the danger of an AIDS epidemic. It was the country's élite, both those who had been deposed and their successors, who were behind this message: Cambodia did not need to remember. Cambodia needed to hate.

As Gerard was saying goodbye to the interpreter he clasped the other's outstretched hand in both of his and I recognized the priest in him, in the feigned warmth and paternalistic air with which he addressed the much older man. He was simply not equal to the situation. He tried his best to play the part, but the truth was that he had not the faintest notion of what sort of game he had got himself into and how he was supposed to behave. He seemed terribly lonely, a loneliness that was only enhanced by the fact that his own spiritual conflict fused with and found its echo in a country that in some unnerving way seemed to consist solely of lonely people.

I was certain that he would keep his promise to stay here for the rest of his life. Irresolute souls are always the most fanatical.

Darkness had fallen, like a door slamming, and I got up to leave, wanting to be back at the hotel before the shooting started. A drunken figure staggering along the road ahead of me was fleetingly lit up by the light of a passing bicycle. Then I turned onto the cart track leading down to the lake.

An hour later bursts of fire from the government soldiers' assault guns were resounding through the night. I thought of Gerard, that knight of a lost cause in a forlorn land, but I no longer felt like laughing at him.

The little town of Stung, 50 kilometres from Kampong Thom, was reputed to be the most trouble-torn spot in Kampong Thom province. The Khmer

Rouge positions were not far off and Stung was regularly bombarded by shells. Only ten days earlier a band of guerrillas had stormed the town, firing at anything in sight and eventually winding up in the market place, where they stuffed their rucksacks with loot before pulling back, leaving behind them the usual dead and wounded.

On the road to Stung I passed a squad of Cambodian soldiers who were in the process of clearing mines. They sat hunkered down in small groups, tiny and neat in freshly pressed, pale-blue uniforms, passing mine detectors over the ground. On the surrounding trees and bushes hung the red warning signs bearing the white skull and crossbones which I had come across so often in Cambodia. The soldiers had the look of children playing some forbidden game. They held themselves quite, quite still, as if even the sound of their voices might set off a mine. Never before had I experienced such intense stillness. With their mine detectors they made tiny tracks for human beings in the middle of a territory that had long been a land of ghosts.

I looked at the houses I was driving past and it occurred to me that the lives of the Cambodian people were much like these huts cobbled together from straw and wooden planks. They endured for a short while; they were flimsy and tended to cave in easily; they left behind no trace of themselves, nor any ruins. Cambodians did not come into contact with the twentieth century until the moment when they stepped on a land mine.

I tried to envisage shells dropping on this landscape of drained rice paddies and grey wooden huts. The idea was every bit as absurd as Joseph Conrad's description in *Heart of Darkness* of a French man-of-war shelling a stretch of coastline somewhere in Africa. "In the empty immensity of earth, sky and water, there she was, incomprehensible, firing into a continent," wrote Conrad of the ludicrous, impotent gesture that is war. Here, too, the earth would open up to receive the shells, the houses move aside, the people fall to the ground. Afterwards, life would go on as before, the shells having fallen like stones thrown into water.

Four or five tanks were drawn up on the rice fields just outside Stung. They all had a rather neglected look about them and their sandy-yellow and leaf-green camouflage made it seem as though the soil and vegetation with which they were meant to merge was reclaiming them. Between the caterpillar tracks and a shady fig tree the soldiers had hung hammocks in which they slept through the noonday heat.

Tanks were not the tools of this war. Men, both in plain clothes and in uniform, drove past on bicycles and scooters, all carrying Russian AK-47 rifles over their shoulders. The AK-47 was the weapon of choice in this war which, like all wars that cannot be won, had replaced the battlefield with terrorism, in an interminable and unstoppable trial of strength in which the death rate was low, the suffering great and the fear even greater.

Everywhere one looked in Stung there were armed men. In a wooden shack from which a barber plied his trade I saw a man stretched out on a bench, having a shave. He had set aside his weapon – a belt containing five hand grenades.

I took a short stroll around the town, which was not much more than a collection of yellow and white colonial houses with rough sandy tracks for streets. I settled myself on a little bench underneath a sign proclaiming that this was a "Drink Shop". The owner of the shop, an elderly woman, fetched me a can of lukewarm Coca Cola. Then she leaned towards me confidentially. "The government, the Khmer Rouge – what difference does it make. They're thieves, the lot of them."

I called in at the Indonesian UN battalion's HQ and was given a guided tour of the premises by a second-in-command whose English was very poor. He showed me the shelters which the soldiers had dug in the sand: holes, a little over a metre deep, covered with palm-tree trunks and sandbags. "All of the townspeople take refuge here when there is an attack," he said and smiled apologetically as if he were sorry he did not have anything better to offer than these makeshift holes in the ground.

Stung also had a police station, set up and run – like everything else – by UN personnel. A captain from the German *Bundesgrenzschutz* received me seated behind his desk. He had only been in Cambodia for three days and was suffering from the tropical heat. The sweat ran down his fleshy face in veritable rivers and he mopped his brow with a voluminous white handkerchief while assuring me, as if taking an oath before a judge, that the main thing was to do one's job properly and that he hoped he would be able to stay long enough to have the chance to become better acquainted with conditions here. Having delivered this ingenuous testimony to his devotion to duty, he announced that as far as everything else was concerned I would have to speak to his superiors in Kampong Thom.

The name Pu Mo Tjak was one of the things that had brought me to Stung. An English UN observer in Kampong Thom had told me about this place inhabited by a group of "displaced persons". "Displaced persons" was the official term for refugees within the country itself, in this case an entire village that had been forced to flee from a Khmer Rouge controlled area. Here was an opportunity to observe these emigrants from the unknown land created by political terrorism.

I had taken a careful note of the name exactly as the UN observer had pronounced it: "Pu Mo Tjak". When I gave this name to the young man in the market-place in Stung who had agreed to drive me out there on his motorbike for five dollars, he corrected me: not "Pu Mo Tjak", but just "Mo Tjok".

Over the hour that followed I was to give a great deal of thought to what happens to the pronunciation of a word as it travels from mouth to mouth, especially when it has been spoken by three different sets of lips. Was it still the same word? Or, to put it another way: was I really going where I thought I was going? The possibilities of mutual misunderstanding were endless, and almost all fatal.

Pu Mo Tjak was a safe area, which means it is outside Khmer Rouge control, and only ten minutes from Stung – so the Englishman had said. Only when we had been driving for three-quarters of an hour and my guide's monotonously repeated assurances that we would be there in a couple of minutes had begun to sound like an admission that not even he knew where we were, did I start to feel uneasy.

The road ran alongside a river with banks of red clay, past little clumps of straw huts sheltering from the sun in the middle of a palm grove and over bow-backed bridges whose loose planks rattled under the motorbike wheels. With their graceful arches the bridges spoke of engineering skills which, like Cambodia itself, were fragile and evanescent in their beauty.

We headed away from the river and carried on across deserted rice paddies, along roads that were nothing but the beaten tracks the farmers followed on their way out to the fields. As the motorbike threaded its way between the bushes and the odd palm tree I repeated Andrew's warning to myself. Always keep to the major roads, he had said. This could not even be said to be a minor road. I was only a few kilometres from Khmer Rouge country and why were there no longer any houses or people to be seen? I gave myself up to the contemplation of phonetics, and it crossed my mind that phonetics might prove the cause of our heading straight for one of Cambodia's four million mines and, a moment from now, of my having my leg blown off.

Then, all at once, we were there. The river came into view again, it was almost dry. Over the years it had carved its way into a flat plain covered with wizened, flaxen grass that stretched all the way to the horizon. The refugees appeared to blend with the landscape; the first things I noticed were their big, high-wheeled wooden carts. They had sought shelter from the scorching sun under improvised lean-tos made from straw and blue plastic sheeting supplied by the UN. The ground was littered with blackened cooking pots, the ashes of dead fires and stacks of firewood. There were naked children running about; old women with heads shaved, Buddhist fashion; mothers in long sarongs and black cotton shirts and men who sat motionless under the lean-to roofs with red-checked Khmer scarves wrapped around their heads as protection against the sun. They sat, eyeing me in utter silence. They had escaped from the dead zone, but they had brought its eerie stillness with them.

They had packed up their village and their lives, taking with them everything that could be loaded onto their big ox-carts. They called to mind a tribe of Indians roaming the American prairies, or a band of gypsies whose caravan had escaped the Holocaust. Now they sat in the pitiless sun beside a dried-up river-bed waiting for a war that had lasted for 20 years to come to an end. It was a wait that was nigh-on indistinguishable from death.

These "displaced persons" were there as living proof that yet again, with the age of exploration long since past, our world harbours uncharted territory; no longer white spaces on the map, but black spaces, created by political terrorism; defended, not by insurmountable chains of mountains and impenetrable jungles, but by dogma, blood-lust and modern weapon technology, all of which are once again closing the doors our curiosity had opened. These black spaces are appearing everywhere, spreading until it seems sometimes as if they might join up and blot out the map entirely, in order to turn the planet into a black, imploding star.

But then there are other countries, inaccessible until only a moment ago, which are opening up once more. Islands appear where before there was ocean. The tectonic plates of history keep shifting. The Earth is born again and crying out to be discovered, but the greatest illusion of our times lies in the name it has accorded itself: the age of information.

River Patrol to the End of the Earth

ON THE DAY OF MY DEPARTURE FROM KAMPONG THOM I presented myself at the Indonesian battalion's HQ where the commander – casually attired, as always, in tennis shoes, T-shirt and shorts – saw to it that I was given a good send-off. I never did catch his name, and it was purely by chance that I later learned what became of him. A few days after I left he had stepped on a land mine and had to have one of his legs amputated at the German-run hospital in Phnom Penh. He had walked straight into a mined area that had been marked with all the usual warning signs; but he had been naïve enough to trust the bomb disposal expert who was with him and was killed in the explosion. I heard the story from Rolf, one of the hospital's German surgeons, a tall thin man with a distinctive face and the look of an adventurer. He was full of such stories, each one accompanied by an Olympian laugh, as if the victims of all such accidents who wound up on his operating table were more indicative of mankind's folly than of its tragedy and, hence, did not merit anything other than indulgent laughter.

It was also Rolf who told me that on the very day that I touched down in Phnom Penh on my way from Kampong Thom to Stung Treng, one of the huge Russian Andropov helicopters, with eight representatives of the international press on board, including correspondents from the *International Herald Tribune*, *Der Spiegel* and *Bildzeitung*, had lost its rudder and crashed down onto the runway. The helicopter had not crashed from any great height and none of its important passengers had been seriously hurt, but they were nonetheless attended by Rolf, who made such a favourable impression that he was the subject of a half-page feature in *Bildzeitung*, under the headline "The Angel of Cambodia", an epithet which, of course, merely elicited yet another burst of Olympian laughter, as if to say "If they only knew".

*　　*　　*

The helicopter that was to take me to Stung Treng was an American built Bell 206L with room for five passengers. I know nothing about helicopters, this was the first time I had ever travelled in one, and all day I had been in such a state of tense excitement that you would have thought I had never flown before. In the waiting room, to which I had been consigned along with the other four passengers, a badly adjusted television set was showing a video of an American Ninja film. My companions were two Irish engineers, permanently stationed at Kampong Thom, and two French doctors, a man and a woman, from Médecins sans Frontières. The man was suffering from a south-east Asian strain of malaria known as *dengue* and was on his way to the hospital in Phnom Penh. With inward-looking eyes which the fever had robbed of all animation, he slumped against the woman who, in turn, had placed a protective arm around his shoulders.

The helicopter touched down. It was not much more than a small, white-lacquered glass bubble, but the noise from its rotor blades was quite impressive. Without switching off the engine, the pilot hopped out and ran, doubled up, towards our little party, signalling frantically to us to make for the helicopter and keep our heads down. His face was contorted with the effort of trying to make himself heard above the racket of the rotor blades.

The helicopter pitched slightly and I realized that we were already a couple of metres off the ground. Then it banked and I was pressed against a window the size of my body, so that I had the sensation of being inside a glass sphere. Down below, almost as if I were lying on the bottom of the sphere, grass swept past, then red earth, then upturned faces and a tiled roof. We were already at an altitude of something like 150 feet by the time the pilot straightened up the helicopter. This was air travel on a quite different, human scale from that of the big passenger jets roaring down the runway; invested with all the magic of nocturnal dreams of flying or visions of being a bird. I had no sense whatsoever of being shut up inside a machine and I noted the tension in the pit of my stomach, as though my own will-power were helping to keep the helicopter in the air.

The noise was too deafening for us to hold any sort of conversation. The only way of communicating was through the headphones with little microphones attached which all of us were wearing. I could hear the pilot explaining to one of the Irish engineers how the helicopter was much more manoeuvrable in Canada (which was evidently where he came from) than here in Cambodia, where the heat and humidity tended to restrict its movement.

We flew across parched, dusty-grey rice paddies; a vast monotonous landscape 2,000 feet below. The low flying height gave a feeling of swooping through the landscape rather than over it and offered a magnificent and detailed view. It was rather like one long landing approach, that odd sense of intimacy fleetingly induced when the vista presented above the clouds, which always seems to me to be reserved for the gods, not mortals, suddenly gives way to glimpses below of people's homes and gardens. Except that here there was only an empty landscape, waiting for the rainy season, with no visible signs of life apart from the small clutches of wooden huts in the villages, and an occasional white-washed pagoda.

The pilot pointed to the left, where a road cut through the countryside, straight as a die. An irregular pattern of bomb craters ran the length of it. "Americans," said the pilot. "It looks like they've been chasing a convoy of trucks. Up north there's a place that's as full of holes as a Swiss cheese. *Jesus Christ*, bomb craters as big as houses. They really went for it."

"I wish to leave a scar on the landscape here," said Perken, in André Malraux's novel, *La Voie Royale*, 40 years before the Americans turned his words into reality on an unimaginable scale. And so 600,000 people had lost their lives in America's undeclared war against Cambodia, in which half a million tonnes of bombs were dropped, three times as many as in the entire final phase of the battle against Japan during the Second World War, and every one ostensibly discharged in defence of the Western values embodied by the corrupt and superstitious general Lon Nol. He had seized power in a *coup d'état* and, even during the short time when his popularity was at its peak, could not drum up more than 35 per cent of the vote. This had been the bloody prologue to the Khmer Rouge's reign of terror, a crime that had now effectively been forgotten, overshadowed as it was by the spiral of crimes that succeeded it.

To make a scar on the landscape. Not a track, not a mark, but a scar: the solution to a wounded and desperate masculinity whose barren motivation lay in the fear of age and impotence. In the character of Perken, Malraux was anticipating the twentieth century. Because the twentieth century it was that stretched out 2,000 feet below me: impotence and fury, bomb craters amid the emptiness of the rice paddies.

Far below, a red sandy track hove into view, with two sunshine-yellow dots moving along it: Buddhist monks, out for a walk and shielded from the sun by their parasols. After the sight of the bomb-scarred landscape this seemed, in some way, healing and, at the same time, tragic. As if the only way for this country to find peace was by turning its back on the twentieth century.

After a brief stopover at the airport in Phnom Penh, where the other passengers remained, the helicopter flew northwards. We made a pass over the royal palace. Way beneath us I could see the tennis court which had now been sitting there waiting for almost 20 years for Prince Sihanouk's return. For a while we followed the course of the Mekong river, before heading off across dense jungle. It was late in the afternoon. The blue-grey clouds fringing the horizon had acquired a golden rim. The sun itself was hidden behind the cloud. The scintillating semi-circle of the rotor blades above our heads stood out like a cipher against the sky. Then the horizon and the more distant stretches of forest began to fade into an indigo haze. The dark-green jungle below floated in the semi-darkness.

"Do you see that mountain over there to the left?" the pilot's voice came over my headphones. I looked in the direction in which he was pointing and made out a blue shadow rising up above the jungle. "I'm going to climb to 5,000 feet now. The Khmer Rouge have a fortified position on the top there. But at that altitude they don't have a chance of hitting us. The gravity makes the shell's trajectory curve."

"I was shot at once," he went on. "Not here, somewhere else. I flew in low over the treetops and suddenly I was out over open country. I saw the smoke. Then I heard the shots. It was a heavier calibre than an ordinary AK-47. That was the first time it dawned on me that this is no joke. The bullets whizzed just past me. I don't know how he could have missed. He was straight ahead of me. I must have been right in his line of fire."

In Canada, Paul had flown for many years for the Canadian Helicopter Corporation (CHC), which also handled a certain amount of helicopter transportation for the UN in Cambodia. The company's slogan was "where the road ends, we begin", and Paul had always taken those jobs that involved making landings in difficult terrain: putting out forest fires, geological expeditions, patrolling nature reserves and the like.

"Interesting work," he said, "but from a financial point of view, there's no sense in what I'm doing now. I did give it up at one point, for my family's sake, and became an estate agent. On the sale of just one house I earned the same as I do in a month now. So what am I doing here? Love of adventure, I guess."

Up ahead the Mekong River came into view once more. Directly in front of us I saw the airport, a strip of black asphalt surrounded by ochre earth and a circular helicopter pad on which sat two of the huge Russian Andropov helicopters painted the conspicuous white of the UN.

We were met by a couple of aircraft mechanics. "That was a near thing," one of them remarked to Paul, "it'll be dark in five minutes."

On a chair outside the wooden shack that passed for an airport building sat a UN soldier clutching a can of Heineken. I went over to him, introduced myself and showed him the identity card I had been issued with at UN headquarters in Phnom Penh. The soldier looked up at me, but made no response. He wore a Dutch flag on his sleeve and a smug look on his small face, its deep flush contrasting sharply with his sun-bleached crew-cut.

"I'm a reporter," I said at length.

"That's your problem." He drank his beer slowly, then belched. "We've got a nice little place up here, and we're very happy with it." He eyed me, as if I was the only troublemaker he could think of in the whole of Cambodia's unspoilt idyll.

I turned to walk away.

"Hey," he said, waving me back and pointing with his beer can towards the airport building, "you'd better book your return flight now." He raised the can as if to drink my health. Then he gave a gloating grin: "Reporters come bottom of the list."

Stung Treng was a small town of grimy concrete houses so ill-suited to the tropical climate they seemed to be mouldering away. Together with a filthy market, where the rubbish piled up in archaeological layers, the houses lent the town a grubby and neglected appearance, more outpost than town. Large, vacant patches of waste ground were everywhere. On the dirt roads there were few private cars, but plenty of small, see-sawing two-wheeled wagons drawn by scrawny horses.

A short step from the centre of the town lay a number of large, airy houses on tall stilts. They were mostly unpainted, unpretentious, but beautiful, with broad flights of steps leading up to covered verandahs that ran the width of the buildings' first floors. Inside, the rooms were spacious and cool. These houses exemplified a traditional Cambodian building style attuned to the climate of the country. It was a style which had fallen into decline when, in the brief flirtation with modern civilization granted them before the horror engulfed them and put an end to all building, the Cambodian middle and upper classes became infatuated with the raw materials of progress: concrete, corrugated sheeting and breeze block, and had opted to live behind walls of damp, crumbling concrete rather than in these exquisite constructions.

The UN headquarters, which lay a little way outside the town, was nothing but a collection of prefab barracks, the sections for which had been flown in on the Russian Andropov helicopters. Inside, each one contained a fully equipped open-plan office complete with canteen and staff rooms, so that you could have been forgiven for thinking, as you stepped inside and felt the chill of the air conditioning, that you had been transported to modern business premises in the West.

Captain Strapolini from the UN's Uruguayan battalion, who had the task of supervising the election proceedings in Stung Treng, was a perfect gentleman and, in marked contrast to the reception I had been given the previous evening, he regarded himself as my host and responsible for my well-being – even if I had invited myself. He had set aside the day to drive me around Stung Treng and organize my visit in such a way that I would get as much out of it as possible. He was a short, plump man with a thick black moustache and a habit of rounding off all his sentences with an apologetic little moue and a shrug of his shoulders, as if the world were forever setting stupid, but irrefutable, obstacles in his path.

When we came to my request to join one of the river patrols up the Mekong River which I had heard regularly ran into the Khmer Rouge, the apologetic little moue flashed across his face again and I expected him to turn me down.

"We soldiers are only observers and we carry no arms when we are on patrol." Captain Strapolini shrugged his shoulders as if he would be the first to deplore this fact. He reached for a calabash on the desk in front of him, put the silver drinking straw sticking out of this spherical object to his mouth and sucked with great gusto. The beverage he was imbibing in this fashion was, as he had explained a moment before, *maté*, a traditional Uruguayan herbal tea. He gave a sigh of contentment before continuing.

"Oh yes, we used to chat to the Khmer Rouge. But three days ago they fired on us at a checkpoint further down the river. So now we've stopped chatting." He pulled another face. "This is an interesting, but sometimes dangerous, job."

Captain Strapolini had been stationed at the South Pole for a year before coming to Cambodia. Down there the temperature had been 60 below zero, here it was plus 40. The change was – he hunted for the word in English. I felt moved to help him find the right expression, believing myself by now to be something of an expert in the motives, above all boredom, which led men to have themselves posted to this God-forsaken country.

"Refreshing?" I suggested.

"How did you guess?" said Captain Strapolini, looking relieved for a moment, as if I had freed him from the burden of having to explain something much more complicated.

He then picked up where he had left of, and proceeded to describe the problems he faced. "We are trying to give them the chance to build a country from the ground up. But you cannot imagine the corruption here. For example, this region is full of illegal sawmills. Whole tracts of jungle are cut down without any kind of check being kept or permits issued. The sawmills are owned by the local Party bosses, all of whom support the ruling Party. And do you know who they use as unpaid labour? Soldiers!" He shook his head, pulling the corners of his mouth down melodramatically. Then he flung his arms wide as if to say: But what can you do?

"Or what do you think of this?" he went on. "Many of the soldiers run around out of uniform – or wearing different uniforms. Armed, of course. There was one soldier from the government army who was going about in a Khmer Rouge uniform. When we stopped him he simply said: 'But everybody knows me. Nobody would mistake me for the enemy'."

*　*　*

On the bow of one of the river patrol's two rubber dinghies someone had written the words *El Demonio de Mekong* with a Magic Marker. I had envisaged a proper boat, but all they had were two inflatable rubber dinghies, each fitted with an outboard motor. This was the extent of the international organisation's authority on the Mekong river; as the Magic Marker inscription suggested, it was not much more than a pleasant joke, which must have been something of a trial for the Latin American soldiers who had their famed machismo to contend with.

Captain Strapolini had outlined for me the duties of the UN soldiers. Armed with the authority invested in their uniforms and that alone, they had the power to stop all traffic on the river and search the craft they pulled in for weapons. Furthermore, there were rumours of government soldiers exacting illegal toll fees from passing boats and here, too, unarmed as they were, they were forced to resort to polite warnings and – in a land where, for 20 years, the voice of the guns had been the only one to be heard – wagging the finger. The thinking behind it was, of course, logical: those who had the job of bringing peace, could not be armed with anything other than the power of their example. Nothing, then, could have been more fitting than to set out on river patrol in two easily punctured rubber dinghies.

We took our places in the dinghies, in which we would spend the following eight hours, while the powerful outboard motors sped us up to the border with Laos and back again. The party consisted of two Chileans, two Uruguayans and a Cambodian interpreter who had learned his Spanish at the Cambodian embassy in Havana.

Along the first stretch, the Mekong River was broad and brilliant green, with dark jungle looming on its distant banks. Then the river narrowed and tight bends began to appear. The current was strong, at some points spiralling downwards into tiny, swirling funnels; elsewhere the surface was smooth – straining, so it seemed, under an inner pressure – only, a moment later, to erupt once more into foaming whirlpools. The dinghy's high speed had lifted its nose into the air and the boat seemed to skim the surface, quite unaffected by the turmoil beneath. There was still a couple of months to go before the start of the rainy season, but rocks that jutted up out of the whirlpools with tall concrete piles set on top of them, indicated that when that time came the water level would be seven to eight metres higher than it was at present. The roots of the immense trees that grew along the bank and some way out into the river stopped high up the trunks, which almost immediately ran into the stout branches in such a way that the tree seemed to consist of a bundle of slender trunks twisted together in the middle by some powerful fist; fantastic and disquieting forms, emphasizing the hostility of the river.

But under the vast arch of the sky the colours were gay and reassuring, the vegetation a vibrant shade of green, the river nothing but one enormous, sparkling, lively reflection of the dazzling sunlight. Now and then a butterfly fluttered across the water, always just on the verge of mistaking the foaming, snow-white coronas of the whirlpools for large, inviting flowers. Birds with ice-blue breasts swooped down over the sun-spangled surface in graceful arcs and came up again with no visible catch in their long, narrow beaks.

A constant stream of canoes slid past, heading in the opposite direction. Sometimes we stopped them and checked their occupants' papers while the soldiers searched for weapons. A canoe with a family of seven on board floated out of the current at the head of a small bay. In the bottom of the canoe lay a half-eaten fish and the remains of a meal of boiled rice wrapped in banana leaves. There was something poignant and utterly innocent about the small party's lunch on the river, a glimpse of Cambodia different to that which had represented the political reality for the past 20 years; not unspoilt idyll, but something strong and solid and lasting; the cornerstone of life.

For reasons which I cannot quite explain, even to myself, I am often moved by the sight of people eating; and especially by solitary individuals who, bowed over their meal, seem to rediscover a dignity which may otherwise be hard to discern in them. I remember an old man whom I saw eating alone in a humble restaurant in one of the poorer districts of Naples. All of his attention was focussed on his meal, which he ate slowly and fastidiously. Afterwards he sat there for a long while, lost, it seemed, in blissful reflection; as if he were not only digesting the food, but also the moment he had just lived through. I formed the notion that he had planned this meal with care, and had been looking forward to it for some time. What he had presented me with was the capacity for joy.

Most people are in possession of this capacity when sitting bowed over a plate. They draw in upon themselves, upon the moment, the fundamentals. They let life in. One only needs to look at the Chinese with their food bowls, the way in which they carefully select one morsel after another with their chopsticks, deliberate and concentrated in their quest. Their actions have an instinctive superiority about them, a dignity quite at odds with their hangdog movements at work, round-shouldered, shuffling, as if the whole point was to make oneself as unnoticeable as possible. At meal times, with their rice bowl in front of them, they command an inner peace. They do honour to themselves.

I looked into the bottom of the canoe and I saw in the remains of that meal an aura of care and generosity. I understood why the Khmer Rouge, with their unerring, totalitarian instinct for everything that can strip people of their dignity, had decreed that all meals were to be taken collectively. Eating a meal is a private and intimate act – like reading. In a country of illiterates the dictatorship chose to crack down on unsupervised meals. The remains of a meal in the bottom of a canoe in a bend in the Mekong River – 15 years earlier they would have been incriminating evidence. Now they represented a hope.

Captain Strapolini had told me about the problems the people on the river had with the underpaid and often starving government troops, and the bandits who posed as soldiers. The illegal toll fees that they demanded from the fishermen were often so hefty – as much as $300 per boat – that they made it quite impossible for them to carry on their trade and ended by wrecking their lives. Ruthlessly they took all they could get, and were ready to underscore their demands with the help of the only thing of which there was no shortage in Cambodia, the gun. The line between soldiering and banditry had long since become fluid, while the UN were powerless and had to confine themselves to making reports. Some elementary pact of trust between human beings, the pact that allows a society to function, appeared to have been broken in Cambodia. That brief glimpse I had had, in the bottom of a canoe, of another Cambodia, was it really a strong enough cornerstone?

At one spot on the riverbank, a group of people had set up camp on the grey sand in the shade of the trees, into which they had retreated, seeking shelter from the midday sun. A woman squatted before a campfire where a blackened pot rested on three rocks. A baby lay sleeping on a straw mat and fishing nets had been hung to dry on the nethermost branches of the trees. They would live like this for weeks at a time while they fished the river. Or perhaps they always lived like this. It was a life as basic as any that has been lived since man started to walk upright.

But life was no less basic for their tormentors, the soldiers, whom we came upon a little further upriver. They had parked themselves on a sand spit that ran out into the river from the bank. From here they had a good view of the river and the passing canoes were within range of their Kalashnikovs. The soldiers, too, had sought refuge from the midday sun among the surrounding trees, where they had made themselves comfortable in hammocks from which they rose warily when they caught sight of our dinghy approaching the bank. Their assault guns had been standing embedded in the sand. They picked them up and slung them over their shoulders before preparing to greet us. They positioned themselves a little way off, their faces impassive. One of them ran a finger along the barrel of his Kalashnikov, and promptly drew it away again. The metal was hot from being out in the sun. Again the finger came back, tentatively, seeming to have a probing life of its own. Another touch and another little jump. It was no more than a nervous reflex.

One of the UN soldiers put out a hand and smiled broadly. There were handshakes all round and cigarettes proffered. These the Cambodians accepted, drawing on them greedily. The interpreter exchanged a few words with the soldiers. They gave grim little smiles. Then their dusky, almost battered looking faces reverted to the impassive look of a moment before. None of them wore boots, they stood barefoot in the burning sand. Their shirts hung loose over trousers that stopped short well above their ankles. Their weapons alone revealed that they were soldiers.

They were here to make sure that the fishermen did not use dynamite when fishing the river, they said in reply to the interpreter's question.

But had they not been squeezing the fishermen for money?

Once more the nervous one started fiddling with the barrel of his machine-gun. One of the others answered: "Yes, we have. We have asked the fishermen for money. But they don't have to pay unless they want to."

"What happens if they don't want to?"

"Then we won't harm them."

"Try to understand." It was the edgy one suddenly speaking up, as if anxious to defend them against some unspoken accusation. "We have nothing."

One thing differentiated the barefoot fishermen from the barefoot soldiers: the Kalashnikov. The soldiers on the Mekong River were not troops in any army, fighting in the name of any nation or ideal. They were soldiers in the only war waged in Cambodia; the most elementary of all wars, that of survival. It was the fight for life, in its rawest form that spoke through their blank, sunburned faces and the itchy fingers which needed constantly to seek reassuring contact with the burning metal of the gun barrel.

Another round of handshakes, and cigarettes, then we left. Some time later we heard shots far off in the distance, but by the time we passed the sand spit again, as we headed downriver, the soldiers had gone.

Over the last stretch of the journey, we had Laos to one side of us, Cambodia to the other. The sky was overcast and blue-grey clouds were building up over a landscape of jungle-clad ridges and steep hills, as a foretaste of the rainy season. We pulled in alongside a muddy bank, where a herd of water buffalo had wandered out into the river. From the top of the bank a group of women and children regarded us without stirring. I suggested to the interpreter that we clamber up and ask them what they thought of the changes their country was undergoing.

The women looked up as we reached the top of the bank, but made no move to rise from the squatting position in which they had been crouched all this time. Their jaws moved monotonously as they chewed on betel nuts that made their cheeks bulge. Now and again they aimed a great jet of spit at the ground, which was already spattered with blood-red stains.

This was a quiet spot, they said. It was many years since there had been any war here, and they uttered the word "war" as if, after all these years they had not only forgotten the war, but also the very meaning of the word. They gazed into space and spat, in confirmation. Oh yes, they were looking forward to the election. (The choice of words was so clichéd that I suspected the interpreter, an erstwhile diplomat who, for the last 30 years, had loyally served successive rulers of Cambodia – with the exception of the Khmer Rouge – of putting words in their mouths, or at least improving on what they had to say.) They had not yet made up their minds who they would vote for. Again they spat and, for a moment, they resembled the ideal citizens in any democracy, peerless and self-sufficent, well aware that when you came down to it, it was they who pulled the strings. Representatives from a couple of the parties had visited the area. But then it was so far out of the way, most politicians did not think it worth the trouble to come here. Then they spat again and rocked gently back and forth on their haunches, seeming to imply that they had had quite enough of all these questions.

Had they felt intimidated, I continued. Intimidated? They shook their heads. Propaganda, yes. Pressure, no. Their expression now was one of superiority, and they tittered, as though the idea that anyone should take it into their heads to threaten then really was too ridiculous. There was something totally unbowed about them, as if they had been squatting there, chewing betel nuts for ever, with death's great scythe, as it swept over Cambodia, never descending to their level.

Was there anything they needed, I asked in conclusion. No, no, they said, they had all they needed, and they spat one last time on the red earth, setting a full stop to the conversation.

"Their needs are not great," said the interpreter, as if the women had just said something strange that called for an explanation. But I had already worked out their last reply for myself. They had been saying it all along, with their unperturbed squatting and the red gobs of betel juice with which they not only spat out the bounds of their territory, but also seemed to demonstrate a proprietorial attitude to life. They were neither strangers nor refugees on this Earth. They lived at the end of the earth and considered, themselves, that it was no bad place to be. They had next to nothing and wanted for less. That was their secret, which gave them strength and enabled them to live in peace.

Pure Evil

I NEVER DID COME FACE TO FACE WITH A MEMBER OF THE Khmer Rouge.

My search ended there on the Mekong River, but I suppose it had truly begun a couple of years earlier, in a village a few hours' drive from the Croatian capital, Zagreb, when I met Captain Martinkovic. Martinkovic was a Serb and a member of a troop of irregulars calling itself "The White Eagles" which at one point played a key role in the war in the former Yugoslavia. Martinkovic had been found lying in a drunken stupor in a village where his men had just killed 45 defenceless old people. I had seen the corpses, laid out on the floor of a chapel, side by side in one long row, their bodies covered in wounds and bruises from the beatings they had suffered, proof that for none of them had dying come easy.

Captain Martinkovic had been captured by Croatian soldiers and it was they who presented him to me. Witnesses had confirmed that Martinkovic himself had taken no hand in the killings. He had selected the victims and viewed their agonizing end, Slivovits bottle in hand. He was 56 years old, a convicted felon and alcoholic, and his face – swollen from the blows he had been dealt by his gaolers – betrayed that this was a man who had long ago lost the key to anything worthwhile within himself.

I never did get to the bottom of the reason for his actions. These killings were so senseless, and yet deeds such as Martinkovic's seemed to be a constant in history. One could cite war as the reason and spread one's arms wide in despair: such things happen. One could search for an explanation in the Captain's own history and unearth the social or psychological roots of evil. That called for a comprehensive knowledge of his life story and I was not sure that, even then, the answer one would arrive at would be a satisfactory one. The leap from an unhappy childhood or adverse social circumstances to the atrocities I had witnessed seemed to me to be so untranslatably great that no explanation would cover it.

It was a question of responsibility. But it was also a question of the nature of evil – assuming that it had such a thing. That was how I had read Jean-Paul Sartre's remark about the purity of evil, "its horrifying, irreducible purity". Evil could not be reduced to anything else. It could not be broken down into traumas, neuroses, wounds inflicted in childhood or social inferiority complexes. It was its own creator and producer, an independently welling spring within humanity, a sort of chemical element within the soul, perhaps not in all people, but certainly within the species. And yet, as a definition of evil this last only serves to perpetuate the riddle of it, not solve it and thus I could go on and on hammering on the same closed door. My desire to meet a member of the Khmer Rouge had merely been a naïve attempt to get that door to open and had I achieved this, in Stung or on the bank of the Mekong River, the result would no doubt have been no more than a repeat performance of my encounter with Captain Martinkovic; but one more confrontation with the impenetrable aspect of evil. I had created an insoluble dilemma for myself. I tried to make sense of evil by employing that faculty of reason the denial of which gives rise to evil. It was, after all, the job of reason to analyse things, to break them down into their individual components and trace them back to their original causes. But an element could not be traced back to anything, nor be converted into fractions. It was an indivisible unit: Pure evil.

Some time after my return home I received a letter from a Dane, Svend Petersen, who had worked for the UN and been stationed in Stung at the time when I visited the town. He apologized for the fact that we had not met. "I could easily have organized a meeting for you with a high-ranking officer in the Khmer Rouge. I regularly came in contact with the local commanders in Stung, and even with a few of the famous/notorious generals," he wrote. He had enclosed a little book about his experiences while stationed in Cambodia which he had published himself under the title "– where the ten commandments do not apply".

The book recounted how for a while he had had a Cambodian mistress who suddenly disclosed on one of their nights together that she had once been an executioner for the Khmer Rouge. She had come to him dressed in all the superficial mystique of Asia, had massaged his back, sung love songs for him in her reedy voice and given herself to him in the tropical night, beneath the bridal veil of the mosquito net. But under the surface she had harboured another, deeper mystery.

One night, in a follow-on to the intimacy of lovemaking, he had asked his mistress the fatal question about the time before '79. She had been a soldier, she replied. But not at the front. Other duties. Then out it comes. She had been a member of a death squad. She had interrogated and tortured prisoners. She had slit the throats of many of them. With others she had laid open the stomach with two slashes and pulled out their entrails. On the very bed where they have just made love she demonstrates how she bound their hands behind their backs, squeezing their wrists with a kind of cuff until the bones in the wrists were crushed and the opening in the cuff was no bigger than the opening in a bamboo flute . . .

At this point in his account Svend Petersen finds it necessary to break off and cover the rest of the page with exclamation marks, question marks and full stops, along with quite a few other symbols from the keyboard not normally employed in a linguistic context. He creates total typographical chaos, with the intent of expressing a confusion for which he has no words. He simply cannot get it to fit. She has lain in his bed. They have made love. He regards her as a woman full of warmth and happiness and vivacity. He tries to translate her actions into something he can recognize. She has described her early years as an executioner and mass-murderer as matter-of-factly as he would have related how, after taking his school-leavers certificate he had served his apprenticeship as a metalworker and fitter with Vilhelm Pedersen & Son in a small town in the north of Denmark, before going to work for a company called Jofa, where he made furniture out of steel tubing. Tubing no thicker than a bamboo flute. At the age of 18 he was working on steel tubing. She was working on wrists.

Svend Petersen's Cambodian mistress had apparently put her past as a mass murderer behind her, just as we put the agonies of adolescence behind us; almost as if being an executioner were a passing phase in the life of every human being.

Here Svend Petersen gives up, and comes down on the side of the here and now. His mistress, the one-time executioner, smiles happily at him. He puts his arm around her shoulders. "I have touched every single part of her body," he writes. "I have kissed those fingers again and again!

How could I have experienced such ecstasy with her? How could we have experienced such ecstasy together? We just could!"

In his letter to me, Svend Petersen writes that his story of this encounter with the female executioner "puts a very different slant on genocide etc. than the debate currently surrounding the executioners, guards and so on in the concentration camps during the Second World War." It is tempting to say that the phenomenon which Svend Petersen has witnessed first-hand is the banality of evil which the philosopher Hannah Arendt described after having attended the trial in Jerusalem in the early sixties of one of the men responsible for the extermination of the Jews, Adolf Eichmann. Hannah Arendt came to the conclusion that there were no diabolical depths to Eichmann. He was not a monster; neither a pervert nor a sadist, but horrifyingly normal. Arendt attributes the evil to the bureaucratic system which enabled someone like Eichmann to be party to a crime as vast as the extermination of the Jews without ever being confronted with the results of his actions or the horror in the eyes of his victims. Eichmann had nothing against the Jews. He did not hate them. On one occasion, when faced with a filled-in mass grave over which the blood of the dead had formed a veritable lake, he was physically sick. He was not an insensitive person. He was not evil. He simply lacked empathy and imagination, and this, although not in itself a crime, may be a contributory factor where crime is concerned. Eichmann was incapable of appreciating the consequences of his actions. He could see only one thing: his own desk and the opportunities for advancement associated with it. That was as far as his sense of responsibility would stretch.

But Captain Martinkovic had never sat behind a desk. Neither had Svend Petersen's Cambodian mistress. They were not, as Eichmann was, remote administrators of massacres. They were active participants. The results of their actions were only an arm's length away; the length of their own arm. For them, suffering was not a figure in a report. And yet nothing had held them back. Did that make them inhuman – unlike Eichmann who was, in fact, a normal human being in an abnormal situation; not evil, merely averagely lacking in imagination? Or is it the case that Svend Petersen's Cambodian mistress is just as much of a human being at the moment when she slits her victim's throat or hauls his entrails out of his slashed stomach as she is when she is singing love songs for her lover under the mosquito net, since evil is but another option open to mankind, a choice, just as good is; and that, like the heart, the soul, too, has its chambers, such that the tender mistress can live right next door to the executioner, inside the same person?

At one point in her life Svend Petersen's mistress opted for evil. Later, she opted for something else. Or perhaps she was satiated. Or just tired. Either that, or the potential of the situation was becoming exhausted. Was she an evil person, now living the life of a good person, was she still the same, or had she changed? Is a human being like an earthworm, which can take being cut in half?

Had she made any choice at all? Was she 18 when she became a mass murderer, as Petersen believed, or perhaps no more than 13 or 14, like the majority of her comrades in the great brotherhood of genocide? How old does a person need to be before one can reasonably say that they are capable of making a choice?

She smiles happily at him. He puts his arm around her shoulders. That's just how it is, he says. How what is? Life? Evil? Does that mean that he forgives her – but who is he to forgive; he, who has only experienced her caresses? Or *is* that just how it is – the banality of evil, of life, a chance encounter in the pressure chamber formed by normality, in which all differences are levelled out, where actions do not have consequences and crucial choices fade from view because they are so . . . so unreal when measured against the attraction between two bodies?

She smiles happily at him. He puts his arm around her shoulders. Is it a pact of oblivion they are entering into, is it mercy they are invoking?

"It was all too human," we say of a deed which we feel we ought to condemn, but which, at heart, we can well understand. For us, the two words "human" and "understandable" are synonymous. Those things we understand are human and vice versa; and when we recite the old Roman saying: that nothing human is foreign to us, we mean it as an exercise in tolerance and an incitement to the broadening of our knowledge of human nature.

Those actions which we cannot understand, on the other hand, we label inhuman, thus implying that evil is something foreign to us and that in practising evil we do not realize ourselves, but something else.

Is that the truth of it? Or is this where we go so fundamentally wrong?

The Woman under the Rain Tree

TOSCA WAS DUTCH, A POLITICAL SCIENCE GRADUATE AND A vivacious woman who was a great favourite with the officers of the Uruguayan battalion, not merely on account of her appearance – her striking mass of curls and long skirts appealing to their somewhat traditional ideal of womanhood – but also for her professional qualities. And she returned their innumerable compliments, always paid in the most respectful tone of voice, by describing them as "perfect gentlemen" or "chivalrous, in a wonderfully old-fashioned way".

Captain Strapolini had insisted that I meet Tosca, and it was clear that he regarded her as one of the few attractions of Stung Treng, if not the only one. When he introduced me to her at the house in which the so-called "electorate mobilization group" was quartered – one of those large, old-style Cambodian wooden houses on stilts with the dim, cool rooms – he treated her with a perfect balance of respect and camaraderie.

Tosca's father was an opera lover and cannot have been a superstitious man, in giving her the name of Puccini's unfortunate heroine as a christening gift. Tosca believed herself to be a Sunday's child, all thanks to her father, and to be able, at no more than 30 years of age, to regard oneself as a child of fortune, one needs a certain kind of ballast and self-confidence. But there was a warmth to her energy and openness which left me convinced that her belief in being Fortune's darling was a self-fulfilling prophecy.

As a political scientist, Tosca had made a special study of the establishment of administrations in the Third World. Cambodia, where she had now spent almost nine months, provided her with a unique opportunity to observe and to witness the emergence of an administration. She was working on the registration of voters and she and her staff held mobilization meetings at which the rules of democracy were explained to prospective voters. There were meetings for women, for illiterates – at least 60 per cent of the population were illiterate – and for the police and officers in the government army. The last two groups were the most difficult, since it was they who would pose the greatest problem for the forthcoming democracy. They considered politically motivated violence and the intimidation of civilians as a natural part of their work, indeed this *was* their work: the protection of those in power from the general public, not the other way round.

Tosca's assessment of the situation was realistic and pretty pessimistic. She did not believe that either the ruling Party – which had its roots in the Communist tradition and had been appointed by the Vietnamese army of occupation – or very many of the other parties which were standing for election, were genuinely disposed towards a parliamentary democracy. So her message to the military was that here they had a once in a lifetime chance to win international support and recognition. Provided, that is, that they allowed the election to take place in what she called "a neutral political atmosphere".

As far as a free and fair outcome of the election was concerned she was sceptical. There were four major parties plus an untold number of smaller parties, none of which stood any chance, all making a bid for power; but one of the main parties not only happened to be in office, it also controlled the administration, the judicial system, the police and the military. The UN had been given the task of guaranteeing all of these bodies autonomy, but this had come to nothing. Likewise, a matter as crucial as the disarmament of the diverse rival armies had turned into a complete fiasco. The ballot itself would, of course, be secret, but after 20 years of war, so terrorized were the locals that word had spread, eventually growing into a firm conviction, that the ruling Party had sent up spy satellites capable of revealing who had voted for whom.

"You have to understand," Tosca said, "that in everything the Cambodians do, fear is the key factor."

That evening an election meeting was held on the outskirts of Stung Treng. A television and a video recorder played a vital part in attracting an audience. Scores of children followed the proceedings as if hypnotised, never once taking their eyes off the screen. Behind the children, who had settled themselves on the ground in front of the television, stood a crowd of women, one or two of them carrying babies in their arms. A few men looked in, but none of them had the patience to stay for any length of time. Darkness fell while the programme was running and the fitful, flickering colours on the screen danced across the dark, half-naked bodies. A gust of wind set the palm trees rustling.

The programme came to an end and a bare light bulb shattered the darkness. I noticed a woman standing a little apart, almost invisible under the dense foliage of a rain tree. She had been standing there throughout, still as a statue, with a baby in her arms. I have no idea who she was, nonetheless, over the months that followed, as my travels carried me further and further away from Cambodia, I often thought about her and the evening on the banks of the Mekong River when I had seen her standing under the rain tree. My eye had been caught only by her unnatural stillness and an air of physical endurance which I found impossible to define. But as time went on it was this stillness and endurance that my thoughts returned to again and again and which I tried to understand, feeling as I did that it harboured a patience which I had overlooked or not apprehended during my time in Cambodia, but which was, in fact, a key.

I left Cambodia. Time passed, the Khmer Rouge stepped up their attacks, the UN troops in Phnom Penh were placed on emergency alert, there was talk of a possible evacuation, the airport at Siem Reap was overrun and once again the temple city of Angkor became inaccessible, as it had been for decades previously. Then came the election. More than 90 per cent of all Cambodians voted, a bigger turn-out than for the majority of elections in any western democracy. And while I delighted in this unexpected outcome of the Cambodian tragedy I thought of the betel-chewing women at the end of the earth and the woman under the rain tree and her endurance. As she stood there, silent in the night, with her child in her arms, a decision had ripened inside her and she had gone to the polls and voted. And nothing would ever be the same.

The motionless woman under the rain tree was not, as I had first thought, a pillar of salt, who had cast a glance over her shoulder and been paralyzed by the sight of her country in flames. She was simply waiting.

What I had seen and not comprehended was the patience of the living.

VIETNAM

Arrival on Earth

Parting is the little sister of death.
To one who respects the rationale of fate,
there is in moments of parting a singularly grim,
nuptial-style awareness.

OSIP MANDELSTAM

Who then has cut the moon in two,
One half imprinting itself on a lonely pillow,
The other lighting up the road?

KIM VAN KIEU

Motorized Flowers

THE SUBURBS OF SAIGON WERE LIKE ALL SUBURBS IN THE THIRD World: a chaotic jumble of buildings; additional floors, some finished, some only half-finished; painted or bare concrete; enamel signs and small shops, piled higgledy-piggledy one on top of the other. It was a while before I realized that these suburbs were, in some indefinable way, different. There were no tower blocks. This was the Third World as it had looked in the early 1970s. By then the cities had begun their uncontrolled growth, coming to resemble one another more and more the world over. Even so, something must have happened since then, because, on the ride into the centre of Saigon I was aware of the divide. Time had stood still, and it was, of course, the Vietnam War that had been the watershed.

There were a few cars on the roads leading into Saigon, but zig-zagging in and out between them were, it seemed, thousands of little Honda scooters. The closer we came to the centre, the more of them there were, many of them ridden by young women in long trousers and white silk tunics slit up the side. Their delicate faces were framed by glossy, blue-black hair that hung down to their narrow waists. A good number of scooters carried two women, one on the pillion elegantly side-saddle, an arm round the waist of the driver who carried a primrose parasol to ward off the sun. The young women wove in and out of the traffic like motorized flowers and I forgot the architecture and abandoned myself to the sight of them.

I had never been able to hear the word "Vietnam" without the word "war" coming after it, as if that were the country's full name. To me, Vietnam *was* a war and I could not envisage its history or identity beyond the battlefield. I had been expecting to find a country that was half ruin, half war museum and altogether an accusation. Now I began to suspect that I was going to have to revise all of my ideas. In China I had not been ashamed of my ignorance. Faced with that country's 5,000-year-old history it would have been foolish not to admit it. Cambodia was still living in the shadow of the colossal tragedy the country had brought upon itself, but in Vietnam I had honestly considered myself well-informed. And it was the Vietnam war, photographed as it was from every angle, that had left me with this sense of satiety. It was a trick played on one by the mass media. You think yourself well-informed because a photographer has been close to the action.

These were not, however, the reflections I was indulging in as I contemplated the primrose-yellow reflection cast by a parasol over the swan-white tunic and graceful features of a young Vietnamese girl. I had quite simply forgotten where I was. A new dimension to my trip had been suddenly revealed to me and this fleeting glimpse of grace would prove to be a foretaste of my time in Vietnam.

A Chink in the Wall

SAIGON'S CITY CENTRE CONSISTED OF SHADY AVENUES LINED BY acacia trees that endowed the town with a peculiar green light which I was to encounter repeatedly in almost every town in Vietnam. All of the city's larger hotels are located around the square in front of the Hotel de Ville and along Nguyen Hue Boulevard, where it cuts down to the Saigon River, its wide central reservation planted with flowers and knots of trees. Here were clamorous crowds that seemed to scent blood whenever a foreigner appeared. The cyclo drivers (in Vietnam a rickshaw is called a cyclo or *zich lo*), immediately started calling out, and giving chase. They could keep this up for ten minutes, all the while repeating the same exasperating cry. There was something alarming about their persistence, it began to feel as if it was less about the hiring of their cyclos than the need for their aggression to find a suitable target, and that they were looking for a fight rather than a customer. The merchants whose stalls overrun the broad pavements of the boulevards shouted and yelled, and the shoeblacks sprang up from their pitches and pointed accusingly at the toes of your shoes. Not even the beggars behaved normally. In most countries they endeavour to arouse one's pity, seated or slumped on the pavement in apparent apathy, but on Nguyen Hue Boulevard in Saigon they came charging towards you, arms and legs flailing, while yelling menacingly and brandishing, almost as an afterthought, a mutilated limb, usually a half arm or an empty trouser leg. Some had lost both hands, others both feet as well, although this did not stop them from advancing at a fair lick, with a rolling, hobbling, but astonishingly effective gait. If you could just stand still for a moment and collect yourself, you could surely summon up the obligatory compassion and offer some money, since even in the interplay between beggar and alms-giver certain rules apply, but these bellicose beggars did not allow you a minute's peace. The rampaging cripples appeared to be involved in some grotesque theatrical performance which only succeeded in scaring the wits out of you with its unnatural vitality. All I wanted to do was to run away and that was, in fact, more or less what I *did* do each time I had to cross the square in front of the Hotel de Ville making for the Rex Hotel, to whose fifth-floor roof garden I repaired in search of a bit of peace and quiet during my first few days in Saigon. I could emerge from one of the calmer sidestreets at any time of the day, to find the square quite deserted, but no sooner did I appear, hoping for a quiet crossing, than the mouth of Hell opened and spat out a gallery of irate, screaming, loping creatures who looked as if they had escaped from a painting by Hieronymus Bosch.

At the Brodard Café, on the corner of Dong Khoi Street, a beggar crawled through the doorway dragging a flaccid and useless leg behind him. When he reached the centre of the room his face metamorphosed into a hideous grimacing mask and he proceeded to bang his forehead against the floor, howling at the top of his voice. The doorman came in off the street and with a waiter tried to haul the man away, but the beggar – a hefty character with a bulldog face and a crew-cut that showed off his thick bull neck – let himself go limp and immovable, while making the most horrendous faces and clutching at the trouser leg of one of the diners. He appeared to be suffering the most profound spiritual anguish, a doomed man pleading for his salvation at the gates of Hell – until, all of a sudden, he got to his feet and nonchalantly left the café, grinning exultantly as he counted the handful of notes that his neat bit of acting had earned him.

I had fallen prey to the malaise by which I was invariably seized on my arrival in a strange city, and now I sat several storeys above the town, nursing my despair and surveying the two stucco elephants and the revolving crown of coloured electric bulbs that served as decoration on the Rex Hotel roof garden. I had copies of *Time* and *Newsweek*, which were easily come by in Saigon, in order, as they say, to familiarize myself with what was happening in the world. But my need to sit with my nose in a magazine or a book was a sure sign. This was how I had always reacted whenever I felt scared or intimidated. At this particular moment I felt like a deep-sea diver who had lost both his lifeline and his airline. Cambodia had left me feeling depressed and I could not have said whether this depression was the country's or my own.

I do not belong to a generation for whom the war in Vietnam had been a momentous experience. It had been going on for some years by the time I was old enough to take an interest in the world about me, and the protest against it seemed to me to be the monopoly of an older generation; one which they jealously guarded, as if this war and the interpretation of it were in some way private property. I accepted that this was the case and was against the war as a matter of course, with all the conformity that so often lies behind the most ostensibly rebellious adolescence. I remember May Day 1975 on Copenhagen Common, where a representative of the Viet Cong proclaimed the Communist victory from the platform. I wandered restlessly around the park, looking for anyone I knew. I was in the habit of counting how many people said "hello" to me, and each year the number grew. I had only been living in the city for a couple of years and had made few friends, so I invested a good deal of energy in creating a life for myself. If the truth be known my so-called political involvement was primarily a means of carving out a place for myself in the world. Although the news of the victory registered with me, it was as if the events that followed had nothing to do with me, but were instead the Vietnamese's own business. The image of the chaos on the roof of the American embassy as the last helicopter took off was of more interest to me than the future of the planned economy. It was easier to identify with a nation battling against its oppressors, because in the uneven nature of the fight all their deeds swelled to heroic proportions. On the other hand there is nothing very romantic about the winning side. Victors must be practical and are seldom given the chance to sport haloes. Besides which, the victors in Vietnam would soon prove to be neither noble nor practical.

The humiliated West was hell bent on punishing Vietnam for its defeat; victorious Vietnam became one of the most isolated and shunned countries in the world and soon found itself also one of the poorest. Obviously such a devastated country could not get back on its feet unaided, and since the only major power to offer a helping hand happened to be the Soviet Union, Vietnam wound up hitching its little sampan to the sinking *Titanic* of Soviet communism.

First came the pogroms against those Chinese who had settled in

Vietnam, then the mass exodus of boat people by the million. Vietnam seemed not only to be cut off from the world, but also cut off from something within itself, the generous spirit of reconciliation without which a ravaged and divided land can never recover.

The Vietnamese army invaded the neighbouring country of Cambodia and China responded with a punitive expedition into North Vietnam which the Vietnamese repelled with their customary, belligerent professionalism. The courageous little country that had defended itself against the Great Power of America had itself become a great power. Vietnam's brief post-victory history seemed to consist of nothing but defeats: first economic and political, then on the moral and public relations fronts.

Both those who had been opposed to the American war in Vietnam and those who had defended it saw themselves confronted with ethical dilemmas that presented a challenge to anyone who had grown used to judging everything according to the imperative either–or of war. Opponents of the Vietnam war were forced to acknowledge that the oppressed could also be wrong, but that this did not give those who had supported the Vietnamese any moral right to resort to the easy way out offered by disillusionment. Because the wounded, the threatened and the needy – which the Vietnamese, living amid their bomb craters, defoliated forests and gutted cities, continued to be – were still entitled to help, simply because they were human beings and not just the upholders of mistaken ideals.

In a way, those who had declared themselves to be supporters of America's armed intervention, found themselves faced with the same dilemma. When they refused to admit that the war was lost and, instead, attempted to prolong it by other means: the weapons of isolation and economic boycott, which were just as effective in what was becoming an increasingly integrated and mutually dependent world economy – they, too, were responsible for the measures taken, in its desperation, by this besieged and solitary nation.

But the Vietnam issue had become a prisoner of the war and its mythology of black-and-white. Those who had once been against the war either fell silent or persisted in churning out fallacious, glamorizing propaganda. Those who had been for it, viewed every outrage committed by the Communists as triumphant proof of the justification of a war, the barbarity of which they still refused to recognize.

Surely there can be no better example of the trap in which the war and the subsequent wave of anti-communist feeling had caught Vietnam than the outside world's reaction to the Vietnamese invasion of its neighbour, Cambodia, at Christmas 1978. On his return to Phnom Penh in 1991, Prince Sihanouk was forced to admit that "had it not been for the intervention of the Vietnamese, we would all be dead". But, during the first ten years of his exile in Beijing this same Prince Sihanouk had sided with the exiled leaders of the ousted Khmer Rouge to form a united front against the Vietnamese; a front which won international recognition and support that extended from capitalist USA to Red China, and which not only won the Khmer Rouge seats in the UN, as the only legitimate representative of the people whose executioner it was, and whom it had starved, depraved and murdered, but also ensured them of continued access to the money and weapons that enabled them, from the border regions where they had dug themselves in, to go on with their killing. For ten years, the Vietnamese army represented the only barrier between the Cambodian people and total annihilation, and the only difference between the genocide of the 1970s and that which the Khmer Rouge had plans to pursue in the 1980s was that where the first had been carried out in total secrecy and only came to the knowledge of the outside world at a later date, the second would have taken place not only with the full knowledge of the world at large, but indeed with its financial backing and under the political aegis of the UN, all because support for the Khmer Rouge happened to be an element of the political blockade of communist Vietnam.

People spoke, rather, of the supremacy and inviolability of the nation State, as if this were a higher ideal than the inviolability of a people, and ignored Hannah Arendt's warning, after the Holocaust, that "if genocide is an actual possibility in the future, then no people on earth can feel reasonably sure of its continued existence without the help and protection of international law." Instead, the UN promised aid to the executioners, in an instance of *realpolitik* so execrable that perversion, rather than cynicism, is the only word that covers it. In the case of Cambodia this left the Vietnamese army acting as sole surety for the existence of that utopian international code of law of which Hannah Arendt spoke, since, whatever the motives behind the Vietnamese decision to invade the country might have been (and they were by no means idealistic), had it not been for them there would be no such place, today, as Cambodia. Consequently, the Cambodians are not the only ones who owe a debt of gratitude to the Vietnamese. We, the rest of the world, ought also to be grateful for the fact that they acted while we turned a blind eye.

During those dark years, the Vietnamese also, however, made a number of practical moves which showed that their victory over the USA had done more than just lead them down a blind alley. Having realized, after ten years of abortive experimentation, that the planned economy spelled disaster for their country, as early as 1986 they introduced a series of reforms which were tantamount to the institution of a market economy and which led, in just a few years, to Vietnam becoming the world's third largest exporter of rice. This was the same year in which Gorbachov's policy of *glasnost* began to manifest itself in the Soviet Union, although it then amounted to no more than moralistic appeals to Russians to drink less vodka, while the system itself looked set to go on for ever. Sitting in the roof garden of the Rex Hotel, I read in an issue of *The Economist* that, since 1987, Vietnam had boasted one of the most liberal legislations in the world when it came to foreign investment, although this had not yet produced any result.

The world played a waiting game, remorseless as always, while Vietnam concentrated all its energies on its fight for survival, drawing yet again on its people's untold reserves of stamina.

Every evening I enjoyed a beer down at the end of Nguyen Hue Boulevard, while I drank in the sight of the traffic on the river and the riot of colour unleashed by the sunset over sky and water. Little ferry boats carried pedestrians and cyclists across the Saigon River, seeming constantly to be on the point of slewing round in the stiff current and disappearing downstream like runaway spinning tops. On the opposite bank a forest of advertising signs rose up against a backdrop of derelict warehouses, moss-grown concrete walls and rickety, rusting iron chimneys. Toshiba, Fuji Film, Sony, Philips, said the signs, distant as satellites in orbit around the Earth; not so much signals to those consumers who were, in any case, nowhere to be found, as invocations and entreaties from a country yearning to break out of its isolation.

Reunification Palace sits in the centre of Saigon, encircled by a large and beautifully laid-out park. I recognized it from the newscasts. It was through the wrought-iron gates at the entrance to the park that North Vietnamese tanks had crashed on April 30th 1975, the day that saw the fall of Saigon and the end of the Vietnam War. Back then Reunification Palace was the Presidential Palace. It had been built in the mid-1960s after the previous presidential residence, a building in the French colonial style, was bombed by a deserter fighter pilot from the South Vietnamese air force, and since 1967 it had been home to General Nguyen Van Thieu, a man whose pathological distrust of those around him was matched only by his own unreliability as an associate. Five days before the fall of Saigon he had fled the country, his suitcases stuffed with millions of dollars, leaving it to one of his generals to capitulate with the Communists.

By one of history's many coincidences, the man who accepted the surrender was not a military commander, but a journalist who had been covering the fall of Saigon for the North Vietnamese army newspaper. For once, here was someone at the centre of a historic event who was, in a purely rhetorical sense, up to the job and, in a typically modern paradox, it was this professional observer, dispatched simply to report on the situation, who would end by creating history, Colonel Bui Tin, editor of the newspaper *Quan Doi Nhan Dan* told the South Vietnamese General Minh: "There is no question of transferring power. Your power has crumbled away. You cannot give up what you do not have."

After making his mark on history instead of simply writing about it, Bui Tin sat down at the absconded president's desk, a fitting space for a journalist in the age of the mass media, and completed his piece on the fall of Saigon and the end of the war. Afterwards, he walked out on to the lawn in front of the palace and lay down on his back on the grass, to spend the rest of that historic day gazing at the heavens.

Now the Vietnamese had done the same with General Thieu's former residence as the French had done with Versailles, the Russians with the Czar's Summer Palace and the Chinese with the Forbidden City. They had turned it into a dubious national monument simultaneously sending out two conflicting messages: see how much we as a nation are capable of! – and: see how our rulers lived at our expense! It is characteristic of all puritanical revolutions, as all three – the Republican revolution in France, the Leninist in Russia and the Maoist in China – were, that they felt the same need to put the splendour enjoyed by their fallen overlords on display to the nation, but were in two minds as to the edifying effect produced by the sight of those gilded halls. Visitors were supposed to be both filled with patriotic pride at the creative powers of their country's historical figures and morally outraged by their extravagance.

How, then, did he live, this General Thieu, whose rule had been an orgy of corruption and who, throughout his eight years in power, as his country stumbled from one military calamity to the next, did nothing except line his own pockets and those of his family and friends? I could not have been more surprised, on entering the three-storey-high Reunification Palace, to find that not only had General Thieu lived in beautiful and stylish surroundings, but that the interior designer who had created the setting for such a corrupt and incompetent general had also come up with a prototype for his country, a lovely and liberated utopia that pointed the way to that future as a modern nation which Vietnam had shed so much blood in one abortive experiment after another to attain.

More often than not, those countries in the Third World which opted for capitalist development committed an act of spiritual suicide that manifested itself most clearly in their vast, burgeoning cities, in which ever-increasing multitudes of people were thrown together in ways that closely reflected the anarchy of the market economy which constituted the prime mover in these chaotic societies. The stagnating Communist regimes, on the other hand, half-strangled as they were by their own lack of dynamism, and abandoned to the whims of their corrupt despots, had been unable to come up with much more than caricatures of society, but they did have one thing in common with their capitalist counterparts: both social models found it necessary to do away with their own cultural traditions. Of the history that had preceded them, they wished to leave little except the self-same ashes to which virgin jungle throughout the Third World was reduced once the bulldozers of progress moved in. Nor did any ecological criteria exist for how to relate to bygone civilizations, with their wealth of insight into human nature and myriad solutions to the problems of existence, and both capitalism and communism nurtured the same disdain for everything that was not modern. And while these two social systems were busy usurping one another, in a sort of political witches sabbath, this one feature formed a link between them: their mutual, all-consuming rage against tradition.

That was why Reunification Palace came as such a surprise. It was elegantly and simply furnished with an almost Scandinavian purity of line and a delicately attuned balance between such modern elements as tubular steel and large expanses of plate glass, and animate, organic materials such as wood and brocade, which represented the Vietnamese tradition. It was a piece of utterly modern architecture, but its sublime aesthetic effect had been achieved only because history had been accorded its rightful place. There it sat, in the centre of Saigon, like a living disavowal of the harsh, single-track mentality of the concept of progress.

Vietnam had travelled in a wide and arduous circle all the way back to the days before its victory over the USA and now here were the advertising signs on the bank of the Saigon River, extolling the very model of progress that had been rejected almost 20 years earlier. And yet the alternative had been there all along, tucked away in Reunification Palace, disguised as interior design – an optical illusion and a puzzle. General Thieu had had the puzzle staring him in the face day in, day out, but he had been too small, too stupid and too grasping to solve it. For decades the Vietnamese had been the children of Karl Marx. Now, once more, they ran the risk of becoming the children of General Thieu, of Philips, Sony and Toshiba; a nation that dreamt only of stuffing its suitcases with green dollar bills, unless, that is, they could solve the puzzle of Reunification Palace and reunite tradition and modernism.

The courtyard of what was then called the Museum of American War Crimes (although it later changed its name to simply the War Crimes Museum) was filled with hardware: tanks, various types of fighter bomber, and a helicopter fitted with a machine-gun. The Vietnamese had a thing about weapons. Their war museums, of which I saw quite a few during my visit, all consist of huge piles of scrap metal, made up of downed aircraft and buckled tanks, and they strut about among the heaps of scrap as if to say: "Look what we did! See what we are capable of!" They are a warlike people, but it is an unusual brand of bellicosity. The sight of a cannon does not appear to give them any particular sense of power. On the contrary, this intoxication with power only seems to hit them at the sight of piles of scrap metal, as if it were not so much that the weapons were an extension of their lithe, reed-thin bodies, but that their bodies set the bounds for the weapons. Inherent in this is a myth that is not hard to decipher. They themselves believe that they won the war with their bare fists.

The lion's share of the museum's documentation took the form of photographs taken by Western photographers. There was one picture of a Viet Cong being thrown out of a helicopter from a great height because he "had refused to co-operate": the body like a streak in mid-air, in free fall towards the earth, silhouetted against a backdrop of grainy clouds. An American soldier standing on the battlefield, one hand clutching the shattered remains of a Vietnamese. He had a firm grip on the shoulder of the dead man; there was not much left but the shoulder. The head, the shoulder, an arm. The rest had been blown away. What he was holding was one quarter of a human being. The dead man's facial features were still intact, the soldier smiling at the photographer as if posing with a hunting trophy: one enemy less. These were the after-effects of war: the napalm victims; landscapes in ashes, with the trees of the jungle like burned-out matches; the deformed infants.

It occurred to me, as I was walking round the museum, that this was not only the documentation of a war crime. It also documented a crisis of conscience. It presented a portrait of an American nation caught up in the war and beginning to have doubts about its own actions due to the fact that the war correspondents, in their unremitting search for truth, had offered its citizens a glimpse of themselves in a mirror. Displayed near the exit was a photostat showing one of the massive peace demonstrations held in Washington in the late 1960s and, underneath it, a message of thanks to those Americans who had not followed their leaders, but had supported the Vietnamese in their struggle. It was a most oriental piece of propaganda, akin to the type of martial art in which one's opponent is allowed to do all the work, turning his strength against himself until in the end he collapses, crushed by his own weight.

An array of American combat medals mounted behind glass were accompanied by the words: "To the people of Vietnam: I was wrong. I am sorry." Beneath this stood the name of the sergeant who, ridden with shame, had presented his medals to his former enemy. But I did not see this, because my eyes had started to stream with tears – so much so that I had to go outside and hide myself among all of those war machines with names such as M-41 and M-71, which I would never learn to tell apart.

The photographs of the victims of murder and torture in Phnom Penh's Security Prison 21 had left me totally numbed. The dead in S-21 had lain like drowned men at the bottom of a well and the horrors they had undergone had created an insurmountable barrier between them and the living. They had been rendered dumb, as we had been rendered deaf. I could tell that they were human beings, but that was as far as my ability to empathize went. Suddenly, however, here in the Museum of American War Crimes, a voice had spoken, and a chink opened up in the otherwise impenetrable wall of terror, in the only way possible: by someone accepting responsibility and saying that behind an event that had taken on the proportions of a natural disaster and the unbearable weight of a tragedy, stood, not blind fate, but human beings; a voice which had the courage to admit: I was one of them. I am guilty and I beg you to forgive me.

Standing in the museum courtyard I was suddenly convinced that the whole thing was an expertly stage-managed Vietnamese propaganda ploy. Were the sergeant's words not too facile, too stereotyped? Would he not have expressed himself in much more personal terms; tentatively, haltingly perhaps, trying to find words for something so difficult? And why was there no photograph of him?

Only much later did I learn that the sergeant did exist. His name was William Brown and he had fought with the 173rd airborne brigade, 503rd infantry regiment. But no matter whether he existed or not, his words embodied a certain truth. There had undoubtedly been a great deal of hate in this war, as in all wars, but it was not hate that was to be its legacy. Strangely enough, there was something rather magnanimous about the Museum of American War Crimes. By exhibiting a humble sergeant's prayer for forgiveness, the Vietnamese demonstrated their own willingness to forgive. They were large enough to recognize that the enemy was not a homogenous mass, but that the nation that had brought down so much death and destruction on their heads was made up of a conglomeration of individuals, all of them different – good and bad, friends and enemies – in such a way that being American was not synonymous with being the enemy, but synonymous with being human, for good or ill.

I rarely cry, but there have been times when I have been moved to tears by some big-hearted gesture that has unexpectedly stirred something within me, as a reminder of potential untapped. To some extent, the American sergeant who presented his medals and his apology to his enemy was offering up himself, a belief he once had cherished, some crucial years of his life and what many of his countrymen might even go so far as to call his honour. But it is the sort of self-sacrifice that sets even the weakest man above his adversary. I have the feeling that it was the power of example which moved me to tears that day in Saigon.

I was treated to one final lesson in the Vietnamese attitude to the war some 30 to 40 kilometres outside of Saigon in the so-called Cu Chi tunnels – a labyrinthine network of low tunnels totalling 350 kilometres in length, dug out of the hard, red clay over an area that stretches from the suburbs of Saigon all the way to the Cambodian border. Tens of thousands of Viet Cong soldiers holed up here in a subterranean city equipped with field kitchens, running water, bedrooms, dining rooms and schoolrooms. By means of exits camouflaged by grass and leaves they were able to make stealth raids on the unsuspecting Americans who had set up an army base in the middle of this area and who spent months trying to figure out how it was possible for them to be shot at in their tents in the middle of the night. It was from the tunnels of Cu Chi, too, that the Tet offensive was launched in the spring of 1968. Viet Cong soldiers penetrated right into the grounds of the American embassy, and despite the fact that the Viet Cong suffered huge losses in this offensive, which was carried out simultaneously in all major towns in Vietnam, it still represented the moral and political turning-point of the war. The Cu Chi area was flattened by bombs, defoliated and set alight with napalm – though so fierce was the heat from the blazing jungle that it unleashed a tropical storm which dowsed the flames. Dogs were sent down into the tunnels, but the Vietnamese sabotaged their sensitive noses with pepper or laid false scent trails by washing themselves with American soap or donning seized uniforms to which the smell of their former owners still clung. After ten years of futile attempts to destroy the tunnel system, it took a massive carpet bombing by the notorious flying fortresses finally, to put a stop to the Viet Cong's subterranean war in the Cu Chi area, but by then the tide of the war had already turned and victory slipped through the Americans' fingers. Sixteen thousand guerrillas had lived in the dark clay, often for months at a time. Only 6,000 of them survived. An unknown number of civilians were killed.

The guide at Cu Chi spoke a barely intelligible, staccato English and had a very offhand manner, as if he could not have cared less whether he was understood or not. But then the place spoke for itself. The Vietnamese had cleared away the top layer of earth from one small section of the tunnel system, leaving it open to view, with just a pent-roof of corrugated iron to protect it from the rain. There was a kitchen consisting of a hearth with three hobs, a common room furnished with a couple of bamboo benches and child-size tables, a section of tunnel, 80 centimetres high and 50 wide, a couple of air vents, a trapdoor cut in the ground – the entrance, no more than 20 centimetres by 40. Getting through this entailed acrobatic contortions and the raising of both arms high above the head.

Nearby lay a two-metre-deep hole, covered by a trapdoor. In peacetime this had been a wild-boar trap, in wartime a soldier trap. Then there was a device known as a nail trap, no more than a piece of wood with a nail sticking out of it, designed for concealment in the undergrowth. In a clearing not far from there the much more impressive traces of the enemy were to be found: a rusting M-41 tank surrounded by newly planted eucalyptus trees with pale, slender trunks and, like a last archaeological relic of the war, two bomb craters as big as houses.

The guide strolled nonchalantly on: pointing here; shrugging his shoulders there; slapping, in passing, the dejectedly listing gun barrel of the rusting American tank. With every gesture, every move he seemed intent on saying: It was nothing. Not because he belittled a war he himself had been too young to take part in, but because understatement was his style. The message he conveyed was: we won this war with underground tunnels, with traps for wild boar, with a nail in the enemy's foot. This was not, in fact, true, since the Vietnamese had also won their war with enormous quantities of Chinese and Soviet weapons, but in their version of it they had made a choice which revealed a truth about themselves. They had elected to identify with David rather than Goliath, with the courage and cunning of the weak rather than the brutal might of the strong.

That they had won this war with tunnels dug out of clay, with nails and with bamboo canes was a psychological truth; by putting them on display when the victory was won, they showed that, when faced with an adversary who had been superior to them in all respects, they had not tried to imitate him or to be like him. They had never accepted the terms of modern warfare and as a result they eventually found themselves dictating their own. They had remained true to themselves. That was the first decisive battle which they won, and with that battle won they were bound to win all the others.

I could not imagine any more convincing memorial to a nation's self-image and pride than the tunnels of Cu Chi. Crouched inside these tiny subterranean passageways, narrow as any birth canal, the Vietnamese became invincible, because they stayed small and opted for the little man's role in the fight against the leviathan. In actual fact, the tunnels of Cu Chi were not a monument so much as an anti-monument, as far removed as possible from the standard, Communist style of monumental art, which always identifies with the strong by paying homage to superlative strength and supermen; the cult of the machine, which is why the similarity between Soviet and Nazi art has always been so eerily striking. It is nothing but power-drunk, bellowing, male lunacy, singing its own praises. The Vietnamese hero was quite the opposite. How could one create monumental art from figures, curled up small and biding their time, whose strength resided not in their muscles, but in their patience?

Nothing could have been more persuasive of this than being allowed to crawl through one of these tunnels. Inside, it was pitch black, cramped and oppressively hot. The earth closed in on all sides; in no time I had lost all sense of direction and had to keep a grip on myself to save from calling out in terror for a light. For every metre I blundered my way forward, I grew more and more frightened. After a hundred metres I was beaten and convinced: it was through channels such as this that invincible revolutions were born.

Back out in the daylight, however, I doubted that the skills born underground in that darkness were also appropriate for winning the peace and shaping a smooth-running, stable society. One thing David and Goliath had in common: both were warriors. Communism was an ideology that seemed to have been made for war and heroism. In states of emergency it possessed a powerful drive. It could move people to do the out-of-the-ordinary, but seldom the ordinary. It had no message for everyday life other than militarization; a mirror image of war, taking the form of endless campaigns against enemies within and without, call-ups and purges. Its language was that of the army, its discipline that of the barracks, its citizens nothing but soldiers on indefinitely extended leave. Its natural state was one of unnaturally sustained suspense. Communism did not know what to do with peace, since heroism does not fall into the category of human attributes promoted by peace. The ultimate failure and collapse of Communism, its corruption and inhumanity, were brought about by its excess of idealism. From a humane point of view, idealism is a state of emergency and no society can live in a permanent state of emergency.

This was the eternal riddle with which all revolutions confronted their supporters. They craved so much suffering, so much self-denial and presupposed such a great faith in mankind; and yet, instead of monuments to everything that was best in mankind, the societies that emerged from this suffering ended by becoming pillars of shame raised to goodness and self-sacrifice.

Perhaps that was the tragic truth about the tunnels of Cu Chi. Having once lived in them, you never left them. You could never again lead a normal life, nor could you build a society that was normal when, to the questions of peace you knew only the answers of war.

Victor Hugo and the Coconut Monk

I CANNOT IMAGINE ANYTHING MORE SUCCINCTLY DIFFERENT from the tunnels of Cu Chi than the Cao Dai Great Temple at Tay Ninh, and yet both are tokens of the diversity of Vietnamese culture and a creativity capable of responding instantaneously to changes in the world around it. Caodaism is a variation of the religious revival that swept the Western world in the years between the wars, manifesting itself in a fascination for oriental religions, spiritualism and syncretistic pseudo-philosophies such as anthroposophy. But in Vietnam this evolved into something much bigger than a sect given to parlour meetings and table banging. Caodaism is a powerful movement with a membership of several million, and its striking temples, built in an extravagant, rococo, comic-strip style, are to be found all over South Vietnam. At times the movement exercised considerable political influence and even had its own standing army of 25,000 men.

Caodism was the religion of the collaborators, its members recruited primarily from the middle classes working within the French colonial administration. The movement allied itself first of all with the French, then with the Japanese occupying force and, thereafter, with the South-Vietnamese government and the Americans. It provided a standpoint for those who never took a stand on anything, renegades caught between two worlds, their own Vietnamese world, which they considered themselves to have risen above, and that of the French, which they could never hope to attain. It was a religion for the half-educated, half-integrated, half-devout, yet wholly uncertain and wholly rootless. Its rituals were strict and inane, its doctrine an incomprehensible mishmash drawn from here, there and everywhere, the result of shallowly read individuals having let their imaginations run away with them. It was at one and the same time unintentionally comical and quite desperate, a combination of Buddhism, Taoism and Confucianism – though Jesus, Moses and Mohammed also had important parts to play in its densely populated Parnassus, which also played home to the spirits which communicated, with the movement's chosen mediums at séances. These spirits included Joan of Arc and René Descartes, both presumably as polite concessions to the French occupying power. There was also William Shakespeare (although nothing had been heard from him since 1935), the father of modern bacteriology, Louis Pasteur, Lenin and the writer Victor Hugo. The last-named was chief among those spirits who had communicated regularly with the founders of the movement, mostly either through a Chinese calligraphy pen or through a spiritualist technique that goes by the name of pneumatography. Victor Hugo was, therefore, the figure most often depicted on the altarpieces of Cao Dai temples, and at the entrance to the Tay Ninh temple the visitor was greeted by a huge painting which showed Victor Hugo standing alongside Joan of Arc and the first leader of the Chinese revolution, Sun Yat Sen.

Services – if that's the right word – were held four times a day. The temple at Tay Ninh was oblong in shape, its interior fashioned like a nave with the choir at one end. There were pillars running down each side and round these coiled huge Chinese dragons painted in bright tones of red, blue and white. The vaulted ceiling was sky-blue, strewn with silver stars; the altar a gigantic sea-green globe at the centre of which floated an enormous, all-seeing eye, like a clam in a tub.

The temple was full of men and women in flowing, white robes, dutifully kneeling on the floor in long rows, the women separated from the men. The men wore a headdress not unlike a mitre, so stiff with starch it might have been made of cardboard. On the front of each hat, in the very centre, sat an eye which looked to be in direct contact with the eye swimming about on the sea-green globe of the altar. The congregation broke into song, every now and again leaning forward to bang their heads against the floor.

My feeling of being in a cinema rather than a temple was very strong and after a while it dawned on me why the Cao Dai movement was not a religion, despite the fact that it was trying so hard to be just that. Its imagery owed its inspiration to choreography and set design as opposed to theology. It provided its devotees with costumes, symbols and physical rituals; gave them an easy answer to who they were, which they needed, since they no longer belonged either to the East or to the West.

There is a very fine line between faith and superstition and many people regard themselves, wrongly, as religious believers when what they are, in fact, is superstitious. Faith entails perseverance in the face of uncertainty, for God is not an intelligible or logical answer to the problems of existence. He is for those who can stand to live with the dictum: I am what I am, while superstition is for those who are looking for answers to everything. The adherents of Caodism were not concerned with the meaning of life, but with their own identity, and in that respect this Far-Eastern ersatz religion that had had its beginnings over 70 years earlier was a thoroughly modern invention which could just as easily have sprung up in the Europe or USA of the 1980s and 1990s.

As I sat there, observing the long rows of white-robed men and women doing obeisance to their nebulous divinity, with a self-imposed discipline which they fancied would help them to evade the arbitrariness of existence, I was conscious of finding them just as ridiculous and pathetic as their spiritual brothers and sisters among all the astrologers, aura readers, vegetarians, healers, witches and Hindus of the West – but only up to a point. Beyond that point I could not help but admire these average, everyday lunatics for the tireless creativity with which they endeavoured to lie their way out of an uncertain existence, and for the almost disarming ingenuity of their self-deception. The Vietnamese, for their part, launched themselves into this with an enthusiasm and expertise no less impressive than that with which they waged war. They were not a nation to accept defeat, not even when it came to the question of the existence of God, where they were not beyond calling Victor Hugo, Lenin and Pasteur as witnesses to their own invention.

The Coconut Monk was another of those enterprising religious crackpots who, after coming into contact with the French colonial administration, felt that he had lost so much of his own culture that it was necessary for him to invent a completely new religious universe in order to make up for his loss. His real name was Nguyen Thanh Nam and he had been given his nickname for having lived for three years on a diet of coconuts while receiving, during deep meditation, the visions which were to form the foundation of a religion intended to marry Christianity with Buddhism. The Coconut Monk had spent some years in France, studying physics and chemistry, and like his compatriots who had studied Marxism on the Left Bank, he had drawn inspiration from his encounter with the West. His new religion was no more than a naïve and, in truth, touching attempt to unite the two worlds and heal a division which he must have felt deep within himself; the division of the traitor and the collaborator, although he might not have put it quite that way.

He had installed himself on a small island in the middle of the Mekong River, and here he lived with his handful of followers. Out on the tip of the island a number of metal structures stuck up into the air; they must at one time have been painted in bright, eye-catching colours, but were now faded by the sun. It had the look of a poorly maintained, provincial fairground with deserted swing-boats and a dilapidated roller-coaster, but it was, in fact, the Coconut Monk's monument to his patchwork religion. Inside an imitation grotto, made out of concrete, stood the remains of the throne on which he had once sat flanked by two elephant tusks, and a concrete platform reminiscent of a helicopter pad was graced by a row of columns encircled by Chinese dragons with gaping mouths which made them look as if they were howling with laughter. Suspended from rusty chains, in the Japanese style, was a large metal globe, a moon – and a model of an Apollo rocket.

The Coconut Monk was 60 when the Americans landed on the moon and it may be that in his muddled mind, which had a knack for making connections between the most irreconcilable things, he discerned a link between the Apollo rocket and his own religion. He may have seen the rocket as a sign connecting man and the cosmos, while the Vietnam War raged, fiercer than ever, around his island. It may be that he simply thought of his own life, and his own journey, and came to the conclusion that the distance between the two cultures over which he was attempting to build a bridge, was every bit as great as the distance between the Earth and the moon and, hence, the Apollo rocket inspired him with optimism. If it were possible to travel to the moon, then why should not his venture also meet with success? Now his religion had sunk into oblivion and his following which, even at its height, had numbered no more than 3,000 devotees, had dwindled away, but the Apollo rocket still hung from its chain, swaying in the breeze off the Mekong River. With the sun glinting off its battered aluminium panels it too testified to the Vietnamese infatuation with the modern world; an infatuation so powerful that it could endow the simplest technological inventions with religious significance.

This was the only evidence that remained of the Coconut Monk's many acts of syncretism and it was a testimonial to great innocence. Preserved within the swaying toy rocket was a kind of hope.

A strange piece of sculpture had been erected in the centre of the concrete platform as a memorial to the late religious founder: a gigantic urn sitting on the back of a turtle, the whole thing executed in porcelain. The urn was decorated, Vietnamese fashion, with hundreds of pottery fragments in every imaginable pattern and colour. Alongside traditional Chinese designs was something that might have been the remains of a French tea-set with a rococo-style, bucolic motif. Other pieces bore pictures of the Coconut Monk and episodes from his life. He was a tiny man with a hunchback and arms like matchsticks protruding from a sleeveless monk's robe. He had the flat-featured face of a frog and his wide mouth, which was wreathed by wispy whiskers, invariably wore a sly little smile which hinted that not only did he have a sense of humour, but that he was also possessed of a degree of self-irony.

There was a caretaker on the island, an old man with thin, grey hair plastered down over his forehead. I asked him how the place's creator had ended his days. He tapped his brow with one gnarled finger, indicating that the monk had wound up in a mental hospital. This may have been the case, but I preferred to think that the Coconut Monk's minor derangement was eventually engulfed by the colossal madness of the war, from which even an imagination as well-developed as his could not protect him.

The caretaker told me that he had been in the police force under the French administration, but I could not persuade him to reveal how he had spent the many intervening years. Whatever it might have been, he had now reached a stage in his life where he was at peace with himself, and ambition had been replaced by an appreciation of simple pleasures. The caretaker, too, had been a collaborator, but unlike the Coconut Monk and the followers of Caodism's bewildering Parnassus, he did not concern himself with who he was or with inventing a new identity. He pointed towards the opposite bank, where he lived on $15 a month. Not much, he remarked with a smile, but on the other hand this island where he worked was "*un petit paradis*", a little paradise. It measured three kilometres in length, supported about a thousand inhabitants and the tip, on which we were standing, was completely taken up by an enormous orchard.

He freely admitted that he was greatly indebted to the Coconut Monk.

He had spent the best part of his life here on the island amid the ruins of the monk's funfair temple, while the sampans swept past on the swift current but rarely landed here. Despite the fact that he had lived on this small island for many years now, he never ceased to be amused by the monk's creations and each time he pointed one out to me he would chuckle and shake his head. "What an imagination," he said.

He invited me to sit in the shade of the trees and placed a bowl of fruit before me. Large butterflies swirled to and fro, drunk on heat, nectar and their own beauty. The caretaker urged me to eat and pointed to each fruit in turn, naming them: papaya, mango, baby banana, jackfruit, sabotje and star-apple. This last got its name from the fact that when cut open its soft flesh, which had to be eaten with a spoon, formed the shape of a star.

Here was a man who had finally come home – to *"un petit paradis"*.

One of the world's most appealing religions has to be the version of Islam practised in Vietnam. There are very few followers of Islam among the Vietnamese – about 5,000 – all of them descended from the Chams, who ruled over most of South Vietnam until the mid-sixteenth century. They had originally been Hindus and both their culture and their religion bore the marks of a strong Indian influence. When they were overthrown by the Vietnamese they either fled to Cambodia or converted to Islam. For some reason, those worshippers of the prophet Mohammed among the descendants of the Chams must either have been very forgetful, or simply not all that interested in religion. They have certainly forgotten most of that otherwise dogmatic doctrine and their way of practising their religion bears most resemblance to the way in which people with very bad memories speak of their past. Their congregations own very few copies of the Koran and none of their priests can read Arabic. Instead of praying five times a day, in keeping with the Koran, they pray only on Fridays. Men observe Ramadan, the Muslim month of fasting, for just three days. When they pray they recite garbled sentences from the Koran of which they cannot understand a word. They practise the circumcision of boys, in symbolic form only the Imam make a number of slashes in the air above the groin of the young men when they turn 15. They would never dream of making the pilgrimage to Mecca, and have a taste for alcohol.

They cannot really be said to cling to their faith. On the other hand, they cannot be said to have abandoned it. They have not converted to any other religion, nor have they gone to the trouble of inventing a new one. While adherents to other faiths either clasp their hands in prayer or kneel on a prayer rug when worshipping their God, the Muslims of Vietnam confine themselves to scratching the backs of their heads, as if trying to recollect something.

Since there are so few of them, I have never met one of these forgetful descendants of the Chams.

I have the idea that they must be happy people.

Man is Like a Bamboo Shoot

ALL FEMALE VIETNAMESE NAMES MEAN SOMETHING. THEY SOUND like poems. It might be Scent of Spring, or Harvest Moon, or Sea Swallow, names rich in poetry and fanciful associations. But when I parted from Tam for the last time I realized that I had never asked her what her name meant. Was it absent-mindedness, or because there was no room for yet another association, yet another ambiguous dream? Like all people who do not believe themselves to be loved she could be demanding and tiresome. Her mood was forever changing, she wept three times a day and laughed twice as often. I knew only the sound of her name. There was no room for more.

Sometimes she would read aloud to me literary quotations which she had copied into her diary.

"Falling in love is searching for happiness in pain," ran one of her quotations. When, on our very first evening together, she placed a bundle of letters from her former lovers in my lap and invited me to read them, I declined. Not so much out of modesty, but because I felt uncomfortable with the situation. It struck me that she was giving me these intimate confessions to read in the same way a servant girl might hand a stack of references to her prospective employer. When I got to know her better I succumbed to my curiosity and one evening I asked her to read aloud from these letters. It was not that she wanted to boast. What she wanted, was to document her losses and her letters made it possible for her to relive them, like an astronomer gazing through his telescope at the radiance of a star which has been extinguished thousands of years ago but whose light still reaches him.

"We are both people who have been hurt," she said, once we had told one another the stories of our lives, but this I brushed off. There had been a time when I had seen myself that way, and doubtless I had given this impression in the manner in which I had told my story. But

I had learned that the one who is hurt has often set out to be stabbed and also knows how to wound. I did not wish to be a member of that brotherhood of victims in which I would be forced to feed off my failures. The navel is the first wound we are dealt, the only one that has its own name and that has become a part of our anatomy. With this wound, life begins, and we have no need to name any others. I did not want my identity to be defined by my scars, or to ride through the darkness on the beam of light from a dead star. And so, right from the start, there was this inequality between us. I was not prepared to enter the room, where she sat alone, and help her to bear her loneliness.

I have sometimes wished I had the courage to say, as Lord Byron did: I do not believe in love. But I do. Most of the time it is about all I *do* believe in. One cannot choose to love. I did not love Tam. Nor do I think that she loved me. But she wanted to be loved by me. We were swept within a hair's-breadth of one another and were never farther apart than at the moment when we were closest, just like two trapeze artists missing their rendezvous in the air.

There was someone I had left before I set out. In this lay the start of my journey. That someone was also the one I loved. In this lay the discovery of my journey. I was in love with my own "no", I had betrothed myself to what was lost, I was bound to a shadow love and was saving myself for someone I had imagined I did not want.

In the end, it is the wounds we have inflicted on others which are the worst. They linger on like a shadow in the heart and never heal. A sharp pang reminds us always of the one we betrayed. One does not recover from a betrayal. There is no convalescence, for time does not heal the wounds we inflict on others. Instead we live in hiding from ourselves and every time we raise our eyes the pain is every bit as sharp. No wounds stay fresh for as long as those we have dealt our own credibility and self-esteem.

Like all people in love I had wanted love to melt and remould me completely – but at the same time I put up a fight. When it came to the crunch, I did not want to lose the worst parts of myself. I had grown too used to them for that. The toughness of my neuroses was also that of my character. I had been offered happiness and yet I had demanded a guarantee that I would, once in a while, be able to feel unhappy. In love I also sought the expression of my worse side, not redemption from it.

That is how love is. Everything looks to find an outlet in it, even evil. And now I lived with the thought of the person I had left; night and day, feeding off each and every moment we had spent together, in something which was in no way remembrance, since nothing was sifted out, everything was reproduced frame by frame. I lived once more through every single minute of the year, during which we had known one another, with all the searing pain of betrayal, with the fierce, self-accusatory yearning of regret, until my shadow love became the sum total of my inner reality, the only stable point in this journey's shifting sands of places and people.

Dong Du Street was full of bars, all bearing vulgar, almost blasphemous, names which could leave no one in any doubt that in a free market economy anything goes, even when the current regime happened to be a Communist one. All of the bars were named after American films about Vietnam, such as *Apocalypse Now*, *Good Morning Vietnam*, *Platoon*. Marlon Brando hung on the walls alongside Willem Dafoe and Robin Williams, and the voice of Jim Morrison rang out across the ill-lit street, which was jam-packed with children selling cigarettes and chewing gum, parked cyclos and prostitutes astride little Honda scooters, cruising up and down the street on the look-out for customers, while young tourists from the West with their shirts hanging outside their trousers tried to find a brief respite from the heat of the tropical night in a glass of cold Anchor or Tiger beer. Saigon was living up to its reputation. Once, this city had profited from the war, and now it was doing so again. Only this time the war had been transformed into a stylistic gimmick, a decorative effect; not entirely serious, even in its provocativeness. But there was an omen to be read in those film posters. The country that had once sent the American soldiers packing, was now asking the USA to return.

But the USA had not returned, even though the whores were back in their places as if they had never been away, still waiting for the GIs to come sauntering round the corner and follow them up to the rooms in the Hotel Saigon on the other side of the street. Many of them looked as if they had been waiting for 20 years, with their raddled faces, taut skin and slight, spare bodies, just solid enough to wear their new clinging dresses which revealed every detail of the bony frames that had supplanted once youthful curves. They were indomitable survivors who had seen it

229

all: war, defeat, re-education camps, peace, the collapse of the planned economy – and now here they were again, sitting at the bar in joints whose names both spoke of new times to come and mocked their mother country's tragedy and loss of faith; tough little sibyls and heralds whose hollow-cheeked, crudely painted faces persisted, with astonishing vitality, in evincing a greed and a rabidity that had never been crushed. They were the living image of both the new Vietnam and the old, which they welcomed back with their red-painted, parched and almost fleshless lips. Good morning, Vietnam! It was not lust they aroused, but an odd sort of respect, similar to that one feels when faced with barbaric idols whose altars still flow with blood.

But the GIs never came. It was not young soldiers, horny and high on mortal dread who filled Dong Du, but no-nonsense, low-budget travellers who had dumped their rucksacks in the cheapest hotels in town and who confined themselves, in all matters, to their obligatory *Lonely Planet* guide to Vietnam with its innumerable, meticulously detailed hints as to how best to hang on to one's cash in a world full of foreign swindlers.

They would have to wait a while yet, the sibyls. They stood no chance of earning their keep from these young men, so stingy when it came to themselves. But then waiting was what they had always done.

A sudden, sharp flurry spread down Dong Du Street. The cigarette vendors drew back onto the pavement, the Honda scooters pulled into the side and the cyclo drivers heaved at their unwieldy vehicles, trying to get them out of the way. An enormous transporter eased its way through the crowd. On the bed of the truck sat a huge, rusty excavator, dry clods of mud still clinging to its caterpillar tracks. High above the crowd, in the darkness that hung between the brightly lit hotel windows, with the glare of the bar neon lights flickering across them, the digger's metal jaws hung half-open, like the lolling, panting mouth of a dying Tyrannosaurus Rex.

A workman in grubby shorts stood on the roof of the excavator, making sure that the partially raised grab did not collide with the low-slung electric cables. On the rear end of the transporter squatted two men with blank, expressionless faces. The immense vehicle lumbered through the street in slow motion, surrounded by the blue fumes of burning diesel oil and lumps of dried mud raining down onto the asphalt. It was like a gigantic, metallic apparition; a mechanical monster that had materialized out of the night in a clash between two eras: the hearse of Communism making its way to the cemetery. Then the vehicle disappeared around a corner, the crowds overran Dong Du Street and, in the heat of the tropical night, the whores' Hondas pounded the lumps of mud to dust against the black asphalt.

Tam worked at *Apocalypse Now*, a dimly lit bar that opened straight onto the crowded street without the inconvenience of any fourth wall. She took the orders, nipping back and forth between the bar and the handful of tables, only stopping now and then to try, by dint of friendly and encouraging arm-waving to foist off one of the place's ageing sibyls onto one of the *Lonely Planet*-reading lads. She did not look like the other girls in the bar. She wore gold-rimmed glasses and a sweater that reached to her knees. Beneath this she wore a pair of tight leggings that ended just above her ankles. She could have been a student at any Western university and she moved around the room with a casual, aloof air, as if she just happened to have popped in to give a girlfriend a hand on a busy night.

I had barricaded myself behind a couple of American current affairs magazines and sat sipping absent-mindedly at a Coca Cola. Tam stopped by my table and started leafing through *Newsweek*.

"Can you read that?" I asked in English, unaware of how rude my question sounded.

"Of course," she hissed.

"Take it then, you're welcome."

She put down the magazine and looked up. Her face was narrow and fine-featured. Behind her glasses her eyes were large and dark. "I'd rather have something else," she said.

Two days later I returned to *Apocalypse Now*. It was Sunday and Tam was clad in a crimson velvet *ao dai* – a traditional Vietnamese women's tunic worn over loose-fitting, wide-legged trousers. Her mass of curly hair hung down over her shoulders. She stood very close and looked up cheekily. "Tell me how to win your heart," she said.

It sounded like the first line of a song. "You don't have to ask," I replied, "You've already won it."

Later I was to learn that the similarity between Tam's question and a line from a song was no coincidence. She owned a little songbook, *101 American Pop Songs*, complete with music and chords. One evening she sat with the book in her hand and sang from it in a thin, little voice. I listened to the chorus. "Tell me how to win your heart." She was singing, not for me, but for herself and an unknown lover. She was lost in a dream which could never come true, since the fulfilment of one dream automatically gave rise to a new and still bigger dream. Her longings were self-accumulating; their perpetually postponed conclusion, the unfulfillability of her dreams.

But when she sang she was also practising her English. Practising for the future. She had what millions of Vietnamese in the past 20 years had risked their lives to obtain. A passport and an emigration permit.

That was one of her many secrets.

In the beginning I wondered, given the place in which we'd met, whether she was a prostitute. Then I began to wonder why I was wondering. Would it have bothered me if she was, or was it that, during these past months, I had become so distanced from myself that I did not care? Did I give any thought to what others would think? But which others? There were no norms here by which I could be judged. When you travel alone you travel unseen and in darkness, including that within yourself. And what about me? Had I no principles? No pride? In honesty I would have to say that I did not know. She never asked me for money and I never gave her any. I did not know then that unhappy people will sometimes behave like prostitutes, giving themselves away in return for the small change of a little attention. I ought to have known. There have been times in my life when I have done the same.

I awoke at first light, every bone in my body aching from having lain on a thin, narrow mattress spread on the floor. She was still sleeping, lying on her side, her small face half hidden by coal-black hair. In sleep, her eyes did not close completely and a white line showed beneath the thick eyelashes. In the pallid light of dawn her skin seemed much darker than the night before. I crossed to the window. Two cream-coloured masts and a wheel-house slid gently past over treetops and red-tile roofs and to my sleepy eyes it looked as though the ships on the Saigon river had sailed up on to land.

The building in which Tam lived lay close to the centre of Saigon. It was a large, concrete-grey block of flats that had known better days and at night the stairwells lay steeped in darkness, making it necessary to light one's way with a cigarette lighter. Caught in its flickering glow, dogs and cockroaches scattered, and beneath the worn stairs of bare wood a bottomless pit seemed to yawn. The stairway was broad and the corridors leading off it had been built to the same vast scale as if, behind its grimy walls the block of flats harboured a ghostly, labyrinthine palace.

In the darkness I had very soon lost my bearings. Stairs and corridors kept giving way to one another while the glow of the lighter swept up and down dirty, peeling walls. Eventually, Tam stopped in front of a door and produced a key. The room behind the door was lit by one drowsy bulb hanging from the ceiling. Sleeping figures were spread out on the floor and on a large bed. In the centre of the room lay a tiger-striped cat with three suckling kittens. An elderly woman was hunkered down next to it. She looked up incuriously as we walked through the door. "My landlady," said Tam.

Her own room was sparsely furnished. Against one wall stood a large cupboard. Set out on the floor were a gas ring, a couple of pots and a small box of joss-sticks. On top of the box sat a white porcelain statuette of a fat Buddha with a wide, beaming smile. Over in one corner two mattresses lay side by side under a mosquito net. Through the netting I could make out the outline of a woman's figure.

Tam said a few words to the other woman in Vietnamese and she came out from under the mosquito net. She was small and slight, about Tam's age with short, well-cut hair and intense, narrow eyes. She gave me a quick smile before sitting down on the floor facing Tam. They began talking to one another in vehement whispers, as though not wishing to be overheard. Now and again, as they talked, the woman stroked Tam's arm with a gentle, soothing hand.

After a while they both turned to me and smiled. Then they brought out a bowl of apples – pale-yellow, small and sour – which they cut into slices and dipped in salt.

Her name was Khieu. She came from Nha Trang, a town on the coast. That is all I know about her. We never spoke to one another, she did not speak English, and yet she went everywhere with us. She was there when Tam and I had breakfast together at the Brodard Café on Dong Kai Street; during our shopping expeditions to Ben Thanh market; on the evening when we ate frogs' legs at Maxim's; on our journeys around the Mekong delta. And when Tam made her favourite dish, *tom chua tseit ljoc* – sweet and sour shrimps with boiled pork, wrapped in rice pancakes and dipped in hot peanut sauce and sweet, spicy fish oils – Khieu squatted next to her and moistened the thin, little pancakes in the sauces before lifting them to my mouth with chopsticks, so that it seemed I was in the company not of two women, but of one who was all the more irresistible and steadfast in her seductive arts for being equipped with four arms instead of two. At night she slept on the mattress next to ours, separated from us by a sheet draped over a cord that Tam had strung across the room. When at last she realized that their separation was inevitable, I saw her cry inconsolably, whimpering like an animal in pain; a Siamese twin separated without anaesthetic from her other half. But Khieu and Tam were not twins. The feelings they entertained for one another were not, I think, of a sisterly nature. Khieu loved Tam the way Tam loved men, with a hopeless longing that was only fuelled by its own vain attempts at fulfilment. She was beyond all jealousy. She lived a life of total subjection.

"I was a victim of the war," said Tam one evening. "And what did I get out of the years after the war? Loneliness." She looked down at her lovely, slender hands. Khieu regarded her wordlessly with her fierce, dark eyes. "I seduced them all. I've changed address as other girls change clothes."

"But why?" I asked. "Why does it have to be like that?" The resignation in her voice shocked me.

"Do you know what a black biography is?"

I shook my head.

"I grew up on the Cam Ranh Naval Base outside of Nha Trang. My father was an officer in the South Vietnamese army. My parents were Catholics. Later on they got divorced." She faltered for a moment, as if considering her next words. "I took a teacher training course. I used to teach Vietnamese. Then, two years ago, I lost my job during one of those purges that are carried out every now and again. I was branded by my past. Oh, you can't imagine what they're like, those humiliating interrogations where they twist everything in your past." She clenched her fists. "My past wasn't revolutionary enough. Daughter of an officer who had fought on the wrong side. Catholic. *That* is a black biography."

She gave a bitter, theatrical laugh. "And then it turns out that my father isn't even my father. Isn't that just the funniest part of the whole thing? My mother had been unfaithful to him. My real father was a Filipino naval officer stationed at Cam Ranh. I never met him; obviously

I knew nothing about it. Then in 1972, when I was seven years old, my mother told my father the truth. Not long afterwards they split up. I never saw him again. But I have forgiven her. She was lonely and unhappy. It was wartime. She seldom saw my father and never knew where he was. Anything could have happened. He could have been killed. All she wanted was a bit of comfort. And I was the result."

She paused for a moment. Then she said vehemently, clenching her fists in her lap yet again: "I've forgiven her. But I cannot love her!"

"Why not?"

"Because she is selfish. She thinks of no one but herself. When the North Vietnamese came we were meant to be evacuated to Vung Tau. Everyone was trying to get on to the last planes out of there. We had made it as far as one of the helicopters, my mother carrying me in her arms. This black soldier reached out for me. People were screaming, going crazy. We could barely hear him shouting: 'Just you, honey – there's only room for you! You're the last one. Come on! Welcome to America!' As soon as my mother realized what he was saying she lowered her arms. I was swallowed up by the crowd and the next instant we had been elbowed aside by a mass of frantic people all struggling to get at the helicopter. Then the door slammed shut and the helicopter began to lift off. There were people clinging to the undercarriage, and others hanging onto them. We watched the helicopter fly out over the sea with a whole gang of people dangling from it. Then they began to drop off, one by one, like ripe grapes. But I could have gone with it. I could have been on that helicopter. I could have had a life in the United States. But she would not let me have it."

She broke off for a second or two and sipped some green tea from a tiny china cup. Khieu leaned towards her and brushed her heavy hair back from her face, as if encouraging her to continue. An oil lamp burned with a clear flame in the sultry evening air and at the foot of the white porcelain Buddha two joss-sticks glowed in the half-light with a scent as sweet and stupefying as that of an over-perfumed body.

"When I was 17 I tried to get out of Vietnam. Along with my aunt. But we didn't make it. We were tricked. We were taken out on a little boat and put ashore on an island where we were asked to wait. But the contact boat that was supposed to carry us out into international waters never turned up. Well, then" – she spread her hand in a gesture of regret – "then I became a schoolteacher and got married at around the same time. A few years later I discovered that my husband was making arrangements to marry another woman. I could have charged him with bigamy. Instead I decided to give him back his freedom. Luckily we never had children." She stared into space, the light of the oil lamp reflected in her eyes. Then she squeezed them tight shut and her whole face contracted. She put her hand to her mouth and a huge sigh worked its way up from her breast. "I can't have children," she whispered through her fingers. Her shoulders heaved and the tears began to run down her cheeks. Khieu put her arms around her and Tam buried her face in the hollow of her friend's throat, shaking uncontrollably.

After a while she looked up, wiped her cheeks with the back of her hand and smiled shyly. "Do you know what the worst thing is about not being able to have children?" she asked me, then answered the question herself: "You can't pass on the eyes of the one you love to posterity. Like the stars they will be put out, instead of living on in a new face. Eyes are jewels. They should be allowed to last as long."

It was Tam who had suggested that we should hire a car and visit the island of the Coconut Monk. Driving through the Mekong delta I noticed how the dense vegetation that surrounded the road on all sides never reached a height of any more than two to three metres. I'm no botanist, and have no idea whether this fact was due to the type of plant life growing there, but I fancied that this stretch of countryside, which had been one of the most heavily bombed in Vietnam, had been replanted after the war and that the height of the trees and bushes acted, in exactly the same way as does a child's height, as an accurate measure of the length of a new life: the number of years for which peace had reigned and for which a new, a resurrected, land had been in existence. Were you to fell one of these trees, their green leaves glinting in the sunlight, its growth rings would lead back to the year zero, to the doomsday of Agent Orange, napalm and the bombs. Here was a war-torn, devastated nation fighting back with the only thing it had, the indomitable luxuriance of ravaged nature.

Our car sped down the long, straight roads at a good steady pace and only rarely did another vehicle heave in sight, driving in the opposite direction. To me it seemed the only sound was the rush of the tyres over the asphalt as if, with its engine off, the car was being propelled forward by some bizarre form of inertia. It was high noon and there was not a soul to be seen. The driver sat still as a statue, staring straight ahead. All the car windows had been wound down, but so overpowering was the heat that not even our speed seemed capable of generating a breeze. Khieu had fallen asleep on the front seat. Tam slept with her head in my lap. Her long, white dress with its pattern of great red and green flower petals covered the whole seat. With her face hidden by her unbound hair she resembled a crumpled flower, stupefied by the heat. I was struck by a strong and quiet and utterly physical sense of peace, as if a noise that had been sounding in my ears all my life had been stilled, and for the first time I heard true silence; not only heard it but felt it in every part of my body, as though muscles that had been tensed for an eternity had only now relaxed.

Careful not to wake her, I stroked Tam's hair, an action that embodied a gratitude I did not understand. It would be a long time before I grasped what my hand had known at that moment: that it was her I had to thank for that unwonted sense of peace. She had laid her head in my lap and fallen asleep. I can conceive of no more trusting act. She presented me with her trust, her vulnerability, her defencelessness. She presented me with my return to earth, the first true arrival of my journey.

Events have their own geography. It is called history. But what do you call it when you travel around the world with no thought for geography and with neither history nor its events as a guide, only people? Is there some invisible history of encounters quite unrelated to the dictates of topography or the long shadows cast by violent occurrences? I am thinking not of Saigon. I am thinking of Tam. I am thinking not of the Mekong delta and the road to the island of the Coconut Monk. I am thinking of that moment with her head cradled in my lap. Within the map of the world there is another map of the world.

I never told her what that moment meant to me. At the time I did not feel that it had anything to do with her, only that it was a very private moment, elicited by the peace of the afternoon. I was far too preoccupied with myself to see that she, too, was involved. But it is the gentle weight of her head in my lap that stays in my memory.

One morning, Tam did not turn up as usual for breakfast at Brodard's. We did not spend every night together. The heavy front gates that provided the only access to the block of flats where she lived were locked after dark. They were minded by a surly watchman who might have to be cajoled and pleaded with for more than half an hour before he was finally persuaded to open up. Tam claimed that he reported the comings and goings of the building's residents to the police. Sometimes, late at night, we simply said goodbye at the gate and made a date to meet the next day. We never slept together at my hotel.

This particular morning, Tam had sent Khieu on ahead. She was waiting for me at the Brodard and ordered breakfast for me as soon as I had taken my seat at the table. With a smile and a hand on my arm she gave me to understand that Tam would arrive shortly. An hour later, my patience exhausted, I called the waiter over with the bill. Khieu sent him away again and a moment later he reappeared, bringing another pot of tea. I resigned myself to waiting. Half an hour later I had had enough. I left some *dong* on the table, more than enough to pay for breakfast, and walked out the door. Khieu ran after me and grabbed my arm. "No, no," she said. They were the first words I had ever heard her say in English.

Just then I caught sight of Tam. She got down from the passenger seat of a cyclo and produced some money for the fare. She had twisted her hair into a knot at the nape of her neck, a hairstyle that left her face looking naked and defenceless. I could see that she had been crying. When she saw me she burst into tears again.

"I'm scared," she said.

Bewildered, I placed a hand on her shoulder. "What's happened?"

"We can't stay out here on the street. I have to go straight home again. I only came so that you wouldn't have to wait. You'll have to follow behind with Khieu. It's not good for us to be seen together."

Back in her room she turned her reddened eyes to mine. "I'm scared," she said again. "He wants to kill me. I can't stay here any longer. I have to get out of Vietnam."

I took her hands in mine. "What's happened? Who wants to kill you?"

"Do you remember the guy who came over and spoke to me the other night in *Apocalypse Now*?" I searched my memory and came up with a picture of a stocky, broad-shouldered man in his late twenties with a grin that was both ingratiating and intimidating. He had said something in urgent tones to Tam, who had abruptly turned her back on him. He left immediately afterwards. When I asked her who he was she shrugged her shoulders dismissively. "Nobody."

The next day there was a knock at the door of her flat. Neither of the two women responded. Then Tam raised a finger to her lips, signalling to me to be quiet. Tam and Khieu exchanged glances. The knocking continued, as if the person on the other side knew they were there and was determined to break down their resistance. This was no ordinary caller. The knocking was heavy with obscure menace. The women looked at me and giggled softly. I could sense their unease. At long last the stranger on the other side of the door gave up. I had not connected the stocky man in the bar with the threatening knocking. But now I did.

As if reading my mind, Tam went on: "He was back again this morning. Oh, you don't know how powerful he is. You don't know what he is capable of." She started crying again. "He has threatened to mark me for life. He says he'll kill me." She covered her face with her hands as if to defend herself against a knife slicing down through the air to slash her skin.

"He wants me to tell him I love him. He says if he sees me with other men, I'm dead. I met him a couple of months ago. But I can't love a man like him. What would you say if somebody held a knife to your throat and ordered you to say you loved them? I told him I didn't love him, but that I respected him. But even that's not true. I'm afraid of him, which is something quite different. He demands protection money from the bars on Dong Du Street. That's why he comes into *Apocalypse Now*. He'd also like to get money out of the girls who work there. You don't know how strong he is. He can do whatever he wants. He can have people killed if he feels like it. He doesn't care about prison or the police. That's how much money he has. He could buy off the lot of them if he had a mind to. He really scares me."

She broke off and squeezed my hands. I did not know what to say. I felt helpless, and more of a stranger in her life than ever before. To me, it all seemed unreal. Tam had evidently read something else into my silence, because suddenly she blurted out: "Oh – you don't have to worry, he thinks you're seeing Khieu."

She stared into space and said, as if to herself: "No, I cannot stay here any longer. I have to get out of the country now. I'll need to get my ticket changed."

"Your ticket?"

"Yes, my ticket to Australia."

She opened her bag and took out a plane ticket that she proceeded to flick through.

"Australia – who do you know in Australia?" I asked.

"My husband," she said. "Who else?"

"You're married?"

"Yes, of course." The words were uttered so firmly, it was as though she wanted to arm herself against an unspoken accusation. But there was also a hint of triumph in her voice which seemed to say that now we were equals, and at long last she was in a position to reciprocate the reserve she had always been conscious of in me. She too had her ties.

"If you don't believe me" – she rummaged in her bag and produced a bundle of envelopes that she tossed into my lap – "see for yourself."

I opened one of the envelopes. Inside was a marriage certificate issued at the Australian embassy in Hanoi. Her husband's name was Francesco. The two other envelopes were addressed to Tam and bore Australian stamps.

"I have to go to the travel agency now." Her voice was dry and practical, but her eyes were still swollen from weeping.

I stayed where I was, on the floor of her room, holding her marriage certificate and the two envelopes. Khieu curled up on the one mattress with her legs drawn up underneath her and a stony expression on her face. I did not feel jealous of Tam's far-off husband, nor did I feel in any way cheated by her. If I had interpreted the faint note of triumph in her voice correctly then I would have to admit that she was right. In some way we were now on a more even footing, owing each other just as much or as little. But, more than anything else, I was confused. I was a stranger to this society and did not know how seriously to take the threats made against her. She had a husband, and a ticket out of Vietnam, but only now – under threat of being beaten up and even killed – had she made up her mind to leave. What was it that tied her to Saigon? What hopes had she pinned on this town, which had been nothing but the end of the line in a biography she herself described as "black"?

I opened one of the two remaining envelopes. It was a letter from her husband written before their marriage. He began by taking her to task because he had not heard from her for some time. He was now considering cancelling his planned journey to Vietnam. His tone was phlegmatic, rather like that of an accountant balancing two emotional columns against one another: debit and credit. He then went on pompously to describe how busy he was (apparently he had a small business), the stiffness of the competition, and ended by saying that he needed a woman to help him. In closing he wrote that he thought she was very beautiful, but apparently felt it necessary to qualify this slightly by adding "even though you have bad teeth".

It could hardly have been for his charm that Tam had married him. She had done it in order to get out of Vietnam, but if that were so then why had she not left long ago? The letter also provided an answer of sorts to this question. Life with this petty-minded character did not look exactly tempting and it may have been that she kept deferring her departure because she knew that the price she would have to pay for escaping from one trap would be to step into another.

An hour later she returned. She seemed depressed. "I'm leaving on Saturday," she said. She showed her ticket to Khieu, who flung her arms around her legs and burst into tears. Tam sat down and put her arm around her. They were both crying: Tam with sobs that made her shoulders shake, while Khieu's weeping turned to long, drawn-out moans of pain.

It was Friday morning, the day before Tam was due to leave. We had arranged to meet at the Brodard. It would be our last breakfast together. I had decided to set off for the north of the country that same day. We could no longer be seen together in public and Tam's departure from Vietnam gave our final hours together the same kind of empty feeling that one senses on a station platform just before the train pulls out. There was nothing more to be said, nothing more to be done. For days I had been a spectator at a drama whose meaning was lost on me. Now it was time to say goodbye. But life is not theatre, and the running order of the play is not always observed. We were not finished with one another yet.

When Tam walked into the Brodard accompanied, as always, by Khieu, she appeared transformed, yet again. She was wearing a coffee-coloured, ankle-length skirt and a large cream shirt which subtly accentuated the fragility of her slim figure. She gave me a big smile and placed a glossy, gift-wrapped parcel in front of me. "This is for you," she said. Inside the parcel was a diary on the title-page of which she had written a little proverb: *Happiness is not a destination one journeys towards, but the journey itself.*

There was also a guide to translating Vietnamese into English, packed with standard phrases and common words, and also containing poems from the classical tradition. She opened the book at a particular page and handed it to me. "Try to read this."

Next to the sentence "Support the socialist system" was another, underlined in red and in the margin next to it a little red heart: "Your arm is softer than a silk cushion." She smiled at me.

On the way to the bus station we passed Tam's house and she asked the cyclo driver to stop. "I want to be alone with you for the last time," she said. Khieu was told to wait outside on the pavement with my bag.

An hour later we were still lying side by side on her mattress. "You have plenty of time. There are buses running all day to Dalat." She sniffed at my hair. "Phew! Your hair smells as if you've been sleeping on the street."

"But I just washed it last night," I objected.

"Smell mine." She leant over me and covered my face with her long hair.

Half an hour later she whispered to me: "I could change my ticket. Take me up north with you. Let me see my country one last time with you."

This set the pattern for our relationship. We should have parted in Saigon, but set off together for Dalat. We should have said goodbye in Dalat, but carried on to Nha Trang, and it wasn't long before we found ourselves in Danang. Tam had a tremendous craving for love; seduction had become a way of life, a means of survival. She needed proof that she could excite love. But she never received it and so she kept on trying. She was given proof of my frailty, of my compliance, but not of my love.

I asked her, once, how she could marry a man she did not love. "Don't make me cry," she replied, "it's my fate, I am an unlucky girl."

It is the kind of question that ought not to be asked. Never ask someone if they are unhappy unless you are prepared to take responsibility for their happiness. She was a child of the war, of a time bereft of love; or rather, perhaps, a time fraught with overwhelming desires; fierce, short-lived passions, the kind that are fostered by war, when no one knows what tomorrow will bring. She had taught herself to survive.

She was a survivor, but she also wanted to be loved and this she fought for with all the dogged resolve of the survivor. But the men whom she endeavoured to win over saw only the survivor in her; the calculating element in her seductive wiles was not lost on them, and they made the most of these for a while, but they did not surrender. What they were looking for was a contract, not love; a fair exchange, nothing more. When it comes to love, no one is inclined to save those who are drowning. Those who grope around blindly rarely manage to get a grip. No one wants to be a straw for someone else to clutch at. People in love want to be everything to the other person. Being a straw is not enough.

There was one man whom she spoke of as being the great lost love of her life and by the way she spoke about him I could tell that she had been seeing him while she was arranging to marry Francesco. But the object of her unrequited love, a German engineer living in Stuttgart had told her that he could offer her neither marriage nor a life in Germany; for one thing, because living together does not require a piece of paper and for another "because you would find life in Stuttgart dull in comparison with the interesting and varied life of Saigon". She quoted this sentence to me and asked whether I could detect the cynicism in it. He had offered to keep her and to stay with her when he was in Vietnam, where he was going to be able to spend more and more time, and she would also be able to join him on journeys abroad. After this letter she finished with him. She was looking for love and contract rolled into one, but her instinct for survival kept bringing her into contact with designing, mean-spirited men.

Although she herself may not have realized it, she *had* had one happy affair – with a young Austrian. He had been in his early twenties, and hence some years younger than her. He had sent her a photograph of himself, crouched down with his rucksack in front of him. With his short, curly hair and plump cheeks he looked like a little boy. He had written a letter to her in which he thanked her for "the best week of my life". He was too young for her to cherish any hopes of the relationship leading anywhere. They had simply spent some time together and enjoyed each other's company without any ulterior motives.

There were many things I did not understand when Tam and I were together, many things I still do not understand. But I noticed how I, too, became mean-spirited, and tried to arm myself against her. It started out as a romantic adventure and it ended in claustrophobia. Or, rather, it was constantly fluctuating between these two states. There were times when her emotions seemed to lie idle – maybe she was bored – and, being at a loose end she had, perforce, to keep finding excuses for rows, and the making up that followed.

She might suddenly forbid me ever again to lay a finger on her. "From now on we are brother and sister," she fumed. "Okay, I'll never touch you again," I replied. A moment later she took my hand and placed it on her thigh. I let it lie there. "Ha-ha!" she laughed triumphantly. "You said you wouldn't touch me, but you're doing it all the same. You are weak, and I am strong."

After a whole day of this I had been smitten by her aimlessness and was utterly exhausted. All I wanted was to be alone and I told her that we were going to have to part company. She had a husband who was expecting her and I had to be moving on. She cried. "You made me cry," she said afterwards, but there was no note of reproach in her voice. Rather, she sounded relieved, as if something had been brought to fruition, a pattern fallen into place, and Fate taken its normal course. Or perhaps it was just that at such a moment she felt like a woman and looked upon me as a man. She became meek and self-effacing and displayed all of that Asian aloofness which I had never experienced at close quarters, to the point where I began to long once more for her to be her old, unpredictable, tempestuous, passionate self. She surrounded and besieged me with the full force of her soft, yielding femininity, which was every bit as alien and captivating to me as the Vietnamese countryside. I felt as clumsy and confused as a circus elephant being trained for the ring, well aware that it was her slender fingers that directed my every move, until I surrendered and asked her to travel on with me.

I read the poems in the book she had given me in search of clues as to what, apart from the war, made Tam the person she was. There were poems with such titles as "Mother, I Want a Husband!" or "Lament of a Wife whose Husband has Gone Off to the Wars". Would I find her, in lines such as these? "At my age I am still alone. Always alone. If ill luck should have it that I let my chance pass me by, what shall become of me? The green spring is over so soon. I believe man is like a bamboo shoot, ageing fast." Or here, in the lament of the forsaken wife: "He left me here with a broken heart. Why am I not a horse, that I could keep him company? Why am I not a boat, that I could bear him across the water? The running water cannot take my sorrow with it, nor the freshness of the grass spirit away my pain . . . Wherever you go, my lord my soul will follow you like a moonbeam."

A woman's lot: to suffer and to yearn. And Tam: a moonbeam on the hunt for another moonbeam, rediscovering the lost or missing one in whoever came along only, when she reached out her hand, to discover that there was nothing there but moonshine, bathing it in its cold light. She was lost in an altered, partially shattered world; her only resource, her femininity merely served to intensify her impotence and her anguish. Some Vietnamese begged on the streets. Tam reached out her hand and asked passers-by to still the hunger in her heart.

We parted in Danang. Her tears spoke of disaster. She had played and lost. She had played her husband, won a marriage certificate – and lost. She had played me and won a little every day – another couple of kilometres, some countryside, a few hours and nights – and lost.

"Take me with you to Hué," she said, "just to Hué. Then I'll go back to Saigon." But I knew that in Hué the drama would be re-enacted and she would ask to accompany me to Hanoi. And in Hanoi . . . She would chase that moonbeam to the ends of the earth. There was nothing I could do. I did not love her and she was too preoccupied with her own fate to be capable of loving anyone else.

I put out my hand to touch her. "Don't touch me," she said, beseechingly. "Don't ever touch me again. We are never going to do anything together again."

She was not trying to start another row. Her voice contained no threat. She was simply stating facts. The next morning I would travel on to Hué in a rented car and she would return to Saigon to embark on the journey that would end with her husband in Australia. We would never see one another again.

She curled up in a ball on the hotel bed under the room's harsh, violet fluorescent light. Beneath her thick, curling hair, glinting in the artificial light, her face was sunk in olive shadow. Her white shirt gave off a phosphorescent glow. It was stained red where she had spilled watermelon juice down it that afternoon. Now the stains looked like blood. I felt ashamed of myself.

I left early, in the grey morning light just before sunrise. Tam stood with her face averted as the car drove off. I leaned out of the open window and looked back at her. I still felt ashamed, but I also felt as if a weight had been lifted from my mind. Then, suddenly, she turned around and began to wave. There was something easy and undaunted about her wave, as if she had just regained her dignity and we were at last equals. She was no longer asking anything of me. I waved back.

A morning mist hung over the rice fields and a grainy blush of pink tinged the eastern sky. Silhouetted against the dawn sky, long lines of farm workers walked slowly along the road, on their way to the rice fields.

"I am very happy to meet you," said my driver, stroking my arm as if I were an old and long-lost friend.

"Vietnam – much hardship," he said a moment later, as if to himself.

"Were you a soldier?" I asked.

"Not me – I'm too scared."

That evening, when I opened my diary I found that Tam had left a little note in it, along with a photograph of herself. On the back of the photograph there was an inscription: *My darling. I have a dream, a wonderful dream . . .*

Nothing else. She had not signed her name, but I recognized her handwriting.

The brief, half-finished dedication was dated the previous October. It was not meant for me at all.

Would I Could Own the Face of Eternity

AS A TRAVELLER IT IS NOT THAT YOU ARE INVISIBLE, RATHER that you become visible in a particular way. Everyone looks at you, or no, they do not look, they *stare*, but they stare at you as at a stranger and they do not expect a stranger to abide by *their* moral precepts and standards, nor do they know anything of *his*; they may even entertain the suspicion that he has none. When we say that a stranger lives by a different etchical code what we really mean is that he has no ethical code at all – ours being the only one there is. And do not we ourselves prefer to visit brothels and commit our crimes in foreign parts? The fact that no one there knows us makes it easier for us to forgive ourselves.

Being a stranger means being free, and experiencing the weightlessness of the self. There is no longer anyone to tell you who you are – and so you are no one. If André Malraux was right when he wrote that "Europe believes that whatever does not imitate its reality represents a dream," this explains what is so appealing about Asia, the chance to journey through a dream, to cut loose from your own identity and conscious will and abandon yourself to other forces; to immerse yourself in the murky waters of the unconscious and become invisible, even to yourself. The dream of adventure and action pure and simple, of being ruled by impulse, of being moulded and tested beyond the limits of all that one already is, to be reborn part-felon, part-child. That is why travel is the medium of youth, a floating venue for self-exploration and new beginnings. For the older traveller, it can be a depressing and humiliating experience to discover that the character you believed to be so well-established and stable is, in fact, nothing but an imprint of its surroundings. But you may also find yourself freed from an old, outmoded role; from a life that took a wrong turn. It is tempting to go chasing after your youth, to roam through nostalgia in search of chances lost, and there is always the risk that you will find them. Incognito as you appear in foreign surroundings, anything is possible, and the youthful appetite for life is resurrected, no longer innocent, but transformed into perversion and complacency. Well, why not? There's no one to see.

A resentful freedom is the result. Feeble souls cannot cope with being given a taste of their own potential. Robust souls can, but use this freedom to explore inhibitions and their necessity at a certain stage in life. It is salutary to be faced with one's own anonymity, for in the eyes that gaze straight through you, there lies a truth. You look at these other people, imagining yourself to be their yardstick. Then you discover that it is they who are yours, and you are cut down to size.

I set out with no nostalgic illusions; I was not on a quest for my younger self and the limitless potential of youth. I was not looking for liberation of any kind and I fancied that I knew my own limits. Nonetheless, Vietnam revealed itself to me as a land of parallel universes, continually presenting me with new ways of being, other identities, a whole string of possible selves. I was struck not by the delirious freedom of youth but by something quite different and more powerful: by a sense of my own thoroughly plastic malleability. I could be a murderer, a thief, a corrupter of minors, this country offered me the lot and in my anonymity, which hung like a protective cloud around my actions, I was conscious of my own response. I was beguiled and enticed: it seemed that all these impulses were lying, ready and waiting, inside me. Vietnam was a land where I could become lost inside myself, a land of inner opportunity, and I did get ever so slightly lost and I committed one small crime. (But aren't petty misdemeanours related to the major crimes to which they inevitably lead?) At any rate, I crossed a line drawn in the sand; one that had been there all my life.

I have always made one rule when travelling: no physical contact with strangers. But in Vietnam, strangers constantly made physical contact without my feeling threatened. On the contrary, their touch moved me and made me happy, because I saw it as an expression of benevolent and generous tenderness. Vietnam was the only country on my travels where I never felt lonely. With every touch another layer of the onion fell away and I drew closer to the surrender inherent in the acceptance of one's own anonymity. It did not matter that they touched me. They were welcome to do so, because I trusted them, or rather my trust grew out of these caresses. There was a woman in a small town in the north-west of the

248

country, on my arrival late one night at a hotel, who came over to me, put her arm round my waist and stroked my arm reassuringly. I never saw her again. I have no idea why she should have bestowed this mark of intimacy upon me but I am grateful to her for doing so. There was a young girl who hung out at a restaurant in Hué where I often ate. She always came over to my table and stood for a while chatting to me in English. Then one day she bent down and kissed me on the cheek. She was practising her femininity on me and I was aware that I had been kissed by a woman, even though the lips were those of a child. I felt a strange longing for this budding woman, a longing which was not, and yet was, sexual; like lusting after an image or something unseen, the woman she had not yet become but of whom she had, fleetingly, given me a taste. To her, too, I was grateful.

All of this somehow ties in with what happened at My Son: my small crime. That too involved a longing for something untouched, the desire to possess and be possessed, to be swallowed up by something great; a dream of permanence in the midst of impermanence.

My Son lies about 60 kilometres from Danang. Once it had been to the Chams – later to prove so forgetful – what Angkor had been to the Khmer: a spiritual and religious centre and, above all else, an architectonic achievement. For more than 1,000 years this city had been inhabited and then, in a way so characteristic of Asia, it was abandoned and what we mistakenly refer to as time could start the job of demolishing it. It was not time that had torn down these temples, but plundering armies stomping back and forth over the temple city, there being very few spots in this long, narrow and war-torn country that had not been trampled underfoot. The last to stomp all over it were the Americans, who razed the thousand-year-old buildings to the ground because the area, a well-protected valley encircled by jungle-clad hills was a Vietcong stronghold. After the destruction of one of the loveliest temple sites, Philippe Stern, an expert on the Cham civilization and chief curator of the Musée Guinnet in Paris, wrote an open letter to President Nixon, in which he begged him to suspend the bombing raids on these unique buildings. Nixon promised, much in the spirit of the neutron bomb invented some years later, to leave the buildings alone and confine himself to killing Vietnamese.

Time would have to find other ways of doing its job.

This was where I came in.

Four or five kilometres outside My Son the road petered out. A couple of booths had been set up here, and there was a policeman sitting underneath a table in the shade of an awning. He asked for my passport and copied down the number of my visa. Then a lanky young man wearing a yellow safety helmet appeared and offered to drive me the last few kilometres on his motorbike.

The green slopes shimmered blue in the heat haze but there was not much left of My Son. There was an occasional pillar of rusty red brick, but mostly it was a matter of wending one's way around bomb craters and flattened buildings. Shattered masonry and stone blocks several feet long lay everywhere. Severed tree trunks jutted out of a small, half-ruined temple. One building, furnished with a corrugated iron roof and grilles across its doorways, served as a storehouse for sculptures and fragments of the decorations that had adorned the temples. A sign proclaimed that the preservation work had been sponsored by the German Mercedes company under the slogan "Preserving the Past for the Future".

The bombs had done their bit, but it was obvious that My Son, unlike Angkor, had never constituted the hub of a great empire. There was an air of tranquillity about the place, so much so that the city seemed almost to have been born out of that tranquillity.

I was the only visitor to the valley. Which may be why it happened. Two guards with rifles resting on their knees sat at the entrance to the temple city. When I returned from my tour of the place they waved me over and held out an object wrapped in newspaper. I caught a glimpse of red sandstone. They beckoned invitingly, grinned insinuatingly, their manner over-familiar. A little souvenir? They smiled ingratiatingly.

My reaction was one of anger. I felt as though they had pawed me and hinted that they could see right through me and knew my secrets. But I wanted nothing to do with their corrupt fraternity. I was not one of them. I felt disgusted and repelled. These were corrupt public servants, selling off the treasures they had been charged with guarding. They were simply extending the destruction set in train by the war-crazed Americans, with the same disregard for the past and history. This sad country, I thought, which had so little and yet was not even going to hold on to the few remnants of its history left once the bombs had done their work.

After my rebuff, the guards changed their tactics. Their fawning manner was replaced by pleasant straightforwardness. Tea? they asked. It was hot, I had been walking around in the sun for some hours, so I accepted the proffered cup. They offered me a stool at a little table. We sat there for a while. They asked the usual questions. I was seized by the urge to communicate and forgot my outrage. Suddenly one of them placed the paper parcel on the table in front of me. I looked down, but by then it was already too late. In the blink of an eye I learned that beauty is the chief accomplice of corruption.

There before me lay the head of a Buddha. It was of red sandstone and the marks of the chisel that once had summoned up the features of its face from the stone could still be discerned like open pores in the skin where sand had silted up over the centuries. The ear lobes were elongated and the ornate curls of the hair arched into the shape of a pagoda. The voluptuous curve of the upper lip tilted upwards in a faint smile and the eyelids, half-closed over the sloping slits of the eyes, gave the face an expression of spiritual exaltation.

I picked it up and grew solemn. It fitted into my cupped hand, while possessing some hidden weightiness that made it seem twice its actual size. It was a wonderful face, so rich in eternity, and I realized that it could be mine. I could live with it beside me every single day for the rest of my life, witnessing each day this smile which seemed to me to harbour a mystery more profound than that of the Mona Lisa. The Buddha, "who has forgotten those things that we experience and experiences things we never attain".

My desire to possess this head was most certainly acute, inasmuch as it was the desire to own eternity and thus insure myself against my own passing. In my hand I held 40 to 50 generations and through this head, so it seemed, I could live for 40 to 50 generations to come. It had all the magnetic force of a moonstone, a chunk of the universe that had landed, out of the blue, into my hand, testifying to a place beyond time. Secreted within it was a glorious promise, and yet it was quite clear to me that what the Buddha was smiling at, regarding with such indulgence from beneath those half-shut eyelids, was nothing other than the sure and certain transience of all things. But so beautiful was this face that it, too, exerted all the seductive power of that same transitoriness. Now I could not bear the thought of never seeing it again. I wanted to stop time.

The back of the head was missing and the throat was just one gash. It must have been mounted on a temple wall as part of a larger frieze and had been lopped off, like the heads I had seen at Angkor. Grains of red sand nestled in the gash. It must have happened long ago.

"Americans," said the guards, pointing at the throat.

"Tenth century," they went on, "cheap. $80."

They had grown cocky now. They had seen the weakness in me.

"$60," I said. I didn't mean it. What I meant was: save me from buying this exquisite head because I cannot cope with the image of myself such an act would hold up to me. But I am powerless to say no. So I am going to leave the decision to chance. Should you back down I will buy the head and leave this place a changed, a lesser, man. But you won't. Because you're right. It is cheap. $80 is nothing for a chunk of eternity. And you're probably only selling it so cheaply because you're having a job finding buyers for your ill-gotten wares in such an out-of-the-way spot. So you'll stand your ground, and I'll stand my ground and in a minute or two I'll take my leave, peaceably and with a clear conscience.

"$80," they repeated. "Cheap."

"$60."

They shook their heads. I stood up, relieved, and made to go.

"$70."

Before I could stop myself I had turned around and nodded, yes.

They wrapped the head in the newspaper again and handed it to me. I thought of the policeman stationed at the road end. "No problem," they said and shook their heads. With a practised hand the man in the yellow safety helmet took the wrapped head and slipped it into one of his capacious pockets. They winked at me. I was one of theirs now. They'd got me.

We drove past the policeman and, screened by a car door, I took possession of the head. Then I drove off, feeling like another person; not a better person, but a better judge of my own character. I had been cured of my clear conscience. I had overstepped a boundary, gone over to "them", the others – the bomb-throwers, the despoilers, whom I had always viewed from the safe side of a clear conscience – and become one small link in the great chain of destruction.

André Malraux cut whole blocks out of Bantey Srei, I took away a tiny sliver of My Son. Malraux's hero, Perken, dreamt of leaving a scar in the landscape; the Americans had realized this dream, drawn up to full industrial scale, and left behind a land as pockmarked as a Swiss cheese. And when enough time had passed people would refer to the traces of war as the ravages of time and no longer see the ruthless hand of man or hear the tramp of the armies' feet. But it was this harsh passage that had found an echo in my little transaction and in some way I was now a more legitimate part of the human race: crossed the border to the lands of destruction and learned that beauty had its price and that the $70 I had paid for it was but a fraction of that price.

Land of Women

LANG CO WAS A LARGE FISHING VILLAGE ON THE COAST BETWEEN Danang and Hué. It sat right out on the tip of a long spit of silver sand which threw a protective arm around a shallow, turquoise-blue lagoon. Electric pylons strode across the mouth of the lagoon and followed the line of the white surf, their high-voltage cables sagging limply, like the rope on a winch momentarily given some slack in the midst of all the heaving and straining to haul the country into the future.

You could walk along the beach for hours without meeting anyone. Fishing boats beat back and forth across the water. From each prow jutted two long spars from which a fishing net was slung. The fishermen stood bolt upright and motionless. An old man ambled past me, skin wrinkled and leathery beneath a straw hat. Hands clasped behind his back, he was enjoying the privilege of old age: leisure, which he spent thoughtfully perusing the sea. Then a fisherman strolled by with a long bamboo fishing pole over his shoulder. A woman emerged from the dunes, trotting nimbly under a wooden yoke from the ends of which dangled heavy bundles of brushwood. In the late afternoon the sands were overrun by troops of naked children. School was out for the day, and they came down to the water to cool off in the surf.

In the morning the beach was drained of colour by the rapidly rising sun. The mountains hovered in hazy blue silhouette, the sand became white as the horizon, the sea turned milky. As the afternoon wore on the colours regained their warmth and intensity. The sand shifted to a honey gold, the sea shimmered with an emerald-green lustre, the mountains faded to a deeper blue and appeared to increase in weight until, all at once, the jungle-clad hillsides ignited in a blaze of colour.

It was the season of the full moon and late in the afternoon, over the sea, the sun produced a pale replica of the lunar disc. In the evening the beach was silvered and crawling with tiny crabs which left lacy patterns in the sand. Groups of young men and women walked together along the shore, white shirts luminescent in the moonlight. The girls' raven hair hung loose down their backs, the night which the moon had put to flight seeming to have taken refuge there.

I was sitting scanning the ocean when a small boy came and sat down facing me. He squirmed self-consciously. Between shyness and curiosity, curiosity won. We regarded one another for a while in silence, until finally he plucked up his courage.

"Might one be permitted to ask your name?" he asked in a thin voice. I stared at him, astonished by the impeccability of his English. I told him my name.

"Might one be permitted to inquire as to your age?" he went on. "I myself am twelve years old. I know that in your eyes I must seem younger, but I have never been very big for my age."

For some time we continued in this fashion, putting the most politely couched questions to one another. His name was Choung, his father was an English teacher; for his own part, he had not yet made up his mind about his future. Having formed a rough picture of my marital, professional and national status, he got to his feet and executed a small courtly bow, not less impeccable than his English.

"I am very pleased to meet you. I will now go and notify my father of your arrival." He took a couple of dignified paces on his spindly legs, then hared off at a boyish gallop.

An hour later he was back. "My father has asked me to extend you an invitation to visit our home."

"Thank you, I would like that very much. When would it be convenient for your father?"

"My father says the sooner the better. For lunch, tomorrow."

I took a present for Choung's family. It was the American journalist Stanley Karnow's book about the Vietnam war, *Vietnam: A History*, which I had just finished reading on the beach. Choung's father was a stocky man with wiry hair and a small goatee beard. He no longer worked as a teacher, he told me as he showed me into the living room where a smiling woman waited with a large bowl of steaming noodle soup. He had given up teaching eight years ago, because he had been unable to support his family on the 20,000 *dong* (about $2) a month which was what a schoolteacher's salary amounted to under the depressed Vietnamese planned economy. His wife had opened a small shop and he now worked there as her assistant. They earned as much in a day as he had earned in a month. It was still not a lot, but enough to live on. They had built this house themselves, having saved up for eleven years.

Choung's mother had settled herself across from us, assuming an easy position with her legs tucked under her. Her figure was curvaceous beneath the baggy pyjamas that are the traditional dress of Vietnamese women. Before long she was setting the tone of the whole conversation with her husky laugh. She wanted to know what conditions were like for immigrants in Denmark. A family from Lang Co had moved to my country. They showed me the address.

"Are there many people in Denmark who are unemployed because they are lazy?" asked Choung's mother.

"Not that many. Most of them are unhappy with their situation and embarrassed by it."

"It is the same here. A lot of young people are unemployed. But maybe Denmark is a good country for those who are lazy. Vietnam is not an easy country for lazy people. Hard work is the only way to survive."

"It's worst in the country areas," her husband added. "Hard work and rice three times a day. Many people have no more than five years of schooling. And there are those who cannot read or write."

"First there was the war," said Choung's mother. "Then the government wanted to control everything. But the economy is in a bad way. It's the women who keep the whole thing going. Just look at him." She laughed and nodded mockingly at her husband. "You may look like a man. But you're not a real man. You're a woman."

I expected Choung's father to be furious at this outspoken comment on his failure to live up to the duty imposed on him by his sex, to be the breadwinner. But he merely laughed good-naturedly. "Oh yes, I'm a proper housewife!"

This was clearly a long-standing joke between them. With her head for business, she laid the foundation of the family's financial situation and he had accepted the new division of roles. Yet his influence on Choung showed that he was still the head of the family and his son's role model.

I thought of the women I had seen walking along the country roads early in the morning and the countless, gracefully bobbing straw hats that dominated the market places. After a wartime economy and a planned economy, Vietnam now had a female economy, and Choung's mother and father were doubtless not alone in practising this bantering exchange of roles.

In Stanley Karnow's book I had read about the country's first two national heroes, both of them women. Trung Nhi and Trung Trac were sisters who had taken up arms against the arch-enemy, China, and kicked their invading army out of Vietnam. They had just two years in which to reap the benefits of their victory, before they were defeated; at which point they both committed suicide. Two hundred years later the Vietnamese rose up once more, again led by a Vietnamese Joan of Arc, and history repeated itself: victory, defeat, suicide. With her short, powerful limbs and throaty laugh, so full of warmth and self-assurance, Choung's mother looked a true descendant of these heroines.

In my mind's eye I saw all of these Vietnamese women whom I had paid little attention, simply because Tam had overshadowed them. Sturdy women and slightly splay-footed, accustomed to heavy loads. Like Choung's mother, they laughed a lot; laughter that might be read as a testimony to their strength. Unlike the men, the women in the market place did not lose their temper if you caught them cheating. They simply laughed knowingly, as if you had just shown the first signs of intelligence.

When we parted, Choung's father presented me with a booklet entitled *Introduction to Vietnamese Poetry*. It had been printed in Saigon long before the reunification of Vietnam and it closed with the words: "Modern Vietnam is still waiting for its poet."

A couple of days later Choung saw me to the railway station. I had borrowed his father's bicycle. We cycled across the bridge spanning the lagoon and cut across the rice fields, heading towards the densely forested mountains that rose ahead of us in all their lush, green profusion. We turned off the road and followed the sandy track leading to the station. The one platform was packed with stalls and heaving with people. I bought a bottle of water and found somewhere to sit, worn out by the ride through the sweltering heat. In exuberant voices the women cried their wares, white teeth flashing in inviting smiles. A couple of men wandered past, glassy-eyed and unsteady on their feet. One of them raised a bottle to his lips and the white of his eye turned yellow for a moment as he swallowed. I thought of what Choung's father had said about the unemployed.

The train to Danang pulled in on the opposite track and was swiftly besieged by women holding up their baskets to the passengers who leaned out of the windows. After a while, as business tailed off, the women sat down for a chat in the shade of the railway carriages. One of them crawled in under a carriage and coolly made herself comfortable on the rail between two wheels. I stared, aghast. Then the train to Hué rolled in alongside the platform and blocked my view. The carriages were wooden and painted green; goods wagons converted to carry passengers, with benches built down the sides. The broad central aisle was crammed with bicycles and scooters. A conductor showed me to a carriage in which the seats were arranged facing one another in compartments constructed from bare wood, dark and shiny with wear.

I took my seat and bid a cheerful hello to the Western-looking couple sitting opposite me. They did not answer. I could hear from their conversation that they were French. Both had remarkable noses and pompous, rather aggrieved looks on their faces and they were in the midst of a bitter quarrel. Each time the row came to a head one or other of them would pointedly stick the sunglasses, that both had dangling from chains around their necks, on his or her very striking nose in order to register indifference to their partner's arguments. For the most part he remained quietly entreating; she, sulky, the entire lower half of her face and her small mouth twisted out of shape with icy remoteness.

I leaned out of the window and waved to Choung.

"Our parting touches me deeply," he shouted in his little voice. "Don't forget to write!"

A Garden City

IN HUÉ CLOUDS HUNG LOW OVER THE FORBIDDEN PURPLE CITY, for 300 years the official residence of Vietnamese emperors. The glazed yellow brick of Ngo Mon Gate shone, but the green had turned to grey, the blue of the pillars had softened and the red lacquer had lost its fire; lichen, mould and the dehydrating effects of the sun dictated the colour scheme here.

The high walls girding the imperial city were but a shell. Inside there was nothing. The Vietcong had marched into Hué at the height of the war, raised their flag above the Citadel and held the city for three weeks, during which time they systematically executed thousands of their political opponents. Then the counter-attack was launched, with artillery, missiles and aerial bombardments. The crucial battles were fought here, at the very crossroads of history. It was a case of two adversaries from the same native land becoming obsessed with one another; not with what bound them to one another, but with the things that kept them apart. So they destroyed their common history, and their love of the motherland brought about its ruin. The site on which an imperial palace had once stood was now divided into vegetable plots. An archaeologist would have been out of a job amid all those plants and herbs. Not even the relics were allowed to be abundant. So much history and so little of it left.

Well, no, there is a little. In the Halls of the Mandarins they will show you a felicitously restored ceiling; point out the bullet holes in the floor and in a mirror – still fractured 25 years on – that says more about the war than it does about the 300 years of history which were completely erased by the battle of Hué. Outside, all is green: a crumbling stairway overgrown with grass, a stone dragon nestling in clover and lettuces, a lone bronze urn in the middle of a field.

But Hué is not a dismal town. Ruins document the passage of time. Vegetable plots do not, and it was as half-city, half-kitchen garden that

259

Hué had come up with an after-life for itself, a life beyond the devastation, like a tropical Dresden mercifully returned to nature in the wake of the bombings.

In the moat encircling the Citadel rice had been planted and the bluish-green stems of spring onions sprouted everywhere. Opposite the Citadel, on the other side of the Perfume River, a few French houses still stood, relics of colonial days, surrounded by large, well-kept gardens; buildings on a generous scale, with oriel windows, pointed gables and sloping tiled roofs. Every street was an avenue and I guessed that at another time of year the thick shrubs which spilled out over the pavements almost everywhere would be covered in sweet-smelling blossoms. Gardeners had taken the place of town planners, and instead of rebuilding the city after the convulsions of war its inhabitants had preferred, so it seemed, to let it languish in peaceful exhaustion, abandoned to the laws of organic growth rather than the sharp edges and straight lines of architecture.

Like its temples and pagodas, the old walls of Hué were worn and battered, adorned with black lichen and patches of mould possessed of a beauty all their own; the beauty of survival – devoid of illusions, sober, frugal, far removed from the enthusiasms of the past. As with the walls, so with the plant life: allotments as opposed to parkland. The Vietnam war had been waged not just against a people, but against the essence of their being, against the land, its crops and vegetation; a war of extermination of ecological dimensions. Someone had tried to take Nature away from them. This, too, pervaded the allotments and avenues of Hué: a healing of the natural world. I have the feeling that the inhabitants of the city must look with gratitude on all that greenery: we came through it together.

It was a city populated by women. They endowed it with an air of dynamism. All the small cafés in the town were occupied by men slumped over half-empty beer glasses, looking as though they had tumbled out of the maelstrom of cyclists and motorists dominated by purposeful-looking women. Under the thin stuff of their pyjama suits one glimpsed softly rounded forms; an inviting languor lay beneath their deft movements and animated chatter, a tacit erotic promise which did not bring out the lover in you: you did not wander around filled with desire in a city that seemed already to have brought you release. Rather, you went about in an almost soporific state of surrender, devotedly and trustingly allowing yourself to be enfolded by its lush greenery and smiling women. You were barely aware of moving around, feeling more as if you were lying next to the city after happy lovemaking. The hot, humid air; the fine rain falling as intimately as sweat on the skin; voices; glances – all blending into one generous caress; an all-embracing erotic experience in which an entire culture converged on you in a single loving touch.

I ate lunch at a little restaurant that opened directly onto the street. One half of the blue-distempered, soot-blackened interior was taken up by an array of gas rings, pots and woks, and a mound of vegetables. I was the only customer and the two women who were serving promptly sat themselves down at my rickety table, having first decked it with bowls of translucent noodle pancakes, peanut sauce and herbs. While I ate, I was subjected to an interrogation into my marital status. They happily divulged details of their own. The restaurant's owner was a slim, attractive woman of 40 with a long, girlish ponytail hanging down her back. Her skin was white and the thready network of blue veins discernible beneath her collarbone gave her a delicate, vulnerable look. Her friend, who was exactly one year older, was a mournful beauty with heavy black hair coiled into a bun at the nape of her neck. "She is single," announced the proprietress – she the mother of two – and in the same breath went on to ask whether I had ever thought of marrying a Vietnamese woman. She motioned encouragingly at her friend, who responded by modestly lowering her eyes, then straightaway raised them again to send me a coy look.

We were joined by a girl of 15 or so; quite small, nowhere near fully developed, but trying out on her own face the grown woman's repertoire of seductive glances. She made her own contribution to the flirtatious atmosphere by praising the single woman to the skies for her beauty, for her youthfulness, and concluded, with the demeanour of an experienced madame, by assuring me that I had only to say the word and she was mine.

I showered all three with compliments and when they placed a tattered notebook in front of me, declaring it to be the visitors' book of this run-down little establishment I was duty-bound to write my honest opinion. I wrote that the food was as delicious as the women who served it. The owner read this out to the other two, who clapped delightedly. After this they brought me tea and commanded me to wait one moment. Then they disappeared up a spiral staircase at the back of the room. I could hear them laughing on the first floor and a while later they reappeared. All three had put on red lipstick and the proprietress had exchanged her pyjamas for a pink dress. Her friend was now wearing a pair of tight black pants and a loose-fitting shirt, also black, which accentuated the darkly brooding quality of her mature good looks. I knew that as a single woman of 41 she must harbour some tragic secret, but this she had succeeded in turning to her advantage. There was something alluring and provocative about her aura of mystery.

"Now, I hope you're going to come back and eat here again tonight," said the owner, with her freshly rouged lips.

I left on my rented bicycle, dazed and electrified by all that erotic attention being lavished on a customer who had paid not more than 20 pence sterling for his meal. I had been in the hands of two expert businesswomen and though I had seen through their game, there had been so much spontaneous playfulness that I had willingly gone along with it. No doubt this state of flattered and reinforced manliness was to blame for my cycling north, although the place I wanted to visit lay some kilometres south of Hué. I eventually realized my mistake and stopped to consult my map, just outside a bank. A moment later I looked up from the map to find the entire staff, all of them women, clustered behind the glass door, waving and beckoning to me to come inside. I waved back, but so befuddled was I by the attentions of women that I wasted no time in running off.

I returned to the restaurant that evening. The owner was nowhere to be seen and a man with a facial tic so persistent that I thought he might be spastic, ushered me up to the first floor where one or two tables had been set out on a little balcony overlooking the street. The moody beauty was sitting in an adjoining room, watching television. She looked round and smiled. Then she turned her attention back to the screen. I had been outmanoeuvred by a video.

The 15-year-old's interest was, however, undiminished. She invested all of her youthful energies in an extension of the afternoon's flirtation, which had – so it seemed – passed into a more serious stage, inasmuch as she now began to pinch me hard in various parts of my anatomy, primarily my forearm. To her unqualified delight I pinched her back, and we had a splendid evening.

When I turned, on my way down the spiral staircase, to say goodbye to her, she put her arm round my neck and gave me a kiss that was both shy and ardent and which landed on my cheek, although its target had clearly been my lips. I was overwhelmed with tenderness towards her. It was not desire that I felt, but it may have been the germ of physical attraction, an almost metaphysical fascination induced by her innocence, a longing to possess what cannot be possessed, something akin to the moment when I held the Buddha's head in my hand. Sex, physical lust, focuses on the moment, but in eroticism there is always a metaphysical element, the yearning for eternity, for the arrested moment between two heartbeats. Was it the woman in her to whom I was attracted, or the child in me who was drawn to her? It was the woman in her, but it was also the child. It was the child in me, but also the man. The erotic: the eternal switching of roles. Eroticism is our way of shirking the dictates of procreation. It is a dressing-up game for children who know that they are children no longer. The game we played on the spiral staircase was an impossible one, because she was a child though she did not know it. She played at being a woman, I remained a man. I knew too much, she too little. We could meet on my cheek, not on my lips. In our pinching we were equals, nowhere else.

I rode south, in another effort to find the ancient Royal Tombs. On the way I stopped at Bao Quoc Pagoda which lay on the outskirts of the city, just across the railway line, in a leafy little side street that ended in a flight of steps leading up to the temple. The walls around the pagoda were of a faded yellow, with a red-lacquered gateway at their centre. No sooner had I stepped inside than I was approached by a young girl. She introduced herself as a student of English and asked politely whether I could spare her a little of my time so that she might practise her English on me. While we were talking she showed me the gardens surrounding the temple. Everywhere one looked, on the steps and in the shade of the trees, slender students sat engrossed in textbooks and exercise books. The monastery garden was one large, hushed reading room. One section of the gardens consisted of an area laid out with freshly cast concrete steps, ponds, miniature pagodas and low walls. In its interaction with the little flower beds and the ubiquitous frangipani trees with their silvery bark and snow-white, lily-like flowers, some decorative quality appeared to have been coaxed out of the concrete, allowing its ordinarily drab hue to take its place in a delicately balanced colour scheme.

We came into the little monastery rose garden with its rose-beds framed by hanging orchids and amaryllis in large, terracotta pots. We sat down on the rim of one of the small ponds and the girl student proceeded to point out to me the surrounding trees and reel off their names in Vietnamese. Then she tore a page out of her exercise book and wrote them down for me. "Su' Tree have a pleasant smell. Hoang Tree have a nice smell. Flower is white."

Hué was a city in which the women patiently taught the visitor the names of the flowers and trees, as if one were a new arrival in the garden of Eden.

Ask the Immortals about
the Meaning of Life

I CYCLED OUT TO THE TOMB OF EMPEROR TU DUC, TO THE south of Hué, in a gentle drizzle. Tu Duc had reigned as emperor during the years when Vietnam lost its independence and became a French colony. After 35 years on the throne he died, according to a communiqué issued by the Imperial Court, with a curse against the French colonial overlords on his lips. Tu Duc had been a gentle and refined man by nature, no more than five foot tall with sensitive fingers and a look in his eyes which one French traveller described as "remarkably deep". He had the Buddhist's proclivity for melancholy other-worldliness and, as emperor, was quite unfitted to steering his country safely through its confrontation with the French colonial power. He thought he could save his country by cutting it off from the world and bringing time to a standstill, there, between the sea and the mountains. Instead he lost control over the country, over time, and over his own subjects, who not only revolted against the invading French troops, but also against their emperor. He publicly acknowledged his personal impotence in long, lyrical laments that cannot have moved his hard-pressed subjects to think any more kindly of him. "Above me I fear the decrees of Heaven, below me the trials of the people trouble me day and night. Deep in my heart I tremble and blush and can find neither words or actions to help my subjects. I am without words. My pulse is weak, my body pale and thin, my beard and hair white. Though not yet 40 I am already an old man . . ."

Tu Duc was laid to rest in a setting designed to symbolize the bed of a giant. One mountain represented the pillow on which he rested his head; another was a table set before him; a third, a dragon to his left side; a fourth, a tiger to his right. He lay with his face towards the setting sun, not far from the Perfume River, whose course symbolized the emperor's soul wending its way to eternal life. The mountains and hills to the south-west of Hué were full of such imperial tombs, their monumental scale lying hidden like a secret in the lines of the landscape.

True to tradition, at Tu Duc's burial large sums of money were spent on elaborate carts, boats and palaces made out of paper, all of which were consigned to the flames so that they might accompany the dead emperor to the other world for his use there. But Tu Duc, himself so conscious of the transience of all things – not least his own – would surely, had he been in a position to observe the ceremony, have been of quite a different mind and, rather than viewing the fire on which the paper palaces were consumed as a gateway to the hereafter, would have seen the devouring flames as a picture of this life of his which had just ended. For what were his power, his empire, his coat of arms, his throne, but paper? All of them were seized by an immense, brutal hand, crumpled up and thrown away.

At the entrance to the tomb one was issued with a ticket with a poem by Tu Duc printed on the back. In it he ruthlessly takes stock of his life as emperor: "Ephemeral were wealth and fame. Conquests would be lost finally. Life was burdened by sorrow. Ask of the immortal about it and you'd get no reply. So try to endure your last days and see what life would bring."

The mausoleum was a sprawling complex of pavilions, stairways, a small palace, a lake and a network of little canals meandering through the grounds. A mass of spectacular drawings executed in black mould and patches of mildew fading to blue covered the walls which were a mouldering brick-red, a weather-beaten terracotta and a sere, washed-out yellow with the green patina of verdigris. There were frangipani trees everywhere, their upswept branches rendering them a part of the architecture. Their white bark, which was patched with green moss, echoed the bleached yellow of the porcelain dressed walls. Only at the very top did the trees sport buds and flowers otherwise they were bare. A sun conspicuous by its absence; distant thunder and half-hearted rain; tattered clouds sailing past; the mould-bedecked dragons of the pagodas silhouetted against the slate-grey sky – it was as if the mausoleum were dictating the weather conditions.

I thought of Tu Duc's poem, which had been written in the past tense and gave the impression of having originated somewhere far beyond

266

the grave. The same applied to his tomb, which looked as though it had always expected the rain, the corrosive dampness and the overcast skies. It had not been built to resist. It was fated to decay, its walls only waiting for the black mould and the blues of the lichen to put the finishing touches to its colour scheme; its ornamentation was not complete until weathering made it a harmonious part of the pattern formed by the upstretched branches of the frangipani trees; its silence not veritable until it was underlined by the incessant pattering of the raindrops. Here was an elegant work of architecture deliberately exposing its beauty to decay, knowing that the beauty would only deepen once the stone had gone the way of all flesh. Death and decline are the lot of all things, but here these had been overcome by being employed as a conscious effect in the architectural design. This was the mausoleum of a Buddhist emperor. A human being is destined to die and be forgotten. His work shares his fate and is brought to perfection even as it is crumbles away. Death removes the last stone. Then it is fulfilled.

I spent a day or two cycling round the countryside south of Hué, visiting the Royal Tombs. Everywhere I went I was left with the same impression. None of these mausoleums would last for long. By the time they were pushing 200 they would be in a worse state of disrepair than the pyramids.

Emperor Minh Mang's was possibly the loveliest of them all. Its finely wrought buildings with their muted hues lay on a series of man-made islands connected by little bridges and separated by narrow moats that flowed into a half-moon shaped lake. Amid the green of a countryside which, under the grey sky, was as dense and dark as a Danish forest in late summer, the pavilions and stairways had the distinctive, frail and inscrutable air of superiority found in one who is exalted by the awareness of his own impending death.

The Tomb of Khai Din was a hideous monstrosity. Completed in 1931, it was an enormous concrete pile that ascended a steep hillside by way of grandiose, baroque staircases. Ten thousand men, many of them convicts, had worked on it for eleven years. It was the only display of power permitted an emperor who had lost his country and become nothing but a puppet in the hands of the French overlords. Here was a man who wanted to be remembered. But time did not want to hear about him, for the merciless climate had already clothed his tomb in a cloak of black mould with the result that, only 62 years after its completion it resembled an archaeologist's dream. The monument was greater in its conception than the life of the emperor, but like his name it is now being worn away without grace or philosophizing.

I would never have found the monument to Gia Long had it not been for Lúc. Lúc was a young man who had invited me for lunch at the home of his family, a blue-walled house surrounded by a garden and tall trees and fronting directly onto the Perfume River. He entertained me for long enough with the story of an Australian friend with whom he corresponded and whose name was Robert, although everyone called him Tim. Tim worked as a dishwasher and lived with his mother because it was cheapest that way. Tim was not all that crazy about his job but felt that washing dishes was better than being unemployed. What was special about Tim was that he had once sent Lúc $A100 to help with the purchase of a camera which Lúc had persuaded him he needed. As he still did, he said, giving me a suggestive look in case I happened to have missed the point. All this was revealed in Tim's letters, which Lúc unearthed and urged me to read. My eye fell on a postscript in one of these: "An education is the best investment in the future." I read this out loud and looked pointedly at Lúc, who immediately came to the conclusion that I must be a bit slow on the uptake.

Presumably that was why he had offered to take me to the tomb of Gia Long; to give his subtle hint about my contributing towards his camera more time to sink in. We cycled down a red sandy track that ran alongside the Perfume River to a little village where Lúc first had to introduce me to a friend who was "famous" for his guitar playing. The friend, a tailor by trade and in his early twenties, played us his best-known number, a somewhat shaky version of the Brazilian melody "Lambada", at a tempo about five times slower than the original. He accompanied his playing with a tremulous, all but inaudible hum. While I was watching it suddenly struck me that this was not actually music for listening to, but music for looking at. The tailor played the simple tune with an abundance of outrageously affected gestures and almost unbelievable snaps of his wrists and finger joints while gazing enraptured at his own slender fingers, all of which ended in impossibly long nails. He looked as though he were stitching, needling the music out of the guitar. Lúc, too, stared in fascination at the musician's hands and I realized that the musical village tailor was not so much famed for his playing as for the extravagant flourishes with which he handled his instrument.

With his guitar slung over his shoulder, the tailor followed us the last bit of the way to the tomb, which had been completed by the time of the emperor's death in 1820. "The third of February, I still remember the date," said Lúc solemnly, as if he had actually been there at the time.

Courtiers had placed a wisp of cotton on the tip of the Emperor Gia Long's nose, in order to be able to tell the exact moment when he breathed his last. They had also pushed a pair of chopsticks inlaid with mother-of-pearl between his lips to prevent his mouth from closing when death occurred, the intention being that the deceased emperor's gullet be filled with precious pearls. When the wisp of cotton ceased to flutter, they laid him on the floor in the hope that contact with the earth might revive him. Only after this had been done did they consider him to be dead. On his chest they laid a piece of milk-white silk, in which his soul was supposed to take up residence after death. The silk was knotted in such a way that it formed a figure with a head and four limbs: the soul of the emperor. Mandarins of the three most senior ranks were forbidden to wear red or to listen to music for the next 27 months; for mandarins of lower rank the ban applied for nine months; and for the common people and for the emperor's soldiers, 100 days.

Gia Long's tomb had not yet passed its second century, but the thousand-year-old Angkor Wat looked brand-new in comparison. The silence of mourning seemed to be the only thing to endure. It was said that the mausoleum had once covered an area of 7,500 acres, but now there was not much left except impressions and ridges in the landscape, as if the city of death had reverted to the foundations and trenches from which it had once risen. There were vestiges of broad stairways, symmetrical ponds and little lakes ringed by grassy hills on the slopes of which ancient pine trees stood in lonesome silhouette against a sky heavy with rain. Long-bodied stone dragons snaked their way down the terraced steps, an elephant at the base of the tomb had lost its trunk and next to it a legless horse had toppled over into the grass. To the left of the steps a row of mandarins lay with their plinths in the air, like checkmated chess pieces. On the hillsides, vying with the pine trees, stood two enormous pillars, too far apart now to convey anything about the building of which they must once have been a part. Amid a welter of shattered masonry, bamboo poles and beams meant to hold up a crumbling palace the roof of which had already fallen in, a caretaker lay asleep, stretched out on a table.

Lúc pointed to various spots in the dark-green landscape, so softly undulating that it might have been constructed out of cushions of moss: "There – and there – and there, the Americans dropped bombs." But there was no way of telling whether the humps in the landscape were overgrown heaps of rubble or simply irregularities in the terrain. And that hollow over there – was it the remains of one of Gia Long's artificial lakes or a bomb crater left by the Americans?

It had a strange magic about it, this moss-green stretch of countryside: not even the past lasted long here, even though the past was normally supposed to be the most constant of the three times, since present and future will inevitably end up in its great, greedy maw. In the landscape which had swallowed up the tomb of Gia Long, even the stones seemed to be suffering from amnesia.

Lúc and his friend walked ahead of me, willowy and with an inherent grace in their movements, the tailor with his guitar slung round his neck; and it struck me that, above all else, it was in their elegant bodies that the Vietnamese held on to their 2,000-year-old civilization.

I looked around me at the green countryside. It could be that its fecundity went hand in hand with the forgetfulness. There is often something rather barren about people with good memories, just as there is with nations which worship their own pasts with too much reverence and pedantry. With the Vietnamese, the recollection ran in their veins; they carried the past with them more as physical instinct and invisible laws which determined the delicate development of their limbs and the choreography of their movements than as the result of the efforts of historians or the strenuous endeavours of archaeologists to preserve the evidence of the past.

The ferry which carried us over the Perfume River was a large canoe, the inner side of its hull reinforced with sheets of corrugated iron beaten flat. High up in the stern a young girl in white pyjamas with blue-black hair down to her waist plied an oar three times her own length.

Lúc and the tailor exchanged winks.

"I need a camera," said Lúc.

"Get yourself an education," I replied.

The Snow behind Thien Mu Pagoda

SOMETHING STRANGE HAPPENED TO ME AT THIEN MU PAGODA; something inexplicable and yet significant. I find it difficult to put it into words. I could say that I felt as if I had reached journey's end. In a way, those words feel right, and yet it feels just as right to say that I had reached the beginning of my journey. Or the midpoint of my journey – or perhaps the centre of the Earth since, although my experience was deeply personal, it also struck me as being universal and objective, as if I had suddenly come up against certain fundamental laws of existence. A pleasant languor crept over my movements, as if my body had found its own force of gravity. Could one, instead, say force of belonging? Thien Mu Pagoda exerted a tremendous force of belonging, of a sort one normally only feels in one's childhood haunts – and they, of course, are to be found nowhere except in one's memory. But Thien Mu Pagoda did not make me think of any other place; it did not call to mind anything I had ever previously experienced; not until some time later when something did dawn on my memory and then it was an unknown place which I had only ever visited in my dreams. For me, Thien Mu Pagoda was, at one and the same time, the end, the beginning and the middle. For one moment I looked deeper into life than I have ever done before and I saw it form a figure for which there is no geometrical term, neither line nor curve, circle or spiral. There is one word which covers my experience, even though it does not explain it. The word is happiness. At Thien Mu Pagoda I was happy, for a few minutes and for an eternity and since then I have had the feeling that those moments of happiness which I had experienced before were only a prelude to this, and those moments of happiness that will come along later in life are a kind of after-shock; and that, taken as a whole, they make up that unknown geometric figure that is life.

Thien Mu Pagoda, set on the banks of the Song Huong river, is the most famous pagoda in Vietnam and has become a kind of symbol of

Hué. But that is of no relevance to what happened. The pagoda tower stands 21 metres high, built by Emperor Thieu Tri in 1844 on seven storeys, each one representing a Buddha who had assumed human form. This is not relevant, either, to what I am about to relate. The tower itself is as grimy as a factory chimney, its red walls covered with Hué's ubiquitous patches of black lichen and mildew; it is worn and dilapidated and if it has any beauty at all then it is not that of the monument itself, but that of survival: illusionless, pragmatic. Nor is that of any relevance. In the temple yard stands an old blue-grey Austin – the car which brought the monk Thich Quang Duc to this spot where, in 1963, he immolated himself in protest against the South-Vietnamese regime. Photographs of him travelled round the world eventually winding up in Ingmar Bergman's film *Persona*, in which the heat from the flames finally sets light to the celluloid itself. But not even that is of any relevance.

In the temple yard I could hear the monks chanting. The tempo of their singing kept accelerating, without becoming rhythmical or rousing or working towards a climax. Now and again the singing was punctuated by the sound of a gong whose boom, as it slowly died away, summoned up the silence. The silence hung like an aura around the song, and the chanting of the monks chimed in with it. I walked across the temple yard, carrying on past the temple and into the monastery garden which lay surrounded by low walls and with a view of rolling hills. At one end of the garden stood a clump of tall trees, bald trunks crowned, at the very top, by leafy branches that shook in the breeze. A short flight of steps in pearl- and slate-grey was flanked by short, four-sided columns painted with black calligraphic characters.

The monks' chant droned on behind me, broken now and again by the gong, which lent a hypnotic intensity to the steadily mounting note of their singing. I had passed through this sound and come out, altered, on the other side. I walked across the garden the way, in dreams, one goes through doors: each step a new door, a new room that was not there before, but which from vague outline changes to concrete form; rooms within rooms, landscapes within landscapes, boxes within boxes. I saw a grey tower roofed by green tiles, the dove-grey silhouettes of the trees against the luminous blanket of cloud, white flowers – and then a distant hill dotted with graves. I had that sense of fulfilment. I can go no further. This is the outermost limit, the last landscape. I had never seen it in dreams, because my dreams do not delve deep enough.

For me, a landscape signifies longing. I do not, in fact, see the landscape, I see its horizon. In the monastery garden behind Thien Mu Pagoda I discovered the landscape where all longing comes to an end. I had gone beyond the horizon. No questions had been answered. All had been silenced.

Not until some time later did I realize that this experience had its roots in something from my own life. At the age of four I had spent some time in hospital after a road accident. It was winter and from the window of my room I could look down into a snow-covered garden. The garden was screened in by a row of tall, old birches and one day a hare appeared in the shrubbery beneath the trees. It sat perfectly still for a while, before loping warily out over the virgin white surface of the lawn. It was the first time I had ever seen a hare and amid the stultifying tedium of my hospitalization its presence seemed to me to be a miracle. In typical childish fashion, I felt that its appearance must have something to do with me, that it had been "sent", guided by a will – perhaps its own – but that I entered into the considerations of this will. It had appeared to me and when, a little later, it took itself off, my thoughts went with it. I wanted to know where it had come from and in the images I conjured up in my mind's eye lay the child's dawning recognition of the fact that there is a world beyond himself, one which was not governed by his needs and which might not even know that he existed. While I may have thought that it had appeared especially for me in my mental pictures of the hare's life I also glimpsed a world that was not mine and which I was barred from entering. Where did the hare came from? The answer crystallized into the image of the hare sitting on the frozen, snow-clad field under a leaden sky, where the horizon smouldered white and pale coral as the low winter sun struggled to break through. It was a bleak and barren spot a place where a child would feel forsaken, and yet all of my longing to be gone from that hospital room condensed into this picture of the hare in the wintry waste. If I had to put a name to where I have been when I stood in the garden of Thien Mu Pagoda with a feeling of finding myself in the last landscape, I would have to say that I have been to where the hare came from.

A link has been established in my life between then and now, like an underground tunnel suddenly opening up between two places on opposite sides of the globe. The hare came to me from the landscape behind Thien

Mu pagoda, like a messenger from the future. It left its tracks in the snow that always falls on the hills and dales of remembrance and the tracks had stuck in my memory, so that I would not come unprepared to this moment, many years later, and overlook its importance.

At Thien Mu Pagoda life revealed itself to me beyond those questions I was capable of asking and answers I was capable of understanding and I could walk away from there easier at heart and with a little less yearning.

The Eunuchs' Graveyard

IT WAS MY LAST DAY IN HUÉ AND I HAD CALLED ON MY TWO lady friends for a taste of their delicious transparent noodle pancakes. This time both were wearing *ao dais* and the owner's friend had let her hair down, so that it fell over her shoulders and set off the swan-white silk.

They parked themselves at my table and using chopsticks one of them deftly mixed some mint leaves into my salad. I told them about my visit to the imperial tombs.

"Did you know," said the owner, "that it took 50 cooks to prepare a meal for Emperor Tu Duc and that every day he sat down to 50 dishes, served by 50 attendants? His tea was made from dewdrops gathered from the lotus leaves early in the morning. You'll have to make do with us."

She laughed coquettishly and took up a piece of pancake with the chopsticks. This she then dipped in the peanut sauce before offering it to me. I looked about to be sure no one was looking, then – in a blend of delight and embarrassment – permitted myself to be fed, at once lionized and nannied.

"How could he possibly eat that much?" I asked.

"He only ate one mouthful of each dish," said the lady of the house, lifting the chopsticks to my lips again. "Besides which, he drank a special herb infusion which aided the digestion and whetted the appetite. The name of this drink was 'Five Couplings in One Night'."

"Ah, so it wasn't just one sort of appetite this drink whetted?"

"The emperor had one empress and 103 concubines, so it's no wonder that he needed a little help. Not only that, but he didn't have a very good memory, although he did have a highly developed sense of smell. He couldn't remember the names of his concubines, or tell their faces apart. Instead, he recognized them by their scent."

I laughed and produced a little parcel from my pocket. "I've heard that story before. Look what I've got!" I unwrapped the parcel. Inside were two tiny ivory *flacons* with mountainscapes and pavilions etched into their yellowing surfaces. "These belonged to the concubines of Emperor Tu Duc. They kept their scent in them. They're perfume bottles."

I gave them one each to admire. They studied the little *flacons* with astonishment. "Where did you get them?" asked the owner. "I bought them in the Forbidden Purple City. There's a shop there selling all sorts of old things. The assistant told me their origin."

"Did she say they were ivory?"

I nodded.

She went over to the gas hob and picked up a lighter. She lit the gas and passed the bottle through the flame.

"Hey! What are you doing?" I cried.

"It's a test," she said. "If it really is ivory the flame will not leave a mark. If it does, that means it's only bone." Triumphantly she held up the bottle. "See, nothing happened. It's the real thing."

Then all at once she turned serious. "You must take good care of them," she said, "and only give them to someone you truly care for." Coyly, her unmarried friend lowered her eyelashes.

"Not me, not her," said my hostess. "I'm sure there is someone back there, where you come from, who ought to have these."

When I had finished my meal and was about to say my goodbyes, she told me: "There is one thing about the lives of the concubines I think you ought to know. There were many words which they were forbidden to say: all of the words which carry evil omens or are in some other way unlucky; words like 'death', 'illness', 'blood' or 'blindness'. In fact there were so many inappropriate words that for their first three months in the Forbidden Purple City new concubines did not utter a single word for fear of saying something wrong. Most of them were unhappy and did not live to be very old. What this teaches you is that if love is to last it must be able to cope with all the words a language possesses."

The last thing I did before leaving Hué was to visit the eunuchs' graveyard. The eunuchs are buried in a garden some way south of Hué. All of this stretch of countryside to the south of the Imperial City was consecrated to the past. There was nothing here but tombs, pagodas, monuments; every hillside, every mountain, every river was endowed with its own, half-forgotten, significance. Cycling around this area was like touring the hereafter, or rather that bygone age when the hereafter still figured largely in a nation's consciousness and the worship of the dead had an architectural style all its own. It was a Vietnamese Hades, a landscape of shades where no one now came to offer up the fresh blood of their curiosity to give life to the past.

The eunuchs had paid for this graveyard themselves by collecting money for the restoration of Tu Hien Pagoda, to which the land belonged. That was in 1893. Sixty years before this the Emperor Minh Mang, incensed by the eunuchs' political intriguing, had deprived them of any say in affairs of state and banished them to the furthest regions of the Imperial Palace where they were permitted only to attend to the Emperor's immediate family. By 1893 it could not have made much difference anyway. In his occupied empire, the emperor was himself as powerless as his own dethroned eunuchs and while he compensated for this with an extravagantly corrupt and luxurious private life, the child-men were robbed of the only thing that could have compensated for their half-life: the liberty to meddle in government matters.

In 1893 the remaining eunuchs must have guessed that they would be the last of their kind, although every generation of eunuchs must have lived with just such a premonition of doomsday, incapable as they were of propagating. Maybe they viewed their own extinction as a release; maybe they were seized by the all-too-human feeling that their wretchedness would be easier to bear if they could pass it on to others. No one knows. They left no testimony, only gravestones. But who did they think was going to cherish their memory?

I came upon the pagoda in a grove of slender pine trees. The needle-covered forest floor rose and fell in a succession of little hills and valleys and in one such hollow lay the Tu Hien monastery, surrounded by vegetable plots, a pond – and the eunuchs' graveyard. The graves, 20 of them, were encircled by a crumbling, lichen-covered wall. They were simple, with modest little headstones bearing inscriptions in the old Vietnamese calligraphy, which the French abolished in favour of the Roman alphabet. An ancient frangipani tree hanging over the wall had scattered its lily-white blossoms on the graves. This was the sole memorial raised to the virginal child-men; and in the flowers – which seemed, with their snowy purity, to symbolize the enforced innocence of these men – there lay also a cruel irony, because all through their lives the eunuchs had been forced to wear a flower, embroidered on the chest of their robes. The flower was the symbol of their lamentable status, the Star of David of their missing sex. And now, when nature itself strewed the graves of these forgotten dead, it appeared not so much to be paying them a last tribute as to be making fun of them. Not even in death were they allowed to lose their stigma.

A novice from the monastery appeared at my side. He had buck teeth and wore a pair of huge black horn-rimmed glasses, which looked as if they were glued to his shaven skull. "More graves," he said in English, pointing towards the other side of the monastery.

I started walking in the direction he had indicated and he fell into step beside me. We came past a number of large sepulchres; shards of broken porcelain cups and bowls embedded in the concrete of their walls. The entrance to each sepulchre was flanked by pillars that culminated, at their tops, in lotus flowers.

"Eunuchs?" I inquired.

The novice shook his head. "Reverend fathers," he said, explaining that this was where the abbots of the monastery were interred.

We walked across a large meadow until we came to a wall whose gateway was blocked by withered thorn bushes. The novice dragged aside one of the bushes piled up loosely on the ground and we stepped through to the other side of the wall. At the centre of the enclosure lay a grave-stone for eunuchs with a bundle of burnt-out joss-sticks protruding from a crack in the slab. This was the only trace of the dead. Other than that it was all perfectly straight paths and low, manicured bushes. Here the sterile men had been allowed to fertilize the soil in one of Vietnam's many vegetable gardens, a more merciful fate than being remembered with blossoms.

Perhaps the eunuchs' real misfortune had been that they had had innocence forced upon them, and that for them there had been no escape from it. They had the right to marry one another, but their marriage only provided a framework for two lonely people who had to make do with consolation rather than love, for consolation is a kind of second-hand love, just as intrigue is evil at second hand; and perhaps that is why they were known for being such plotters and schemers, since they were, in all matters, merely onlookers. We have got into the habit of associating innocence with bliss and an affinity with all living things, but innocence equals loneliness and blindness, a terrible immaculacy and isolation from life. And the eunuchs were not a travesty of innocence, but the truth of it when it becomes a chronic condition. We become human only when we have lost our innocence.

Before cycling back to Hué I went to take a last look at the graves. A stray cow stood munching the scattered frangipani blossom and two aged women were going up and down between the graves, gathering brushwood. Beneath their straw hats glowed a couple of roll-ups.

Then it struck me how all-embracing and benevolent this land was, and how much of eternity was contained within its day-to-day existence. Could one conceive of a more beautiful end than to lie here among brushwood-gathering women and grazing cows, once more a part of the great fecund, creative cycle of life? It did not matter now how the eunuchs had looked on death. Death had looked on them and made the decision for them. Despite their sexless state, they too had been absorbed into the process of regeneration.

I observed the contented cow and the old women, for the first time feeling that I was close to solving the riddle of this tormented part of the world. The forgetfulness on which the European has always remarked when confronted with the Asian's want of any sense of history was not a sign of a poor memory. On the contrary, this forgetfulness was in itself an active, creative faculty, just as selective and formative as remembrance. The Asian talent for forgetting was founded on an acceptance of death which, in a way that is foreign to us, rendered the work of the historians and archaeologists superfluous.

Buddhism did not need to rationalize suffering, to explain it or understand it. It took it for granted. Nor would it ever dream of tying together two such irreconcilable concepts as death and justice. The Buddhist did not consider death to be unjust: hence his lack of interest in history. The passion for history, the intellectual study of it and the desire to change it so characteristic of the Western mentality has its basis in an outcry against the injustice which death is alleged to be.

On the other hand, it was not as if the Vietnamese had no knowledge of history. Most of them could count off on their fingers all the times their country had been invaded; but these repeated assaults had shaped their view of history so that they did not see it as a constantly shifting progression but as one long reprise. The invasions were predetermined, as inevitable as the rainy season, sickness and death and, likewise, their own resistance to the successive occupying powers was an unalterable given, an identity they could not deny.

During a visit to Hanoi at the height of the Vietnam war, the American author Susan Sontag observed that the Vietnamese were not good enough at hating and that rather than regard the horrendous things that had befallen them with an indignant sense of injustice they seemed to view them with gentle sorrow. Now they were in the process of forgetting, but I realized that their willingness to forget was not a symptom of casualness. It was the sandpaper with which they refined an outlook on life.

Remote-controlled Death and
Murderous Innocence

HANOI BROUGHT ME MY ONLY ENCOUNTER WITH VIETNAMESE officialdom. I was keen to meet some Vietnamese writers (I did not know anything about Vietnamese literature; Bao Ninh's novel *Sorrow of War* had not yet been published in the West) and I supposed that the Vietnamese Society of Authors must be the correct starting point. I asked the receptionist at the Hotel Dong Do to call the society for me and set up a meeting.

The office of the Society of Authors occupied a room facing on to a little square. The interior was lit by fluorescent tubes whose purplish light combined with the shabby lime-green walls to cast a cheerless pall over the place. Some tables had been pushed up against one wall. A group of women stood in a corner talking. One of them, a heavily built older woman with cropped hair and clad in black pyjamas came over to me. I introduced myself.

"Ah," she said suspiciously, "so you are the Danish writer we had the call about yesterday. What exactly is it you want?

"I would like to meet some Vietnamese writers."

"I'm afraid none of our writers have time. They all have meetings to attend."

"I had the idea that some of them might be writing, in which case they might be a bit more flexible."

"Here in Vietnam no writers sit at home writing. They attend meetings. That is what they are paid to do."

"Well, perhaps I could meet them in the evening."

"You cannot expect our writers to spend their evenings going to unofficial meetings."

"I thought it might be interesting for Vietnamese writers to meet a colleague from the West."

"Are you travelling alone?" Her tone was inquisitorial.

"Yes, I'm travelling alone."

"So you do not have anyone sponsoring you, no organisation behind you?"

I shook my head.

"Usually, writers come here as official guests, with a guide and an interpreter. Then we draw up an itinerary. That is how it is done. That is the normal procedure."

"But if a writer comes here on his own account then the Vietnamese Society of Authors cannot do anything for them, not even give them a couple of addresses? Is that the case?"

The official looked at me in obvious irritation. "Yes," she said firmly, "that is the case."

I discovered more passion for literature in the receptionist at the Hotel Dong Do, an extraordinary and intriguing woman with long, curling hair and beautiful, mature features. Her skin was very white, but there was a touch of the Indian, rather than the Vietnamese, about her aristocratic face, which was forever shifting from one subtle expression to the next. Her thin, plucked eyebrows would pucker, then smooth out again; or they would arch in some sophisticated syntax of hints and allusions designed to reflect a gamut of emotions the significance of which was lost on me. Like her facial pantomime, her English was a fine-drawn, feminine, rather tentative melody, not unlike the sound of feet pattering hesitantly across a bare floor.

I told her there was something about her face that made me think she was not Vietnamese.

She smiled, and by her smile I could tell that she had taken my interest in her appearance as a compliment. "A lot of people have told me that. But you aren't all that European in appearance, either. You have an Asian look about you. You could be mistaken for an Afghan."

"Are you married?" I asked, with the bold directness one gets used to in Asia, at least where personal relationships are concerned.

"Yes," she replied, "I have a child."

I dried up, all at once embarrassed by my own presumption.

"You must be a writer, if you want to visit the Society of Authors?"

I nodded.

"You know, I am acquainted with one Danish author. His name is Andersen."

"Hans Christian Andersen?"

"No, not Hans Christian Andersen. Another Andersen. Martin Andersen . . ." Her voice tailed away.

" . . . Nexø!"*

"That's it! The book about Ditte," and she pronounced the name with a Vietnamese intonation that made it sound like the appellation of some rare and wonderful flower.

"The tragic story of a poor girl," I said with that pedantic condescension which one occasionally falls prey to in foreign countries.

"Yes," she said, "but with a big heart." And she placed her lovely hand on her starched white cotton shirt, just over the spot where her own heart resided.

"Are you familiar with John Steinbeck?" she went on, and the list of writers on whom she was anxious to hear my opinion expanded to include Faulkner, William Saroyan and Hemingway. "I inherited my love of English literature from my parents. My childhood home was full of books. Books are my great love."

"I'm pleased to have met a writer," she said. "My name means Harvest Moon. You can call me that if you like. I hope you will enjoy your stay in Hanoi. If there is anything I can do to help you, please just ask."

In my room that evening I found a vase with seven deep-red roses in bud. By the morning they had opened out.

Hanoi, like Hué, was a city full of intimacy. The capital of the unified Socialist Republic of Vietnam had not suffered nearly so much damage as the old imperial city, because although the Americans had bombed it, they had bombed only the suburbs, and the city centre, built for the most part in the French colonial style, had emerged more or less unscathed from the war. The majority of its buildings were yellow-washed, both those left by the French and the little houses in the winding lanes of the

* Martin Andersen Nexø (1869–1954) was born in Copenhagen and is best remembered for his classic novel *Pelle Eroberen* [*Pelle the Conqueror*]. The novel recalled here is a later, more pessimistic work, *Ditte Menneskebarn* [*Ditte: Towards the Stars*]. It depicts the darker side of capitalism, and the eponymous heroine works herself to death at an early age. [Tr.]

Chinese quarter to the north of Hoan Kiem Lake. The light fell green as in a forest. All the streets were lined with trees and at the point where the city was at its densest their branches formed a green canopy over the roadway. Hanoi was like a wood with streets – or a city abounding in woodland paths; a picture puzzle in yellow-wash and leaf-green in which at one minute you were looking for the city in the forest, the next for the forest in the city.

The traffic in the streets was dominated by the ubiquitous cyclos, whose laboriously pedalling drivers wore grass-green helmets and baggy shirts of the same shade, all adding to the impression of a city bathed in dim and dappled sylvan light. Here and there, children played badminton in the street. The lingering flight of the shuttlecock fitted well with the leisurely, distracted zig-zagging of the traffic. Unlike in the Chinese cities, there was no stream of cyclists into which one could be sucked and in which the pack set the collective tempo. In principle, one drove on the right; in fact, this rule was thwarted by the narrowness of the streets and the easy-going flexibility of the Vietnamese. As a cyclist one could make headway a little faster than as a pedestrian, while keeping only half an eye on where one was going, piloted by an instinctive sense of security. After all, the consequences of any collision in such sedately processing traffic could never be that dire.

As with all old Oriental cities, each street in Hanoi was the domain of a particular trade. One street was full of tool-makers; another dealt in straw mats and bamboo curtains; in a third a profusion of scents proclaimed the site of the spice market; a fourth was devoted to the sewing of religious hangings and Communist banners that gleamed gold and scarlet under the greenery of the trees. Everywhere there were bicycle-borne flower girls selling white lilies, short-stemmed red roses and yellow marguerites. There were streets lined exclusively with food stalls, and even one street filled with stalls that stayed open far into the night specializing in cakes and sweetmeats. And at every turn there were cafés consisting of little more than a sign and a couple of tiny stools set beside low tables at which taciturn, vegetating men had installed themselves. In the evenings, the red and yellow fairy-lights strung across the café facades enhanced the hushed intimacy of night life in the streets of Hanoi.

* * *

In the museums of Hanoi I discovered a different Vietnam. Unlike the Museum of American War Crimes in Saigon they were not dedicated to the victims of war and their suffering, nor was their view of the enemy particularly nuanced. These museums were dedicated to victory, to Vietnamese military might in a glorification of virile power, a display of force which, in all its blatant brutality, seemed to me quite alien to the Vietnam I had come to know. I thought that I detected the influence of the Soviet Union, Vietnam's chief ally during the war and its key collaborator thereafter in peacetime. But as I cycled around Hanoi I asked myself the question: what could be said to be truly Vietnamese? The city's two outstanding features, those which lent it its charm and its identity were the buildings which the French administration had left behind and the warren of narrow streets on the north side of Hoan Kiem Lake which took its name from the Chinese who had once lived there. Could it be that what was quintessentially Vietnamese was impossible to separate from the traces left by the colonizers and invaders? And yet I felt that there was something that was uniquely Vietnamese, although it did not reside in anything that you might see in any street scene. It was the same quality that I had remarked upon in the imperial tombs outside Hué, and in the bodies and gestures of the Vietnamese people: an indefinable elegance, a graceful awareness of the inevitability of death derived from 2,000 years of history; an imperceptible hardiness, closer to that of the reed than of the oak, which had made it possible for them to win the war, not thanks to military supremacy but thanks to an innate intractability.

Ho Chi Minh, the man at the head of the Vietnamese revolution and a 30-year war of liberation, first against the French and then against the Americans, appeared to be that reed; the classic image of the Oriental sage, epitomizing the superiority of the power of the intellect in the face of brutish military might. In appearance Ho Chi Minh was frail, his slightly stooping frame draped in loose-fitting garments. He was a wiry man with a white goatee beard and an air of disarming humility that seemed to belong more to the ascetic than to the man of power. He embodied both external frailty and inner strength; he was half-Gandhi, half-Mao, a pacifist with a machine-gun, who knew how to conduct his war with the same tactical shrewdness as Gandhi his hunger-strikes. But this was not the image that I encountered when I visited the Ho Chi Minh museum.

Ho's museum was an immense concrete pile situated at one end of a parade ground and only recently completed with Soviet assistance, more than 20 years after the father of the country's death. In front of its ostentatious facade stood a vast and equally ostentatious statue of Ho Chi Minh with his hand raised in salute. Photographs in the museum invariably showed him assuming all the familiar dictatorial poses: on platforms, surrounded by children or adults acting like children, grateful and meekly attentive soldiers, farmers and factory workers. His face was never anything but that of the ascetic and one discerned the paradox of his life: that he was a man trapped inside a role, but there was also a role trapped inside a man, because the ascetic expression may also have been a pose, a concession to an Asiatic tradition. The paradox followed him to his death, for it had been his wish that he be cremated and his ashes scattered over the country to which he had consecrated his life. And yet, through his posturing, all his life he had been paving the way for what would in fact be his body's ultimate fate, the dictator's final pose, that of a mummy in a hideous mausoleum, a monument not only to a man who had dedicated his life to his country, but also to a country that had been obliged to dedicate its history to one man.

The top floor of the museum reminded me of an aeronautical museum built in honour, not of a revolution, but the conquest of uncharted space. The effect was ludicrous as that of the stamps issued by banana republics, hailing the achievements of technology on envelopes with return addresses in countries where the people live in huts of mud and straw. Immense glass spheres encircled by Saturnian rings of burnished steel had been inset into walls of brushed aluminium, and on moving closer to see what these satellite-style structures contained, one found only an old pair of Uncle Ho spectacles or a photocopy of a closely written sheet of manuscript or a yellowed pamphlet from the 1920s. There was a rickety table at which he had once sat; a bicycle that had been used on the Ho Chi Minh trail, heavily laden with sacks, and gracing a podium over which one expected to see a troupe of fashion models come striding at any moment. Onto the walls of a labyrinth of glass a series of images had been transposed, depicting the last 100 years of European history as one great Edvard Munch scream of horror – monstrous, frivolous, bellicose and destructive, with a panorama of blitzed cities at either end. Out of sloping walls of white plastic reared the screaming horses of Picasso's *Guernica* and bulls

287

with heads menacingly lowered. It was an existential ghost train; the twentieth century's chronicle of war, revolution and counter-revolution reproduced in an architectural house of illusion.

I saw only one portrait of Ho Chi Minh that I liked. It hung in Hanoi's Museum of Fine Arts among a whole lot of other pictures in which he was seen posing, as usual, with all the trappings of a despotic cult. But in this particular painting the leader of the Vietnamese revolution was sitting alone by the banks of a lake with his bare feet stuck in a pair of large and sturdy sandals. Around him twined an oriental tracery of flowers, trees and birds. Ho Chi Minh's features were sharp and ascetic, his eyes deep-set and piercing. One hand rested in his lap; in the other a cigarette was held between two cocked fingers, and it was to this that the eye was drawn. That distant and yet introspective look in his eye – no, it did not stem from the political leader's weighty sense of responsibility for the future, but simply from the influence of the tobacco on Ho Chi Minh's spirit, the blissfully sublime effect of inhaling. His thoughts drifted aloft like the little spiral rising from his cigarette, which also lent its colour to a landscape that seemed itself to be fashioned out of smoke and reverie.

The Army Museum devoted itself to the Vietnamese victory over the Americans. Its walls were covered in black-and-white photostats illustrating the high points of the war. Fuzzy silhouettes on the march, taken with the joggled hand of the war photographer; white fire, pointing gun muzzles, blazing fighters and bombers nailed in the hail of anti-aircraft fire and immortalized in their plunge out of the skies, crashing down over jungles, rice paddies, villages, like far-off monsters; the Roc, caparisoned with metal plating and now spewing out its soul; pilots suspended from swaying parachutes, falling to earth and transformation into ordinary mortals with recognizable faces – shocked, frightened, with defeat showing in features grown suddenly heavy, as if the fall from the skies also represented a waking from an all-too-innocent dream, from the sedative effect of the instrument panel, the mechanical action of the bombing co-ordinates, the exonerating detachment of remote-controlled death. Only now, dangling from their parachutes with the ground rushing up to meet them, did it dawn on them that they were taking part in a war and not in the games of childhood. The earth, which confronted them with the consequences of the gentle pressure of their fingers on a release mechanism – people scorched, charred, hunted, lost – was also about to make grown men of them.

These pilots who from their high-flying fortresses wiped out people, countryside and the embryos of the future, were the epitome of the twentieth-century criminal. Enclosed within secure high-tech wombs, they could carry on with their deadly game without ever having to confront the damage they did. Only now, dangling from their parachutes, did they drop out of the twentieth century and into one of the moral dilemmas which had, to an increasing extent, become alien to that century.

And yet I found it hard not to feel for the dead and captured pilots. At the moment of their downfall they seemed entitled to be treated with some respect. It is not done to strip a vanquished enemy of his last shreds of dignity, but the Vietnamese had heartlessly pulled the pilots' boots off their feet and collected them in large boxes which were exhibited in the rooms of the museum along with their flyers' helmets.

On the wall hung a photograph of a pilot on an ox-cart, running the gauntlet of a mob of gawking Vietnamese. One had leapt forward and lashed out at him. He sat there helpless, his bare feet sticking out in front of him and his eyes cast down in an effort to deny the reality that now had him in its clutches. Between his legs lay a flyer's helmet, emblazoned with a hand-drawn silhouette of a fighter bomber. This same helmet lay among a whole pile of others in one of the museum boxes. To me, the pilot on the cart looked all too human. To those who had chosen to put the photograph on display he looked the very image of the enemy. (Later on my travels I came across the photograph again in a copy of *Newsweek* and this time the pilot was furnished with a name and a story: "He made it home," read the caption. "Vietnamese shake their fists and hit out at Major William Gideon after his fighter was shot down in 1966. Gideon was released six years later.")

Such fragments of a downed innocence were to be found all over the museum. There were torn-off sections of aircraft wing painted with the emblems of various divisions: Tactical Air Command – a sword with eagle's wings. Strategic Air Command – an armoured fist closed round a red lightning bolt and a twig sprouting green leaves. Mere boys had used their imaginations to decorate these killer machines; boys who had gone on playing with matches for so long that, by the time they swapped them for phosphorus and napalm and 500-lb bombs, they could no longer tell the difference; for what were these machines that had been shot down but shattered toys; an enormous disavowal of one of the twentieth century's many fallacious ideals, that of the unsullied nature of the childish mind, of play and creativity as a measure of human evolution. It would be hypocritical to deny that war, too, involved creativity and ingenuity, or that in its advances technology not only strives to develop ever more efficient methods of killing, but also to develop ever more efficient methods of quashing the ethical aspects of that killing, insofar as more and more emphasis is placed on the playful aspect of war in order to delay the maturing of boy into man so that he never reaches the stage where he can recognize that war – no matter whether it is necessary or just or not – is never anything but tragic.

The museum courtyard was overshadowed by an immense heap of the garbage of war. In one photograph inside the museum I had seen the wreck of a B-52, one of the Vietnam War's flying fortresses. Monstrous as a downed spaceship from some intergalactic stellar war, it lay there on the ground while diminutive men strutted round it, posing like big-game hunters, their surprise as great as their exultation at having bagged Sinbad's Roc. Now here it was, lying in the courtyard alongside the wing of an F-21, both brought down on Boxing Day, 1972, during President Nixon's Christmas offensive against Hanoi. The huge jet turbines glistened in the rain, rusty and green with moss. Ranged alongside these stood an array of anti-aircraft guns: the .100mm that had shot the B-52 out of the skies; a .57mm bearing the inscription *During the years 1965–68 this type of gun shot down 45 US aircraft*; a .37mm with a similar inscription stating that this type of anti-aircraft gun had brought down 124 US planes.

The Museum of American War Crimes in Saigon told of the costs of war, the museum in Hanoi spoke only of winning and the victory of machine over machine. And yet I felt nothing but pity at the sight of all those cannon mouths trained in fossilized triumph on the grey skies over Hanoi. That and shame, a shame that ran deep and made me wish that all of this could be forgotten, if the price of remembering had to be that it was done in such a way. The pointing gun muzzles and the mounds of mangled aircraft parts seemed merely to stand as a shameful monument to the Americans for what they had done and to the Vietnamese for the picture they presented of what had been done. In the brochure supplied along with my ticket I read: "A visit to The Army Museum will be sure to satisfy all Vietnamese and foreign visitors."

"Satisfy"?

The Vietnamese's strength had always lain in their ability to place their struggle in a context akin to that of legend, here to select the roles best designed to engender sympathy for their cause. They were David against Goliath, Odysseus against the Cyclops, Little Claus against Big Claus. Three times in the course of their history they had been able to substantiate this myth, and each time it had become a little less true. In the year 938 a Vietnamese mandarin, Ngo Quyen, lured an attacking Chinese fleet far up the Bach Dang river. It was high tide. Ngo Quyen had driven iron-tipped stakes into the bed of the river and was only waiting for the moment when the tide would turn. The Chinese war junks were holed and had no choice but to surrender to an enemy much less well-equipped and inferior in number, whose best weapon was their guile. Both in the History Museum and the Revolutionary Museum in Hanoi this incident was represented in large, European-style paintings depicting the sinking junks surrounded by a swarm of small craft. The Revolutionary Museum even exhibited a stake, black and petrified with age, that was said to have come from the bottom of the Bach Dang river. It was like seeing the stake which Odysseus used to poke out the eye of the Cyclops, or the pebble from David's sling.

The second occasion on which the myth was borne out and shown to be a little less – though still near enough – true, was in 1954 when the Vietnamese conquered the French army at the battle of Dien Bien Phu, thereby bringing to an end the European colonization of Asia. In terms of manpower the Vietnamese outnumbered the French, who had dug themselves in behind an ostensibly unassailable system of trenches and bunkers. But, even as 1,000 years earlier, the Vietnamese's trump card proved to be their ability to do the unexpected and to achieve the apparently impossible – in this case the dragging of all their heavy artillery up and over a chain of steep hills. Not only did this represent the triumph of guile, it also constituted a victory for the endurance found only where people know that they have right on their side.

The third occasion was on 30 April 1975, when a Soviet-built tank crashed through the wrought-iron gates of the presidential palace in

Saigon. But by this point the myth had already grown hollow, as was illustrated in no uncertain terms by a tableau in the Army Museum in Hanoi in which the self-same tank was exhibited alongside a fragment of one of the gates which had been dragged the 3,000 kilometres north from a city that was the capital no longer to one that had now become such with a vengeance. The gate lay there on the floor, delicate wrought iron crushed under caterpillar tracks. It was no longer a case of guile versus superior force. Here the strong celebrated himself, in a tribute to superior fire-power, in an unalloyed and disheartening iron-clad, armour-plated legend. Almost as if David had only beaten Goliath in order to take his place, and Odysseus only blinded the Cyclops that he himself might become one-eyed.

Scent of Spring and Harvest Moon

WHO COULD RESIST A PLACE BEARING THE NAME THE TEMPLE of Literature?

Van Mieu Temple in the heart of Hanoi was dedicated to scholars and writers who had distinguished themselves in the world of letters. It was the oldest temple in Vietnam, more than 900 years old, and there seemed to me to be a quite literally poetic justice in the fact that a temple to literature should be the one to stand up longest to the ravages of time. After all those war museums and revolutionary museums, bombarding the visitor beyond endurance with their grandiloquent salutes to heroism and the insanity of self-sacrifice, peace was to be found in Van Mieu Temple's spacious albeit run-down gardens. A troop of stone tortoises trailed through the gardens, carrying tablets inscribed with the exploits of those mandarins who had passed the innumerable tests that had to be undergone to gain entry to the imperial court. A large cobbled court-yard was occupied by more turtles, these ones in terracotta, their backs supporting evergreen bushes cunningly clipped into the shape of strutting cranes. The temple itself was under restoration. High up under the heavy wooden beams holding up the building's tiled roof, workmen swarmed over bamboo scaffolding. Black lacquer gleamed in the glare of electric bulbs and minuscule, glittering slivers of silver leaf, drifted down onto the floor. I stretched out a hand and two rectangular flecks of silver settled in my upturned palm.

But not even here could one avoid being reminded of the war. Behind the temple lay the ruins of Hanoi University, blown sky-high by the French during their ignominious withdrawal from Vietnam after the rout at Dien Bien Phu. The celebrated college of the Sorbonne was founded in 1253, Paris University half a century earlier, but by then the University of Hanoi had been in existence for 125 years. It was no despot who had ordered such a heinous act, but the leader of a democratic country

293

that prided itself on being the birthplace of Voltaire and that swore by the universal values of the Enlightenment.

The Vietnamese had neither architectural drawings nor photographs accurate enough to have made it possible for them to reconstruct the university buildings. All that is left today of what was once one of the world's oldest universities are a few lichen-covered blocks of stone lying in the grass.

Two young girls who were sitting on a step waved me over. One of them dipped her hand into a brown paper bag, pulled out an ice cream and offered it to me. Before leaving Denmark I had been warned by a doctor never to touch ices of any description while in the Third World since they are often manufactured under conditions that can be breeding grounds for bacteria. I was, however, of the belief that I had developed a cast-iron stomach in the course of my travels and I was happy to take a bit of a risk in order to spend some time in female company. So I accepted the proffered ice cream. The two girls promptly subjected me to the usual cross-examination on my work, family background, marital status and age.

"Forty! That's impossible. You look much younger," they said with shameless flattery. "You must play a lot of sport."

I shook my head. "No, not at all. I'm far too lazy."

We carried on in this vein for about an hour. Then one of them showed me an application she had written to a foreign company that was looking for a receptionist for a newly opened branch in Hanoi. "You're a writer," she said, "could you help me a little bit with the wording?"

I looked at her application, which had been written on a word processor, making much use of the wide variety of typefaces on offer. I corrected a couple of mistakes and tidied up the wording here and there.

"My great-uncle is also a writer," she said. "He translated Mikhail Sholokhov's *Quiet Flows the Don* into Vietnamese and was invited to the Soviet Union by the author. Would you like to meet him?"

She gave me her telephone number and asked me to ring her that evening.

I walked back to my hotel under a heavy April downpour. The cyclo drivers had put up the hoods on their vehicles, offering their passengers shelter from the rain under large sheets of clear plastic.

Her name was Scent of Spring.

*　*　*

I was invited to call at Scent of Spring's parents' house at eight o'clock in the evening. The real star of the occasion, Scent of Spring's great-uncle, the writer and translator, would also be there. Having accepted the invitation, I began to wonder whether I was invited for dinner. Should I take a gift and, if so, what?

I went down to reception and asked Harvest Moon. If I had been invited to come at eight o'clock then it could not possibly be for dinner, she told me. Besides which, dinner parties were reserved for close friends and family. As far as a gift was concerned, since it was my first visit, I ought only to take something small, a box of chocolates, for example, or some biscuits. She then proceeded to grill me thoroughly on the purpose of my visit. I explained about the elderly writer and his brother's grandchild. It was obvious that she did not buy the part about the writer. "Good luck," she said and smiled knowingly when I left.

I had found a large tin of "Danish cookies" which had been "made in Indonesia", although "to a Danish recipe", as it said beneath the picture of a leaping ballerina from the Danish Royal Ballet. With this under my arm I rang the doorbell of Scent of Spring's family home. Scent of Spring herself opened the door, dressed in leggings and a sleeveless white shirt. The heavy waist-length hair that had been bound up during the day now hung loose so that it covered her shoulders. Her mother appeared and began to set a table for tea. This done, she bustled out again. A moment later her father came in to say hello to me. He was a P.E. instructor with grizzled, collar-length hair that gave him a somewhat arty look.

"He's not very strong," said Scent of Spring, laughing undiplomatically at her father, who apparently did not understand English. "Do you think he looks strong?"

Then it was the turn of her two brothers. They, too, withdrew again as soon as we had shaken hands.

"My family has pressing business elsewhere," said Scent of Spring. "Which is to say, a new video of an American western." We were left with the sitting-room to ourselves. The promised main attraction of the evening was nowhere to be seen.

We started with the family album. I was shown Scent of Spring posing in a wide variety of frocks and after a while it occurred to me that what I was witnessing in these photographs, in which her hair gradually grew

295

longer and her posture more self-assured, was her growth into womanhood. In one picture she was standing next to a girlfriend in a wedding dress. The bride's face was caked with face powder that rendered her skin as white as her dress. Beside her, Scent of Spring stood lost in rapture.

The episode from our meeting at the Temple of Literature was repeated. Again she brought out a letter she had written in English and asked me to help her with the grammar. It was a letter of congratulations to her former English teacher, a Canadian now settled in Singapore with a wife and a new baby. In fulsome yet formal terms she wished them well on the addition to the family and expressed a wish to be godmother to the child, whereupon she immediately asked to be forgiven if her request had offended them with her ignorance of their culture and traditions. She, too, passionately wanted to have a child, she continued. She was now 22 and in Vietnam it was common for women to marry between the ages of 23 and 25, while the corresponding age for men was between 25 and 27. It was therefore natural for her to be thinking about marriage. She was looking for a man who was mature and intelligent and respected her independence, just as he would be prepared to share the responsibility of a child. But she did not know what the future would bring. She had a girlfriend who had married a year ago but who was very unhappy. She had made the wrong choice. "Sometimes I feel as if I'm on the verge of a breakdown," she wrote.

I looked up from the letter. "This sentence is far too dramatic," I said. "It will worry your friend unnecessarily, and anyway I'm not sure that this is quite the right expression for what you are trying to say. I can't imagine that an intelligent, independent woman like yourself would want to give the impression that all you think about is getting married."

She laughed and told me off with mock severity. "I only asked you to correct my English, so would you please stick to the grammatical problems and leave the content of my letter to me."

She had sat down beside me on the sofa and brought her head close to mine while we studied the letter.

"Tell me, when did you actually write this letter? This afternoon?" I asked. I was beginning to think this letter was addressed to someone other than the former English teacher.

She laughed again and wagged her finger at me. "You are far too nosy."

Then she changed tack and her voice grew serious. "I would like to ask you a very personal question. May I?"

I nodded.

She eyed me appraisingly. "Why exactly did you and your wife get divorced?"

The question took me completely by surprise, but I tried to answer it as best I could, well knowing that I was being weighed up.

"I have a reason for asking," she said. "When I speak to people from other countries I get the feeling that they don't take marriage seriously. My parents are faithful to one another and have been together for many years. But they also respect each other's independence. My mother teaches, like my father. Lots of men expect the woman to give up her job. I would never do that just because some man said so. And in any case I don't intend to get married until I've completed my education. I once read a short story called 'The First Teacher' about a young teacher in a little village who shows a girl how to have respect for herself and make her own decisions about her life. That is how I want to live my life."

As Scent of Spring spoke she grew in stature before my eyes. I could sense her strength of will, but I also noted her tone, which was matter-of-fact and businesslike. The letter had provided us with an excuse for a bit of innocent flirtation, but she was also a woman exploring and weighing up her options. What I had entered into here was more than an encounter between a man and a woman. I had become involved in a time-honoured ritual governing congress between the sexes, and one in which Scent of Spring played her part in a most modern fashion. Here was a woman who was getting ready to take her place in the world and this she did with a maturity which was not only special to her, but which was also a part of her cultural heritage. Despite the almost 20 years' difference in our age, I was the one who was being led by the hand like a child through a strange world of ritual in which each step had been carefully prescribed, and at that particular moment I did not think it trite or theatrical. On the contrary, I found it meaningful.

All at once she changed the subject, reverting to her flirtatious tone. "I'll have to introduce you to my friends from college," she giggled. "There's many a good match among them and we'll have to see if we can't find you a Vietnamese girl, because then you would stay here for a long, long time and we could see each other often and have long, interesting conversations."

She dropped her gaze and bent forward so that her face was hidden behind the heavy hair. "I myself am far from beautiful – and besides, I don't know how to cook Danish food." She tossed her hair back from her face and laughed at me.

I had asked Harvest Moon what would be an appropriate time to take my leave and when it came to ten o'clock we said goodnight, with many an assurance on either side of how pleasant we had found each other's company. We agreed to meet again and I was promised that next time Scent of Spring's great-uncle would be introduced.

Scent of Spring's great-uncle lived at the heart of a maze of narrow alleyways and little courtyards. His tiny flat overlooked a grey concrete yard and it was cold and damp. I felt the flagstones chill under my bare feet when I removed my sandals. The room was divided into two by a bookcase. On one side of the bookcase stood an untidy desk, on the other was a more presentable arrangement of wooden sofa and armchairs with tall, slatted backs and flat, cushionless seats set around a low table. Scent of Spring had brought me here around midday and now she was sitting on the sofa, talking intimately with her aunt, who was 29, only seven years older than herself. The aunt, who was still unmarried, was an enchanting and exquisite woman with a small, fine-drawn face, a slim figure and very pale skin. Her black hair was coiled into a heavy bun at the nape of her neck. When she stood up and shook it out it reached nearly to her knees. She was not wearing any lipstick, but her eyebrows were painted in a manner designed to accentuate her wide eyes. She had powdered her face white and touched up her cheeks with pink. The painted eyebrows, plucked in the Vietnamese fashion so that they did not form an arch but merely two straight lines above the eyes, had an almost bluish cast to them. When she changed from her baggy pyjamas into trousers and a shirt I saw how perfectly proportioned this miniature porcelain woman was. Scent of Spring's skin was darker and her cheekbones were more widely set apart. In contrast with her dainty aunt she shone with a wonderful artlessness. She wore her hair hung loose, with two plaits almost hidden among the thick luxuriant tresses holding it back from her face. A pink blouse, fastened with little bows, revealed her still girlish tastes.

Scent of Spring's great-uncle was a fine-looking man, as long as he did not smile, exposing a crooked upper set of teeth. He had a high forehead

298

and wiry grey hair swept back from his face, almost shoulder length, endowing him with an air of dreamy distraction. His face was finely sculpted with the skin stretched taut across the bones and an expression of spiritual clarity so often seen in elderly orientals.

He placed a cup in front of me and filled it with mulberry wine from a long-necked porcelain jug. "This wine is good for the digestion, good for the breathing and good for the mind." I noted the wry and deliberate care with which he chose his words – exactly what one could expect from an ageing intellectual who was in the habit of holding forth to a patient family. Here was a man who obviously enjoyed having an audience and I suspected that he would have behaved in exactly the same way no matter whether he was sitting in his little living room or standing in front of a grand assembly – although I had no idea whether he had ever had occasion to do the latter.

"You should have seen what things were like here only a few years ago. We didn't have enough to eat. There was even a shortage of rice. Imagine, a shortage of rice in Vietnam! At night there was no electricity in Hanoi. And there was very little freedom. Very little. When they shot Ceaușescu in Romania, I was worried. I was afraid that the man in the street would follow the Romanians' example. But the people of Hanoi kept their heads. The Vietnamese have had enough of unrest."

He broke off and pointed to the wall. "It was then that I did that piece of Chinese calligraphy. Oh yes, I've been studying Chinese calligraphy for the past five years" – he gave a smile which managed to be both proud and self-deprecating – "to pass the time." On the wall hung a sheet of white paper inscribed with beautiful, sweeping Chinese characters in Indian ink. "It says: 'I am proud to be Vietnamese'."

Amazed by his frankness when it came to political matters, I asked him how he viewed developments in the former Soviet Union.

"Obviously developments in the Soviet Union have influenced the changes that have been taking place in Vietnam," he said. "But the Russians have always been anarchists. The changes had to come. Here too. An American once told me that we would never be able to bring about the necessary changes because Vietnam has no infrastructure. 'Do you realize what an infrastructure costs?' he asked me. I told him: 'When we took on the French in 1945 we had no boots and no rifles. Nine years later we beat them at the battle of Dien Bien Phu. When the first American bombers flew over Vietnam in 1964 we had no anti-aircraft guns. Eight years later we were shooting down B-52s. As far as the possibilities of our building up an infrastructure are concerned I can, therefore, answer you with an expression well-known to you Americans: Wait and see'."

He poured some more mulberry wine and leaned back in his chair, stretching and smiling a satisfied little smile. "A minute ago, when you laid eyes on me for the first time, would you have said that I looked like a soldier?"

"No, I would have said that you looked a typical intellectual."

"Nonetheless, for twelve years I was a soldier. From 1945 to 1957. Initially I fought against the French, but I have always retained a fondness for French culture. I had friends who were French and I translated Aragon into Vietnamese – not his poems, but his prose, which I find has a poetic quality to it. I also had five years of soldiering in China. I fought against the remnants of Chiang Kai-shek's nationalist brigade."

"Was it tough, being a soldier?" I asked, feeling stupid even as I said it.

He smiled indulgently. "Sometimes it was tough, sometimes not so tough. But that was not a worry to me. I became a soldier for romantic reasons. All of my generation joined up, all of my friends. Today many of them are generals. One of them I see once a week. He was the head of our intelligence service in South Vietnam. It was he who masterminded the storming of the American embassy during the Tet offensive in 1968. He is quite brilliant. But you wouldn't know it to look at him, he looks like a peasant. About once a year I get together with General Giap, the man who won the battle of Dien Bien Phu. He's a busy man, with a head full of schemes. He told me that we ought to prepare ourselves for another war with China. The Chinese are an unpredictable race. We can expect anything of them. Three times in our history we have beaten back the Mongols; and the Chinese five times: twice under the Sung dynasty, once under the Ming dynasty, once under the Tang dynasty and, finally, in 1979 under Deng Xiao Ping."

He paused briefly after this litany of historical fact, then went on: "You know, I don't like living in a country that has a large nation as neighbour. It is far too easy to be evil when one is big. But as Bertolt Brecht once put it, on seeing a Japanese Samurai mask: 'In the long run, evil is a tiresome business.' But I am a great admirer of Chinese calligraphy. It is an art, and as such it also has an inherent philosophy. Oh yes, I do it to pass the time."

He got up from his chair, went over to the bookcase and picked out a book. It was a collection of short stories he had had published in 1972. He had written nothing since then. He hefted his translation of Sholokov's trilogy in both hands. "It passed the time," he remarked casually. He had also translated Babel's *Red Cavalry*. But his translation had never been published. "Babel recognized the weaknesses of socialism right from the start," he said. "But we're not ready for that yet."

His wife had joined us. He spread his hand, in a gesture that embraced the whole room. "I never had any intention of getting married. My friends felt this was an unhealthy state of affairs, so they found me a wife."

His wife, a dumpy little woman with short, grey hair, smiled tolerantly, as if she had heard this story before and put up with it much the way one puts up with the mischief of a child.

Just before midnight I saw his daughter again. She was sitting on a doorstep next to the narrow lane that ran down to his flat. She was all huddled up, occupying as little space as possible, and her pointy little knees jutted straight up into the air. Next to her a young man was huddled in the same position. They sat so close together that they looked like a four-legged creature keeping watch in the night. She was 29 years old, by Vietnamese standards a mature woman, and her emotional life and dreams of romance had been relegated to a doorstep. I slipped quietly by without making myself known.

Intimacies between Strangers

I DO NOT THINK I AM EXAGGERATING IF I SAY THAT NOWHERE has my confidence in my own masculinity been stimulated as much as it was in Vietnam. Instead of becoming satiated, I experienced the opposite. I became insatiable, and that must explain why I started visiting Hanoi's Art Café at times of the day when the place was empty and I could be alone with the café's lovely owner.

Hitherto, I had taken all of the flirting and playful banter in which I had been involved as a gift that never ceased to take me by surprise. Now I set out to court a beautiful woman while egotistically expecting to have my compliments reciprocated and to become entangled in a web of bold questions and answers with all sorts of over- and undertones.

The elegant facade of the café boasted a sign in three languages that here was served THE BEST COFFEE IN SOUTH-EAST ASIA, and Kim was as confident in herself as she was in the quality of her coffee. She knew that she was attractive and although we were soon on intimate terms our conversations often resembled the famous exchange between two narcissists: "Now, enough about me, let's talk about you. What do you think of me?"

The café was furnished with bentwood chairs and round glass-topped tables. A little nosegay of short-stemmed white roses adorned each table, and framed watercolours covered the walls. On the bar there always stood a large vase of white lilies and yellow marguerites. Kim, the owner, was a feline creature with high cheekbones and shoulder-length hair. One could not have told from looking at her that she was, in fact, a doctor who had fallen foul of the government and been dismissed from her last post for having refused to move to a country area far from Hanoi. Instead, she had become a symbol of the new economic liberalization, a successful, self-assured businesswoman who ran her own café and could afford to take holidays in Saigon. She had been divorced six years earlier and now lived alone in a flat above the café with her 20-year-old daughter. Kim came and sat down beside me in the empty café, an iced coffee in her hand. I complimented her on the café's decor and graciously she accepted this bouquet. Then I complimented her on her looks and the way she dressed.

"Many men have told me that," she replied.

When it came to compliments, I realized that no part of this woman had escaped being the object of some eloquent gentleman's praise. Maybe she was tired of compliments, having been paid too many that sounded too much alike. Perhaps she was too inexperienced to play the innocent, to respond to a compliment with surprise, bashfulness or just simple pleasure. For, even if it were an act, such an act is also a compliment, inasmuch as one is making an effort for the other person and I would most certainly have found it more flattering to be the victim of a small deception than to be presented with this dispassionate reckoning of compliments paid.

The conversation flagged. Then she leaned towards me. "A lot of men tell me I am a woman. Of course I'm a woman, I say. What else would I be?" She laughed and threw up her hands. "What do you think of that? I'm more woman than other women, they say. But in what way am I different from other women?"

She gave me an imploring look, as if I were an expert on the subject. In a voice which I did my best to keep matter-of-fact, I described the unique erotic allure of a mature, confident woman who is aware of her attributes and dares to use them. She listened as though I were speaking of some third party and this set the pattern for the intimacy that grew up between us. I abandoned any prospect of having my own vanity gratified and instead I turned myself into a mirror in which she could consider herself from all angles; like the magic mirror in Snow White I answered all of this café queen's self-absorbed questions as to who was the fairest of them all. It came quite unlooked-for, this game that evolved between us in the quiet hours of the afternoon or late at night when the café was closed and she kept my flow of words from drying up with bottle after bottle of the local Halida beer and I have the idea that those exchanges were the only form of erotic pleasure she could get away with in North Vietnam, where relations between the sexes were still in many ways bound by convention and marked by its feudal past.

"Hanoi is a small town," she would say to me, "everybody knows me. They follow my every move."

It was a kind of courtship, but most of the time I had the feeling that all of the things she told me about herself were not, in fact, aimed at me, but that to her I was simply some kind of courier charged with spreading the word of her charms and graces.

"You know," she might say, "it takes you ten minutes to walk back to your hotel. It takes me much longer. I deliberately take my time." She paused. "I do it so that everyone can get a good look at me." Another pause. "I think they're lucky to be given the chance."

Then she would laugh, with not a trace of irony, delighted by her own outspokenness. "I know myself," she said, "I know the effect I have on men. 80 per cent of all men are attracted to me." She looked appealingly at me. "Why do you think it is that the other 20 per cent are not? I don't understand it. Can you explain it to me?"

It was past midnight. Outside the café a couple of cyclo drivers were hanging around, waiting for me to leave. Kim ordered the busboy to switch off the light outside the café and pull down the metal grille over the door. Then she signed to him that he could turn in on the mattress in the back room where he spent his nights. There was a narrow gap at the bottom of the grille where it was not quite closed; outside I could see the cyclo drivers waving at me and making obscene, macho gestures, as much as to say: "We know what's going to happen now!" or "Go for it, boy!" After a while they grew tired of waiting and, as they bedded themselves down in their uncomfortable seats, a hush fell over the street. Kim sat hunched over, her head in her hands. Then she stretched lazily and her cat face twisted in what looked like the beginnings of a miaow. "I was thinking of the men who don't like me. I want them to like me."

I laughed at her.

"I'm a dangerous woman," she said, laughing back. "Dangerous as far as men are concerned." Then, without warning, she grew grave. "After my divorce I said to myself: Never again. I didn't dare. I was too scared. I believe I see things differently now. If I were to find another man I would give up my business. I would do anything for him. Anything."

In making this admission she had lost none of her poise, but there was a warmth in her that had not been there before. And an appeal which she knew could not be answered with the same flippancy as the other questions she asked. It was not an appeal to be loved or idolized, rather it expressed a wish to be able to share a fear and a longing with another person, to be heard and understood, as one sometimes can only be heard and understood by a stranger, because there is a certain vulnerability one can only disclose to someone who is just passing through and will never show their face again. And she had seen this in me. I was just passing through – also through her magic circle. It was the only moment of true intimacy that we shared and suddenly I understood that this was the moment we had been working up to all along and that what we had been indulging in during those early hours was not merely the old game between man and woman, but also the creation of something akin to friendship. We were contemporaries who had conversed, using the code of flirtation and sex, on our age and experience and on the life we had left to us. She was on her feet. It was time to leave. I stepped up to her and put an arm round her waist. I felt the warmth of her body and the smoothness of her skin.

"Good luck," I said.

The invitations to visit Scent of Spring at her parents' home kept coming and once more I consulted Harvest Moon on the etiquette of such matters. On a second visit, she instructed me, I ought also to take a gift, but this time it should be a personal gift for Miss Scent of Spring, a token of my admiration for her. She suggested some French perfume from one of the shops in Hang Bong Street.

After searching long and hard I eventually tracked down a bottle of perfume in elegant dark-green packaging with gilded letters proclaiming it to be *Poison. Christian Dior. Paris.* At a price of 31,000 *dong* – about £3 – I was, however, pretty certain that it could not possibly be the genuine article. "Don't you have any real French perfume?" I asked. The assistant, a stout elderly woman, shook her head.

When I returned to the hotel Harvest Moon was waiting in reception. "It isn't wrapped properly," she said, eyeing the parcel with disapproval. "Here, let me redo it for you." She removed the gift-wrapping and gave me an accusing look. "But this isn't real French perfume. Miss Scent of Spring will be very disappointed."

I shrugged apologetically. "They had none."

Harvest Moon ducked down behind the reception desk and

reappeared with a piece of red ribbon in her hand. "Well, it should at least look decent." She wrapped the box of perfume and tied the ribbon in a variety of different bows before finally declaring herself satisfied. Then she stepped out onto the street to hail me a cyclo. I was not sure exactly what signals I was sending to Scent of Spring along with my gifts, while Harvest Moon continued to pull the strings behind the scenes, caught up in her own romantic machinations.

Scent of Spring's mother was unwell; she had an upset stomach and did not appear. Her father looked in, sat down on the sofa and chatted with me, smiling benevolently all the while, then he shook my hand and made himself scarce. The coffee table was laid with dishes containing slices of cucumber for dipping in *nam* and a kind of rice cake normally only served at the Vietnamese New Year. "I tried my best to find something I knew you hadn't tasted before," said Scent of Spring.

Again we sat side by side on the sofa and although this time there was no letter to be studied and corrected, our conversation soon came round to matters of the heart. For some years she had been seeing a young man a couple of years older than herself. "He's very handsome," she said, as if her fascination with his looks represented an admission of some weakness in herself. But he had also found her to his liking; she had noticed how he enjoyed being seen in public with her. After five years his parents had approached hers with a view to arranging a match. But Scent of Spring had said no. That had been a year ago and she was still not sure whether she had done the right thing. But she could not possibly have said yes. "He wanted to turn me into a housewife," she said. "He could not accept that I wanted to have an education and a career." She lowered her gaze. "I've never spoken of this to anyone before, and I'm telling you, even though we've only known each other such a short time."

I was touched by her trust in me. At the same time I saw that in Hanoi my journey had taken an unexpected turn. As a traveller I encountered undiscovered sides not only of myself, but also of others. They felt free to bare their souls to an outsider. Between our cultures lay a refuge where people could meet and, liberated from conventions, tell the truth about themselves.

It was with the social masks that my fascination had originated, and in Scent of Spring's case it manifested itself as a fascination with an age-old amorous ritual. This fascination did, however, also contain an element of reduction. I oversimplified people by turning them into representatives of their societies. I accorded them an integrity which they might not possess and which blinded me to the cracks through which their humanity sprouted like grass through paving stones.

Scent of Spring began by showing me her mask and, thereafter, her fear of that mask. She did not represent any society, she lived in a society in upheaval and like all people who have to live through a period of transition she had been struck by a more forceful sense of her own naked humanity, which brought with it freedom and the agonizing opportunity of making one's own choices. I had been delighted to detect the patterns of an ancient civilization in our encounters. Now she allowed me to look deeper, and my pleasure in her company was made that much greater.

I continued to see Scent of Spring's great-uncle. He lived not far from my hotel and I had learned how to find my way through the warren of lanes and courtyards that led to his flat. I called on him one evening, bringing a bottle of Bordeaux Supérieur which I had bought for $10 in one of the markets. Through the open door I could see him sitting at his desk, deep in thought. I knocked gently on the door. He immediately got to his feet and came, smiling, to greet me. He put the red wine to one side after scrutinising the label nodding in approval. Then he brought out two cups and the long-necked jug in which he kept his mulberry wine.

In the room next door his wife was sitting in a wicker chair with her legs drawn up beneath her, watching a Japanese film on a black-and-white television.

Scent of Spring's great-uncle nodded towards the television. "It's a Japanese remake of *The Count of Monte Cristo*," he said scornfully. "I am a great admirer of Kurosawa, although I have to admit that I have not seen any of his films. They have never been shown in Vietnam. But I have read about him, and those stills from his films which I have seen have convinced me that he must be a great artist. He played by the rules in order that he might impose his own."

"But why don't they show Kurosawa's films on television instead of this rubbish?" I asked.

He shrugged his shoulders and laughed. "Who knows? Perhaps they got it for free."

He invited me to take a seat in an armchair and sat down across from me on the sofa. His wife got up and turned the sound down.

"Why is it," I asked, "that so many of the Vietnamese people I meet appear to feel no bitterness for all the things that have been done to their land?"

He settled himself more comfortably, his cup of mulberry wine cradled in his hand. "Your question," he said, "reminds me of an interview I once read with Mother Teresa. She was asked 'How do you feel about the past?' 'The past is the past,' she replied. 'That we can do nothing about. So let us waste no time talking about it.' 'Then what about the future?' the interviewer wanted to know. 'The future will come,' she answered. 'That is the only thing we know for certain. So let us not trouble ourselves with it.' 'And the present? How do you see the present?' 'I am but a little pencil in the Creator's great hand,' said Mother Teresa, 'and he writes whatever he wishes with me. That is what I have to say about the present'."

Scent of Spring's great-uncle took a sip of his wine. "A very intelligent woman." He stared into space and I sensed that this was just the start of a long discourse.

"Great personalities who have confidence in their own power never talk about what they are planning to do. And they are not constantly trying to push themselves forward. Picasso said: 'It is the painting that uses me, not the other way round.'"

He drained his cup and offered me the jug of mulberry wine. I held out my cup. It was a good wine, and strong. It was a while since I had taken alcohol and in the warmth of the tropical evening I could feel it having an effect.

"I have read the Bible," said Scent of Spring's great-uncle. "A most interesting book. I have studied Buddhism, Confucianism and Taoism. I won't ever get round to reading the Koran, because it is written in Arabic. None of these have persuaded me or made a believer of me. My wife and children worship our ancestors. I stay well out of it. They have their faith. I have none."

Once again he changed the subject. "It isn't that long ago that for three whole years we did not have enough rice, nor electric power, nor freedom. Now we export 1.5 million tonnes of rice a year, we have all the electrical power we need, while Manila is without power for ten hours of every day. We have also checked inflation. But whether it will last or not no one can say. The future is unforeseeable."

"Yes, but surely now there are grounds for hope?" I said, without placing any particular existential stress on the word.

"Hope is God's gift to people, to enable them to cope with life." Scent of Spring's great-uncle had clearly been inspired by the wine and the opportunity, at long last, to have an audience for his monologues. "Hope is the most precious thing we have been given by God."

". . . says the man who describes himself as a non-believer."

"One should not always give away what one believes in. It is not the same as not being sincere. You do see the difference, don't you?"

He poured more wine. "Three months ago I was speaking to the Mongolian ambassador. When he heard that I had spent five years in China, he asked: 'Are the Chinese really bad?' I told him that in all the time I was in China I had been given food when I was hungry, and something to drink when I was thirsty and that I had met nothing but kindness. 'Ah, but you were stationed in the countryside,' said the ambassador. 'So it must be the Chinese in the cities who are bad.'"

"I answered him: 'In every place I have visited I have come across good people and bad people. The only place where I have had trouble finding good people is among politicians.' Afterwards I asked myself: Now why did you say that? That man is a diplomat and, hence, a politician. So he must have felt that I was getting at him. Nonetheless, I suppose I said it deliberately. I don't like politicians."

I told him about my experience at the Vietnamese Society of Authors. He laughed and took another sip. "For a long time they wouldn't let me join. Then, eventually, they invited me to become a member. I said 'No thanks'. Why should I waste my time with that sort of thing? I've always been regarded as somewhat controversial. But the Party leaders have not bothered me."

"Yes, but there are writers in Vietnam who are being persecuted, imprisoned and their work censored," I said.

"They have been persecuted because they allowed themselves to be persecuted. That is a stupid idea. That one should never do. We orientals have a philosophy which says that one should live in the present."

I could not follow his train of thought. Not that I felt he was ducking the issue, but there was a thread to his argument that I could not grasp.

"But one doesn't always have a choice," I said. "Most people would say it was a bad idea to allow oneself to be bombed, and yet the Vietnamese laid themselves open to bombardment by the Americans. They wanted to stand up for their independence. The authors who are being persecuted are doing the same."

"There's no comparison. The Americans wished to force their way of life on us. That we found hard to accept. Vietnam could not live under a *pax Americana*. During the Second World War the Japanese thought they could intimidate us. By the time I joined the army in 1945 we had taken thousands of Japanese prisoner, though we had next to no weapons. The Americans sent in helicopters, Phantom fighters, B-52 bombers – the whole arsenal a modern air force can command. They, too, thought that they could intimidate us, yet they were obliged to quit our country as the losers. One should never let oneself be frightened. But we have had to pay a price. We have paid with poverty and devastation. And with constraints on writers and intellectuals. That is how things are during a war, people have to stand united. It was the same story when America or France were at war: less freedom for the intellectual."

"Last time we talked you mentioned Isaac Babel and you said that he detected the faults in socialism early on. What faults do you mean? He hardly ever mentions politics."

"No, that is true. He seldom refers to the political system. His interest was confined to the army, but the problems were similar. He attacked bureaucracy and the brutality of his country's leaders. The communists in Vietnam have the same problem. I remember, some years back, reading an interview in the French weekly *L'Express* with a young French philosopher from the Sorbonne. He made a big impression on me, he was only 25. Unfortunately I have forgotten his name. He said that communism was bound to collapse because there was no connection between its theory and its practice. These days it is no longer a question of being either for or against Marxism–Leninism, because in Vietnam these doctrines have long since been abandoned, even if lip-service is still paid to them now and again."

He filled our cups again. I was by now quite drunk, but it was a happy, rather euphoric drunkenness which had as much to do with his company as with the effects of the wine.

"Have you ever been to the Soviet Union yourself?" I asked.

"Sholokhov, whose book I translated, invited me more than once, but I was never granted an exit permit in his lifetime. I did not get there until 1985, when I was invited to attend an international translators' congress. And by then Sholokhov was long dead. Gorbachov had just come to power. Everything seemed to be fine in the Soviet Union, apart from the bureaucracy, which was even more frightful than in Vietnam. I was not happy about being there and I wasted no time in requesting to come home again. I was interviewed and asked what I thought of the USSR. I had just heard one of Gorbachov's speeches and I said that there had been a sentence of his which had made an impression on me: 'It is not enough for leaders to be judged by their words. They must be judged on their actions.'

"It was not a love of Russian literature that made me a translator of Russian literature. It was chance. I had been reading Russian at university for six months before I became a soldier in 1945. In the army we had a Russian manual on military strategy which gave a description of the advance on Berlin. Our general told me that this was an important book and that I should therefore translate it. 'My Russian isn't good enough,' I said, 'I've only been reading Russian for six months.' 'Nobody here has read it for so much as a month,' said the general. 'So you get the job. Consider it an order.' That is how I began my career as a translator. With an order."

His gaze flitted across the television screen, on which the Japanese version of *The Count of Monte Cristo* was still spinning its web of intrigue. "The Japanese have it all," he said. "Everything seems to go well for them. Their economy functions, they export to every corner of the globe, their currency is strong, their standard of living high and yet I do not believe they are happy. They are not free. The life of a Japanese is one long ceremony. Even when he raises a cup of wine to his lips that act is part of a carefully dictated ritual. Me, I drink my wine as I wish, when I wish and as much of it as I wish. Only when mankind has abolished all rituals can it be happy."

He emptied his cup and I sensed that it was time to leave. It was almost two o'clock. I shook his hand. "I hope I haven't disturbed your evening," I said.

"On the contrary, it is me who should beg your forgiveness for having talked so much about myself. Besides, I usually sit up most of the night.

No, not because I need the stillness of the night. I can concentrate under any conditions. I worked on without a pause while the bombs were falling. You have to remember that Hanoi was under bombardment for ten years. We learned to live as if war were a normal state of affairs. We had to."

"So how will you spend the rest of the night?"

"Studying Chinese calligraphy. Practising my brushstrokes. An old man's pastime." He walked over to his desk, which was buried under untidy piles of books and papers covered in writing and unearthed a sheet painted with gracefully swooping Chinese characters. "Here, this is for you. It is a maxim of Uncle Ho: 'A nation's most precious possessions are its independence and freedom'."

Embroidery is their Native Land

DINH THOI VU HAD WORKED FOR SEVEN YEARS FOUNDING a steelworks in Czechoslovakia. He had left just before the start of the Velvet Revolution and returned to Hanoi to take a degree in economics. He had done a fair bit of travelling around Eastern Europe and said he preferred Budapest to Prague, but he had never crossed the Iron Curtain. Nonetheless this young man, who had lived all his life in countries governed by the principles of Communism, seemed to have been born with certain entrepreneurial instincts which would undoubtedly carry him to the top of the new society taking shape in Vietnam. While a student he had become a partner in the Darling Café, which, taking its cue from the Carlsberg advertisements, proclaimed itself to be "Possibly the best café in Hanoi".

The Darling Café was no different from many another public establishment in Vietnam where young men congregated to drink beer; but its menu, with its selection of standard dishes designed to appeal to the childish palates of American college students, and a noticeboard covered in hand-written messages in English, were proof that Hanoi had now become a staging-post on the roving backpacker's route. Vu also organized tours around the north-western corner of Vietnam, along the borders with China – an area which had for years been out of bounds to tourists but which had now been thrown open without any restrictions whatsoever. For $40 a day he supplied a car and a driver. When he accompanied me to the State-owned bank to withdraw the money to pay for my seven-day round journey, he surveyed the large number of staff in the bank with the self-made man's contempt for all government bureaucracy and remarked scornfully: "Look how many of them there are – and how inefficient they are. In the café there are just a handful of us, but we get a lot more done." A businessman to the core, that was Vu.

The driver's name was Tran Dinh Tinh. He used to work for the border police, and his vehicler – a Russian-made jeep – still sported the border police's yellow star on its bonnet. It was battered and ramshackle and even though Vu swore blind that it was only five years old, to my eyes it looked like a veteran of the battle of Stalingrad.

I made a big mistake not arranging to hire an interpreter for the journey. Tinh did not speak a word of English and during the week it took to tour the north-western part of the country I met no one else who could. This meant that I was unable to communicate with anyone other than in sign language. My enforced silence threw me into a strange mood in which, from one moment to the next, I could go from the depths of despondency to a heightened sense of well-being in which I became one with the surrounding countryside. But it was as if everything I felt was rendered in pastels. Like the smoke-coloured mountains I drove through and the white clouds whose shadows sped over the mirror-like surfaces of the terraced paddies I was oddly transparent, as if painted on glass.

After a day or so I discovered that Tran Dinh Tinh did after all have one word of English. It was the word "No", and every time he uttered it he shot his chin out defiantly and compressed his lips – which were unusually thin for a Vietnamese – into a narrow crease of contrariness. The word "No" also came to sum up our relationship since, like an echo of his "No", "No" was the only thing I had to say to him. It developed into a battle of wills which, as such things always are, was about not losing face and giving no quarter. He was continually testing me and after a spell of this I had to make a decision that went against the grain for me. Instead of trying to win his friendship I opted not to give a damn what he thought of me and made a point of keeping my distance.

Almost everywhere we went there would be someone whom Tinh knew, and each time we bumped into one of these characters I had confirmed the impression I had formed early on in my visit to Vietnam that the men often made dull company. They occupied their own self-contained world. The women, on the other hand, were anxious to involve themselves in the world outside. To them a stranger provided a welcome opportunity to learn something new, to the men merely an excuse to assert themselves. All they had were the customary, stereotyped gesticulations of masculinity, the tiresome rituals of drinking cronies and the sodden, invariably ambiguous bonhomie of inebriation which seemed more akin to a ceasefire in the midst of a monotonous bout of bragging. I noticed that they admired the stranger for the power his money gave him while being filled with a sly, unspoken disdain that betrayed itself now and again in outbursts of laughter they thought one did not understand. The men laughed *at* one, weak in their laughter; the women laughed *with* one, confident in theirs.

The landscape surprised me with the strange variety of its proportions. Everything in it was simultaneously grand and minute; it had drama, but on a miniature scale; it was luxuriant without being wild. The little cone-shaped mountains which shot up everywhere had an extravagant air about them, as if nature had launched itself wholeheartedly into an outrageous game involving geometric shapes. The place was overrun with vegetation and in their eagerness to dig in on the steepest slopes the very trees seemed to be striving for artistic effect, half rooted, half flying on the high trapeze. It was a proud and youthful landscape which appeared never to have known the tiredness of erosion, the humble sway-backs of ageing mountains or the pressure of earthly forces in the sluggish shifts of geological metamorphosis. The conical mountains resembled stalagmites formed quietly out of droplets from the sky and when I ran my eye across the horizon the landscape before me looked like the floor of a dripstone cave magnified a thousand times.

Whenever the jeep pulled up and the racket of the engine stilled, the air would be humming with the sound of birdsong. I had hired both jeep and taciturn driver for a seven-day round trip.

The area around Moi Chan was laid out with vast tea plantations, the fresh green of the low, neatly trimmed bushes standing out in pretty contrast to the red clay soil. I have always felt that there was a particular magic about those places where tea is grown, just as there is with fields of flowers. The tea bush is not a food plant and, unlike rice or corn, the care with which it is tended is not taken for survival, but for the sake of taste. Despite the fact that work on the tea plantations is hard and and the pay derisory, I never fail to see the women on the plantations (tea-pickers are always female) moving back and forth across the red earth and stooping over the green bushes without thinking of a woman pottering about a garden wielding a pair of sécateurs. Tea-growing is part farming, part gardening and wholly devoted to the philosophical and poetical pursuits; purveyor of sustenance to dreamers, poets and all others who prefer the company of the moon to the oblivion of a night's sleep. (In Hoi An, a small Vietnamese town south of Danang, I was shown round a house from the eighteenth century, one of the oldest surviving in Vietnam, which had a little courtyard dedicated to "the drinking of tea by the light of the full moon".)

The countryside here, 200 kilometres from Hanoi also marks the beginnings of Montagnard country, province of the hill tribes who people all of this corner of Asia. Their large airy houses are built on stilts and have elegantly curving thatched roofs. Instead of pointed gables the thatch forms a semi-circle and seen from above (more often than not they are situated in the bottom of a valley) the houses could be mistaken for enormous tortoises crawling across the landscape. And it is the tortoise's tempo, too, that the hill tribes have adopted in their progress up the ladder of evolution, on which they seem to have come to a halt at a point midway between the nomadic life and that of the farmer.

This area was predominantly the haunt of the Hmong and Tai tribes, but these two had many physical features in common with all of the other tribes. They were tiny people, even smaller than the Vietnamese, darker-skinned and rounder of head and body than the fine-boned Vietnamese with their willowy limbs and attenuated features. I often saw them walking along the mountain tracks. They were evidently on their way out to work their fields, but rather than letting the track dictate their route they had the air of having merely lit upon it by chance. They were never to be seen alone, moving always in large groups, adults and children bunched together in a close-knit community that was emphasised by the fact that they all wore the same type of clothing, had the same limpid faces and the same unspoiled gaze. Only in their size did they differ, but it was not hard to imagine that the children were simply diminutive adults and the adults overgrown children. I could not help but think that their curious talent for remaining unchanged by their surroundings, by the course of history or by national boundaries, had something to do with their negligible physical size. They were protected by their smallness. They were not big enough to arouse anyone's interest. There was no honour or profit to be gained by suppressing them. They had taken the land that no one else wanted and, furthermore, because they kept moving about it was not even possible to subjugate people who would have disappeared out of the back door even as the invading army was kicking in the door at the front.

These plump, sturdy, composed hill people were closely identified with their costume which, true to tradition, they had worn for centuries, scrupulously adhering to a dress code that enabled one to tell, even from a long way off, to which tribe they belonged. Not even the women's hairstyles admitted any variation. Every tribe was strikingly different from the next, but within each tribe, as far as their appearance was concerned, total uniformity prevailed. While it may not be possible to take their land, one could doubtless eradicate their identity by forcing them to wear other costumes. They have no country to tell them who they are. Their embroidery, the warp and weft of their cloth which is often dyed a distinctive indigo blue, is the only native land and the only history they have.

Every time I slammed the jeep door behind me and the rattle of the engine died away I heard the sound of voices among the mountains. The landscape was not so vast that all sign of human life was swallowed up by it, but in the stillness that reigned here any sound carried a long way. There was an intimacy about it, as if the mountains were speaking to me. I never saw the speakers. They were out of sight on some steep hillside or distant field.

Farther into the mountains, on the fourth day, the air grew slightly cooler. Low clouds sent a pattern of patchy sunlight and straggly shadows scudding over the sides of mountains that melted into a blue haze even when no great distance away. The jungle, too, seemed more blue than green in the altered light. These lofty regions, high up among the mountains, were also populated by tribes other than the otherwise predominant Tai and Hmong tribes. Women from the Huong tribe passed by on the mountain tracks. They wore tall indigo turbans which left exposed a little of their shaven heads, on which only a single lock had been given leave to grow. Their elongated faces were of a deep, smouldering terracotta and their ankle-length skirts, which were dyed the same indigo blue as their turbans, made them look as if they formed part of a picture puzzle which also took in the smoky blue mountains and the sky above them. They gave the impression of having camouflaged themselves to merge not with the earth, but with the sky.

Still deeper into the mountains I caught a glimpse of two young girls from the Cao Lau tribe. They were dressed in black with embroidered streamers and silver coins dangling from their headscarves. When they spied the jeep, with me sitting in the front seat, one of them froze to the spot while the other began at once to scramble up a slope, her eyes bright with panic and her mouth wide in a mute cry of fear. Then the other girl followed her, hands outstretched in helpless terror. This was truly a case of two centuries, or two worlds, coming eye to eye. And there had been the same lack of trust between us as there may be between two different species, predator and prey. Or between certain animals and man.

And yet it was a mistake to think that these mountain tribes were an integral part of nature, living in harmony with it. When the noise of the jeep motor died away for a moment and their voices drifted up to me from the valleys to mingle with the birdsong and the incessant rasping of the insects, and I heard the murmur of the water running down over the terraced rice paddies I could believe it. But then I beheld great swathes of mountainside on which the jungle had been burned away, and could never regrow, and I knew that this was their handiwork. Whole tracts of land had been changed for ever by their habit of burning away the jungle in order to plough the fertilizing ashes into the soil. At first, when I saw the mountains stretching out before me devoid of any vegetation other than yellowing straw and green bracken, I thought we had reached the tree line. But then I noticed fringes of jungle jutting out over vertiginous outcrops of rock even higher up, so exposed that not even the fire could reach that far. Here and there a scorched trunk reared out of the sea of grass like the archaeological remains of another, earlier form of vegetation which these tribes had cleared away with exactly the same callousness that their bigger brothers at much more advanced stages of civilization's evolutionary scale had employed in their campaign against the planet. The industrialized nations did not have a monopoly on damaging nature. The mountain tribes, too, left a trail of ashes across the landscape.

The little towns that nestled here and there among the mountains were different. They had the disorderly, haphazard look of the frontier settlement, built by improvisation and with whatever materials happened to be to hand: wooden shacks, market stalls constructed out of straw and sailcloth, low concrete-walled houses with flat, corrugated tin roofs. We had reached Tuan Giao in the mid-afternoon, and after securing a room at a local guest house I went for a walk down the town's main street.

As soon as I showed my face the whole town came to a standstill. The townspeople, all Vietnamese, stopped dead in their tracks and just stood there gaping – dumbfounded, wide-eyed and open-mouthed. We were kin, they and I, gaping as we did at one another with the same insatiable curiosity. The children, however, were not yet used to the sight of strangers. They goggled at me with the most fearfully intense solemnity and creased their small brows anxiously as they clutched at one another and hudded closer together, quaking with anxious suspense for every step that I took, as if I were some dangerous, unpredictable animal.

First there was this blatant reciprocal gawping. Then all of a sudden the town softened. Moped riders and cyclists drew up and offered me lifts on their baggage racks; navvies working on the road rested on their picks and nodded; men in cafés raised their glasses in invitation and salute; young girls held back a little and clasped each other tightly round the arm or waist before they overcame their fears and their faces lit up in melting smiles that seemed almost to spread to every part of their bodies before eventually culminating in a tentative, melodious "hello"; the old women wagged their heads knowingly beneath the bulky folds of their headscarves as if I were an old acquaintance who had not been here for many years, but whose orbit had now brought me round again, a little like Halley's comet.

On the outskirts of Tuan Giao, at the point where the main street reverted to the open road, a middle-aged man grabbed hold of me and pulled me into his house.

He was holding a baby in his arms and he kept on pulling faces, as though endeavouring to entertain both me and the baby at once. "*Camerade! Camerade!*" he spluttered ecstatically in French, or what I took to be French, for I was not quite certain what language he was actually speaking. He could have been saying "*Camera! Camera!*".

Inside the house I was seated on a bamboo stool about four inches off the ground. I looked around me. Spread about the hard-packed earth floor, half-hidden beneath the white canopies of mosquito nets, were a number of broad pallets constructed out of bamboo cane. In the room next door two little black pigs snuffled about in a bamboo pen. The man's wife, a short stout woman, appeared. She sat down across from me with all the quiet, beaming dignity of a Buddha statue and proceeded to pour tea. "*Merci*," I said, still assuming that they spoke some form of French.

"*Merci! Merci!*" My host threw his head back and roared with laughter and his guffawing acted as a rallying cry, for in next to no time something like 20 to 30 people had crowded into the room. At the front stood the children, surging timidly back and forth. Every time I looked at them they would scatter, squealing and sniggering, in all directions only, a moment later when my attention was elsewhere, to resume their positions.

My host leaned towards me, bubbling with mirth. "*Cinquante-deux*," he said. And then: "*Cinquante-trois*". I thought he must be referring to his age, so I told him mine. He tilted backwards again and dissolved into another fit of ear-splitting merriment. By some miracle the infant, which he was still cradling in one arm, slept on. Once he had got his breath back he leaned towards me once more. "Dien Bien Phu," he said.

Dien Bien Phu was the name of the place where the French had been well and truly routed, not in 1952 or '53, but in '54. Was he – taking me for French – out to remind me, rather rudely, that we were sitting not that far from the spot where my countrymen had been given a sound thrashing more than 40 years ago? Or had he, in fact, been fighting for the French?

I gazed at him in bewilderment. Again he began to guffaw. He turned to the crowd of people who had gathered round about us, his body shaking with laughter and, half-choking, yelled something incomprehensible at them which immediately set them laughing along with him, until the whole house was rocking in one massive convulsion of invisible laughter muscles. Even the children found the courage to giggle and edge closer to me, the laughter seeming suddenly to have brought them up to my level. I too began to laugh. The only one who did not laugh – indeed she retained her placid dignity throughout – was my host's wife. She concentrated on keeping my cup topped up with green tea and sending me the occasional kindly smile of encouragement as much as to say that she was well above such shenanigans and found them every bit as incomprehensible as I did.

I soon gave up trying to converse with my host in French once it dawned on me that his knowledge of that language was limited to the numbers *cinquante-deux* and *cinquante-trois*. I tried speaking English, but soon discovered that the word "maybe" provoked the same peals of laughter as the word "*merci*" had done earlier, presumably because they sounded similar. "Maybe! Maybe!" he shrieked, all but losing his balance and toppling backwards onto the floor, with the baby still slumbering in the crook of his arm.

At length I bid an exhausted farewell to the mirthful house and started back towards the town. His hoots of laughter followed me all the way. I looked round and saw him standing in the middle of the road surrounded by his family, bent double, as if the laughter were a boxer pummelling away at his midriff.

"*Cinquante-trois! Cinquante-trois!*" he yelled across the rice paddies.

The Simplest of all Gifts

IN THE LATE 1950S, FIRED WITH THE EXPECTATION OF REVOLUTION and plagued by visions of measureless catastrophe, a fever-ridden, mortally ill Franz Fanon wrote *The Wretched of the Earth*, his celebrated manifesto for the uprising of the colonized world against the colonizers. In this he nominated Dien Bien Phu – where the French had suffered a decisive defeat in 1954 – as the capital of the new world order to be born out of the native people's rebellion against their colonial masters: "The great victory of the Vietnamese people at Dien Bien Phu is no longer, strictly speaking, a Vietnamese victory. Since July 1954, the question which the colonized peoples have asked themselves has been 'What must be done to bring about another Dien Bien Phu? How can we manage it?' Not a single colonized individual could ever again doubt the possibility of a Dien Bien Phu."

When Fanon wrote his manifesto the population of the earth stood at 2,000 million, "500 million men, and one 1,500 million natives" in the ironic words of Sartre in his preface to the book. Today the earth's population is six billion; a vast, confused mass of humanity without a centre, a capital or any clearly defined aims; and Dien Bien Phu, lodestar for millions in an uprising in which the African felt himself to be brother-in-arms to the Vietnamese has once again become an all-but-inaccessible, out-of-the-way valley in a remote corner of history.

In fact there was no way of getting to Dien Bien Phu other than the one I took: in a jeep that covered the 450 kilometres from Hanoi at an average of 25kph, jolting along metalled roads and cart-tracks dotted with islands of crumbling asphalt – a reminder of other days – when there was some reason to make the journey to Dien Bien Phu or to travel for any distance at all through these mountains, which had briefly rung with the cannon-thunder of history. The mountains had not changed, nor the lives of the people who dwelled among them. As far as they were concerned, history might just as well have been a travelling circus that had raised its Big Top on a field outside town one day, the next day to pack up and move on. The roar of the cannon had not been the cue for profound alteration. History is never more fleeting than when played out on the battlefield.

The landscape was watched over by conical mountains and rugged, thickly forested hills interspersed with low-lying rice terraces and large, thatched houses. Our arrival at the valley in which the famous battle had been fought took me almost unawares. I had pictured the place as being more dramatic, in a deep valley hemmed in by steep mountainsides such as I had peered down into during the earlier stages of my journey. But here the distant, jungle-clad hills from which the Vietnamese army had bombarded the French positions seemed small on the horizon.

The element of surprise in this battle, and the key to the French defeat, had been the Vietnamese's feat of dragging their heavy artillery up the steep, tree-filled slopes of the mountains under cover of artfully constructed camouflage nets. I had seen documentary films in which wiry soldiers heaved and strained at the big guns, slipped and fell, picked themselves up and heaved again. It was a simple and spectacular act of heroism through which they conquered not only the enemy, but also the mountains and the law of gravity. In this sweeping green valley it was hard to imagine.

Dien Bien Phu itself was not much more than a collection of long, yellow-washed buildings with tiled roofs. At the heart of the little town lay a number of knolls and it was around these that all of the crucial fighting had occurred. I walked up one of them and sat myself down near the summit. Known as A1, it was the last hill to be taken, on the momentous day when Dien Bien Phu finally fell: 7 May 1954. The Vietnamese had dug their way underneath the knoll and packed it with a tonne of explosives which they then detonated as the signal to attack. A large portion of the knoll was blown sky-high along with the French legionnaires who had been defending it. Trees grew there now, next to the remains of a concrete bunker and an old, abandoned tank with its gun barrel trained on the ground. The most remarkable thing about the knoll was the memorial which the Vietnamese had raised to the battle. It consisted of an immense concrete "A" beside an immense "1".

There was a good view to be had from the top, and on every hill that reared up out of the valley I saw the same sight: huge concrete letters and numbers announcing the names given to the occupied heights on the general staff map. Nearby were C1 and C2, then D1, and in the distance E1. It was a very prosaic way of commemorating a decisive battle.

The French commander, Castries (Christian-Marie-Ferdinand de La Croix de Castries), being of a more romantic bent, is said to have named the heights after his several mistresses. On his map A1 was "Elaine", C1 was "Dominique", C2 "Claudine", D1 "Huguette" and E1 "Françoise". The less than far-sighted colonel had paid his mistresses a sadly inept compliment and exposed them to ridicule by losing on the field of battle the conquests he had made in bed.

The choice of Colonel Castries was due to one of many misunder-standings that were to determine the outcome of the battle. His superior, General Navarre, was under the impression that the valley was prime tank country and hence he had appointed Castries, the commander of a cavalry regiment, to defend the impregnable garrison. Castries soon discovered that tanks could make no headway whatsoever in the valley, which the spring rain had turned into a sea of mud. Like many a roman-tic hero he found himself in the wrong world. He was a womanizer; beset, in true romantic fashion, by gambling debts; an expert horseman; and, before being transferred to the cavalry, he had earned a reputation as a daredevil pilot with the French air force. Now here was this figure straight out of another age being overtaken by the new, to be defeated not by more modern weapons than those he had at his own command, but by the determination of a people's army to risk everything.

Colonel Castries's image of himself as a cavalier, the one which led him to confuse military campaigns with his sexual conquests, was rudely unmasked when he made his last radio announcement: "*Ils sont à quelque metre du radio d'où je vous parle. Nous ne nous renderons pas.*" ("They are only a few metres away from the radio on which I am speaking to you. We will not surrender.") "And the radio went dead," states the melodramatic postscript in a newspaper cutting from a French newspaper now hanging in the Dien Bien Phu museum. But Castries did surrender. And long lines of humiliated white men who, a minute earlier – thanks to their weaponry – had still been representatives of a superior race, but who were now merely sick, exhausted, wounded and, above all, disarmed representatives of the human race, began to file past the cameras that the Vietnamese had set up in order to preserve their moment of triumph for posterity. This, too, I remembered from a documentary on the battle of

Dien Bien Phu and the memory of it had the power to move me still, sitting there on the top of A1, in the shadow of that sober, unpretentious monument to the battle. Because then, as now, I felt that this was a battle that had been fought on behalf of mankind, in an effort to save the best in all of us; and that the war against colonialism was not a war which transformed men into monsters, but monsters into men. This applied on both sides of the line dividing the victors and the vanquished, inasmuch as the victors, from being natives, became human beings, while the vanquished were liberated from their monstrous fixation with belonging to a master race enjoying special – primarily moral – privileges which guaranteed that they would walk free from any court of law. Now they had been condemned, not only to defeat, but to a life as human beings on an equal footing with everyone else.

On the way out of Dien Bien Phu, down in the valley, I spied Colonel Castries's useless tanks, stranded in the rice fields, their metal reflecting the sunlight in smouldering tones of umber and petrol-blue. They had been there for almost 40 years providing a far more telling monument to the war than any statue of muscle-bound soldiers with rifles held high in triumph could have done. I was reminded of the guide at the tunnels of Cu Chi and his casual slap at the main gun barrel of another tank, that time an American one. This was a similar gesture, a contemptuous slap at the ineffectual instruments of death, these insect-like, dismantled killing machines that had been left to rust amid the green eternity of the rice paddies. And perhaps that was the way with history: a sudden, fierce outbreak of violence, lasting for five minutes, and for the remainder of the day's 24 hours humanity inhabited the great, silent reality of cultivation and self-preservation. The paddies represented the real world, the grand, universal reality of mankind; an expression of its fundamental will. And the tank in their midst represented despair, a cramping of the muscles, the waste product of a fleeting, brief nightmare.

Another heap of mangled metal met the eye in the square outside the large warehouse of sorts that housed the Dien Bien Phu museum. This one consisted of 40-year-old jeeps and trucks, a propeller and half a wing from a downed aircraft, shell casings, a field gun on rubber wheels. Opposite it stood orderly rows of Vietnamese artillery, like chess pieces that have cleared their opponents' half of the board.

Inside the museum, a series of black and white photographs showed how the battlefield had looked once the battle had been won and victory assured: it was like Verdun in the First World War, with churned-up, shell-pocked country from which every trace of vegetation had been erased and was replaced by dead bodies scattered all around; barbed wire; abandoned helmets riddled with bullet holes; drooping standards; the slaughtered earth's substitute for the vanished flora.

There was a photograph of the annihilated enemy on the top of C1, also known as Dominique. One soldier appeared to be asleep with his arms around a sandbag, another lay on his back, arms outstretched, his broad negroid face staring vacantly at the sky. They were soldiers from the African contingent, affording, in a flash, some inkling of the omnipresent tragedy behind the elation of victory. Here the oppressed had had to charge over the bodies of other oppressed people in their struggle for freedom.

In his preface to Franz Fanon's call to arms against colonialism, Sartre wrote ecstatically of the necessity for killing: "to shoot down a European is to kill two birds with one stone, to destroy an oppressor and the man he oppresses at the same time." Meaning, by this last, that the killing was a liberating act which transformed the colonized individual from vassal to free man. How naïve it was, this salute to slaughter. Could Sartre not see that the European was calculating enough always to use other races as cannon fodder, thus allowing the oppressed to murder one another in the name of freedom?

A mere ten years later, history was to repeat itself when the Americans took the place of the French on the battlefields of Vietnam. Three million Vietnamese died, and only 50,000 Americans – the same number as die in traffic accidents in the USA every year; and how many of those slain were, in fact black: men who, during the years when the Vietnamese were battling for their right to be free, were forced to march time and again for the self-same basic rights that democracy otherwise allowed its citizens to enjoy as a matter of course. And they wound up here, on the battlefields of Vietnam, to be killed by an enemy who only wanted the same thing as they did: the right to be human. Did killing a Moroccan, an Algerian or a black American make a Vietnamese free?

I thought of Scent of Spring's great-uncle, an intellectual who had spent twelve years as a soldier and who had spoken of the romance of the struggle for independence. But wherein did this romance lie? And what was one to make of his fascination with Isaac Babel and that writer's depiction of life with a Cossack regiment in the thick of the civil war which would give birth to the Soviet Union? Babel was an intellectual. He described himself as a man with spectacles on his nose and autumn in his heart. He was a man who had turned his life into a sick joke: a Jew who willingly threw in his lot with the anti-Semites and rode with a Cossack regiment whose drive across eastern Poland was to become an unrelieved, blood-crazed massacre of Jews. He spent the whole campaign trying to win the friendship and respect of these barbaric men so full of hate, and on the last page of *Red Cavalry* his dream came true. He had learned to sit in the saddle Cossack fashion. ("The Cossacks stopped following me and my horse with their eyes.") So modest the dream, so powerful the sense of inferiority, so paradoxical the admiration felt by this highly educated Jew who dreamt of being accepted by the murderers of his race.

Babel was one of the seminal writers of the twentieth century and his style – almost reportage in its immediacy, ice-cold, but not without lyrical intensity in its matter-of-fact rendering of detail – was destined to found an entire literary school and be imitated by, among others, Ernest Hemingway, who never succeeded in surpassing it. Babel gives the impression of being sublimely indifferent to the events that take place under his nose. He makes no judgements, does not interpret these events, seems barely to comprehend them, and it is this distance which, in a subtle, indirect way accords his writing style its pathos. But it would be wrong to imagine that this pathos springs from the presence of death on the battlefield, the sufferings of men, their recklessness and self-sacrifice. Rather it is the pathos of self-refutation. So writes an intellectual who longs with all his might to free himself of his spiritual baggage, to escape the moral labyrinths of soul-searching and surrender instead to an elementary man's world of action and intoxicating freedom. The pathos of this style is not the pathos of the warrior, but the pathos of intellectual suicide, the pathos of self-loathing and spiritual flagellation. When a journalist writes in this fashion it is because he is struggling to come to terms with the necessity for objectivity without which his profession would have no moral basis. When an intellectual writes like this, he does so because he is doing violence to his self, his empathy, his right to doubt. He longs to break out into a more simplified reality, into the spring that will release him from the autumn in his heart and the spectacles on his nose. It is a style that would like to be viewed as a salute to a new reality and it is as such that it comes to create a school in the twentieth century, as an expression of the intellectual's fascination with anti-intellectualism.

"You four-eyed lot," one of the Cossacks says to Babel. There they are again, the glasses, in a version reminiscent of the expression "to speak with a forked tongue", to be a liar and a crook. Seeing with two pairs of eyes amounts to much the same thing. You can't trust an intellectual. He is the outsider, able to atone for his position only by removing his glasses and becoming one with the people, that company of noble savages. Which is what Babel does: he atones and becomes one with them, by trading the kingdom of the intellectual for a Cossack horse.

Mortal dread is an intellectual pastime, the bane of feeble souls, which Babel does not see it as his job to describe, despite the fact that he is surrounded on all sides by the stench of death and entrails: "The odour of yesterday's blood and the slain horses drips into the evening coolness," as it says on the first page of *Red Cavalry*. No, the real proof that he has at last become one of the fighting men and shared their life is this: "begging fate for the simplest of abilities – the ability to kill a man". There is the true sign of solidarity, the intellectual's ultimate liberation from himself as the impotent agent of thought and doubt, as he pays homage to violence and makes himself an accomplice to slaughter – and indeed even dreams of taking part in the massacring. Forty years and a world war later Sartre also glorifies slaughter in his show of solidarity with the struggle of the colonized peoples. It is like some barbaric initiation rite. The intellectual's longing for fellowship, his inability to endure his own isolation, lead him to betray the very thing that marks him as an intellectual. For him, solidarity with the masses is impossible without self-abandonment and masochism.

It is wrong to think that such intellectuals want to save the world; they want to save themselves. It is also wrong to think that their choice is an easy one. Should the native peoples have refrained from doing battle with their oppressors? To whom would the intellectuals have given their support if not the oppressed? A situation in which all of the possible options will end up with untold numbers of victims is tragic, no matter who wins, and the intellectual's treachery lies not in refusing to get involved, but in refusing to admit that, no matter what choice he makes, he is a player in a tragedy.

There comes a moment in history, and the Vietnam war is one such moment, where we are suddenly presented with an ethically two-dimensional, fairy-tale world, the simple choice between good and evil; but what we ought always to be aware of is that this moment does not last very long and that things very quickly go back to being much more complicated. As a rule, though, intellectuals do get involved, and even go to war themselves, because they have a weakness for these fairy-tale moments and fancy that they can prolong them indefinitely and live forever in a world of black and white. But they cannot, for no one can walk away unscathed from their own actions.

Nonetheless, in the midst of the campaign in eastern Poland even Babel confided to his diary a story different from the one he published in *Red Cavalry*: "They say they are fighting for justice and they all loot. Life is loathsome . . . I ride with them begging the men not to massacre the prisoners . . . I couldn't look at their faces, they bayoneted some, shot others, bodies covered by corpses, they strip one man while they're shooting another, groans, screams, death rattles . . . We are destroyers . . . we move like a whirlwind, like a stream of lava, hated by everyone, life shatters, I am at a huge, neverending service for the dead . . . the sad senselessness of my life." This was Babel's inner struggle, between the horror he witnessed and felt within himself and his attempt to overcome it through the terse, tight-lipped style that he invented. The twentieth century's great contribution to the regeneration of literary styles: the repression of abhorrence at the sight of death and destruction in a century which has surpassed all others in the article of violent death and destruction.

More than 15 years after the end of the Vietnam War and after many a political let-down, there were Vietnamese writers who finally told the truth about the war; not from the point of view of the intellectual, but from that of the common soldier. The style in Vietnamese novels of war was reminiscent of Isaac Babel's, but the viewpoint was that of his diary, not his art. These novels were not written by intellectuals who had maimed themselves spiritually in order to become one with war. They had been written by survivors, common soldiers who, having been maimed by the war, were attempting to become human once more.

329

The writer Bao Ninh called his novel *The Sorrow of War*. Duong Thu Huong called hers *Novel without a Name*. Duong – a woman and war veteran – has her novel end at the opposite point from Babel, who prays that he may learn how to kill. After the orgy of war, Duong's central character is eventually brought face to face with the vanquished enemy – and lets him go.

Bao Ninh writes: "War was a world bereft of real men, bereft of real women, bereft of feeling. War was also a world bereft of romance . . . in the same strange way, the sorrow that lives on in the soldier's heart was reminiscent of heartache. It was a kind of nostalgia, like the terrible sadness of a twilight world."

Babel believed that he had to free himself from the spectacles that symbolized his intellectual distance, so that he might see man in all his nakedness and become one with war. He thought he could see better with two eyes than with four. These Vietnamese writers, who had lived with the atrocities of war for ten years, had waited another 15 years to complete their war novels, knowing as they did that four eyes saw better than two and that the depiction of the naked individual of wartime craved the distance afforded by remembrance and reflection. They did not renounce their intellectual horizon in order to write about war. Instead, they endeavoured to win themselves an intellectual horizon as a prerequisite for being able to write at all. "How, as a writer, can one possibly seek insight through war?" Bao Ninh asks, and comes up with the answer one cold, dark, spring night when something inside him, something urgent and powerful, pumps life back into his broken spirit: "Something that felt like love. The discovery of some wonderful truth deep within him."

At the time of my visit to Dien Bien Phu I had not read Bao Ninh's or Duong Thu Huong's novels. They had not yet been published in the West, but they had already been written and both writers lived in Hanoi. Duong Thu Huong had spent seven months in prison for distributing documents containing "State secrets". The documents were *Novel without a Name*.

There was a visitors' book in the museum at Dien Bien Phu. I sat down, overwhelmed by the quiet dignity of the place, and wrote: "Few wars can be justified. The battle of Dien Bien Phu is one of the rare exceptions."

I, too, wanted for a moment to live in the ethically two-dimensional, fairy-tale world of war.

"Trung Hoa?" said the driver, eyeing me quizzically. "Trung Hoa," he repeated, and wrote the words down on a piece of paper. Trung Hoa? I looked at him blankly. There was no village on our route by the name of Trung Hoa. Then it dawned on me. Trung Hoa: the horizon, the constant repetition of history, Vietnam's destiny. Trung Hoa was Vietnamese for China, mastodon of an arch-enemy and life-giving source of inspiration, whose repeated invasions had set the tempo of Vietnam's history for thousands of years. We were not far from the border and what the driver was asking was whether I would like to take a look at China.

We crossed the Red River, drifting aslant the current on a large landing-craft nudged through the muddy brown water by a tug with a faded yellow star on its blackened funnel. We were in the middle of nowhere, but frontier towns have a knack of turning the peripheral into the centre of things. Though the town itself consisted of little more than a few bamboo buildings flanking dirt roads churned into mud, nonetheless these shacks were resplendent with signs declaring them to be cafés serving hot cocoa, and women in tight trousers, their hair coiled up, as stylishly turned out as any I had seen in Saigon, drove the mud-filled cart-tracks astride Honda scooters. Everything was coated with dust and rust. The cars, the buses, the trucks and the converted jeeps now doing duty as haulage vehicles – all were models from the '30s and '40s. Then, suddenly, a gleaming white Toyota Corona came gliding through the mud; and as the bamboo curtains across the entrances of the shacks slid back I saw JVC colour televisions and cassette players stacked up like artefacts salvaged from downed UFOs.

The border followed the river for a little way before heading inland. A railway bridge linked Vietnam with China. It was the line from Hanoi to Kunming, but as if symbolizing the relationship between the two countries, on the Chinese side the line was blocked by a wall constructed out of railway sleepers. A narrow opening permitted people to cross over on foot, but there was no one to be seen on the bridge, the Vietnamese side of which was covered with mounds of chippings, as though under repair. On either side of the river fluttered red flags, the Chinese with five gold stars, the Vietnamese with a single star at its centre. Arch-enemies down the ages, now linked by a common ideology, yet still at loggerheads, perhaps because they knew each other too well.

On my journey through the mountains I had never once let slip an opportunity to cross any bridge we drove past. I would ask the driver to stop the car and walking back and forth over them, gazing down from them into the depths, I would enjoy the sight of them and feel their gentle, ticklish swaying in the breeze – more often than not they were suspension bridges. But here was a bridge I could not cross, even though it connected countries which both flew socialist banners and swore by the principle of internationalism. The war between China and Vietnam in 1979 had proved to be an early forerunner of the new age which dawned with the fall of the Berlin Wall and in which those who had once sung The Internationale became the first to renounce the principle of internationalism. From that time on, communists survived only as nationalists.

On both banks of the river danced the same brightly coloured parasols advertising in Chinese characters and Roman lettering the city that had once been the railway line's terminus, Kunming. People could not cross this border, but parasols could, in the osmotic flow of merchandise that the membranes of no border, no matter how closed, were capable of stopping.

That was the new internationalism. Here was the future.

Parting is the Little Sister of Death

HANOI GREETED ME WITH A THUNDEROUS SHOWER THAT SET the trees rustling and drummed on the awnings stretched over the little food stalls on the corner next to the hotel. I had been given a new room, a bigger one with a balcony, but for the same price, and in this I thought I detected Harvest Moon's hand, as I did in the red rosebuds on the bedside table.

I ran out into the rain and made my way from stall to stall in the shelter of awnings sagging heavily under the strain of the collected rainwater, being served with baked fish at one, offal with sautéed spring onions at another, and finishing off with sweetened yoghurt at a third.

Harvest Moon had not been in reception when I arrived, but she was there now. The first thing she asked me was whether I had called Scent of Spring. I shook my head.

"I really am very disappointed in you," she said reproachfully. "She has missed you terribly."

"How do you know that?" I asked.

"Because that's how it was for me with my husband when we first met."

"Yes, but you were in love," I said, annoyed by her scolding.

"No," said Harvest Moon with simple, indisputable logic. "That is how we found out that we were falling in love."

I did call Scent of Spring and we arranged to go for a walk by West Lake the next day. It would be our last day together. But the following morning she rang to say she could not come, that she had slept badly and now had a dreadful headache. She suggested that I call her in the late afternoon.

I took a stroll down to Hoan Kiem Lake, as I often did. I found a seat in a pavilion overlooking the lake and ordered an ice cream. Across from me sat an old man whom I had seen before and had only said hello to. He always seemed to be deeply engrossed in a book and this time, when he felt my eye on him, he raised the book so that I could see its jacket, sending me a friendly nod as he did so. I noticed that it was the same book he had been reading the last time I had seen him, a well-worn anthology of love poems from the French romantic period. He set the book aside. "My name is Nguyen Thinh Young," he said. I shook his hand and introduced myself.

Nguyen Thinh Young was a handsome man with shoulder-length white hair and a wispy goatee beard. "I used to work for a big shipping company," he told me, "I have been to America, Singapore, Europe, all over the world. Oh, I've only visited the ports, but wherever we docked I always had to go ashore and have a look around. What countries have you been to? Have you ever been to Greenland? I often try to imagine what it must be like in Greenland. So cold and quite desolate."

"Are you very fond of poetry?" I asked.

His face lit up and he started to laugh. When he did so his eyes disappeared into two slits and his sinewy old man's body shook heartily. "I must tell you," he said, "that I adore stories about love. Every time I come across a book about love I have to buy it. But my favourites are the French romantic poets – Lamartine, Musset, André Chénier, Alfred de Vigny."

He closed his eyes and began to recite Lamartine's "Le Lac", rapturously and yet softly, his cloud of silver hair standing out like a halo round the high forehead and the delicate skin that stretched taut over his beautifully shaped crown. At his back Hoan Kiem Lake spread smooth as glass, reflecting the cloudy grey sky.

He opened his eyes. "When I am feeling sad I always think of Chénier's "*La jeune captive*". Did you know that he wrote it the evening before his execution?"

And again he recited, eyes closed, in a childishly sing-song rhythm, as if he had once learned the poem by heart at school and been forced to chant it without understanding the words. Even so, his voice had an irresistible lilt to it, like a big wave slowly rolling towards the shore. Eyes open once more, he said: "Poems are the memory of the world."

Nguyen Thinh Young proceeded to speak of his own memory and his love of language. He spoke French and English "because as a sailor you had to", and he could read Russian, though not speak it. Now he was teaching himself German.

"I come here every day to have a cup of coffee and read my love stories. I have developed my own technique for remembering everything I read. Let me explain it to you. I work with comparisons and contrasts. I love to sit for hours on end with a dictionary, learning words by heart. Take your name for example. Your surname is Jensen. To remember your name I think of another name I know well, Einstein. Then I compare the two and find the differences and similarities between them. Now I won't ever forget your name. Jensen."

He sipped his coffee with a faraway look in his eyes and I realized that in his old body he had retained the child's capacity for being surprised and delighted. Here it was my name that had dispatched him into trains of thought. Then he was back with me again. "The one science, though, which is making the most marvellous advances is biology," he said. "Just think. They can take an organ from a dead person and transfer it to someone who is still alive." Aware of the impression he was making on me, he favoured me with an arch little twinkle: "How old would you take me for?" he asked.

"Sixty-eight," I replied. I found it hard to gauge the ages of the Vietnamese.

"Sixty-eight, you say? No, I am in fact 76. See, you have made me eight years younger than I am." And he shut his eyes and dissolved into chuckles that rocked his wiry old body as a mother rocks her baby to sleep.

At the hotel I made another call to Scent of Spring. Her headache was gone and she invited me to her parents' house to spend the evening with her. I greeted her parents, who then made themselves scarce as usual and left us to ourselves. Scent of Spring placed a photograph album on the table in front of me and opened it. It was the same album she had shown me before. "Find the picture of me that you like the best," she said, laughing. "Even though I know that by tomorrow you will have forgotten me."

I picked out a snap which showed her dressed in a long-sleeved, floor-length white silk dress.

"Well then you must have this one, too," she said and handed me a photograph of herself in jeans, as if she wanted to be sure I understood that there were two sides to her.

An hour or two later, when the time came for me to say goodbye, she considered me gravely. "Put out your right hand," she said with the note of assurance in her voice that I had learned to admire. "This is for you," she said, removing from her own wrist a little silver bracelet which she proceeded to fasten around mine. "It is supposed to bring luck and good health. My bracelet will protect you. You still have a long way to go and you are alone, without your family or your friends. I am surrounded by my family so I don't need it."

When we parted I gave her my hand. It was the only physical contact there had ever been between us. There was a line which neither of us could – or would – cross and for the first time in my life I felt that such a line, set by tradition and custom, had some meaning. She had told me that there were times when this observance of decorum made her feel as if she were in a prison, but she had shown – and this she herself was well aware of – that the honouring of tradition also held the key to respect and self-respect. But to say that we shook hands in a spirit of mutual respect sounds too formal, for we shook hands with a respect that was full of warmth and the prospect of friendship, even though we might never meet again. Her manner was evidence of self-respect and I was conscious of how it rubbed off on me. Scent of Spring was a woman in whose presence one grew.

The next morning I said goodbye to Harvest Moon. Her keen eye did not miss a thing. "What's that on your wrist?" she asked as soon as she saw me. I showed her the bracelet and explained that Scent of Spring had given it to me.

"This means that Scent of Spring loves you," said Harvest Moon, delighted to see her schemes bearing fruit.

"No," I replied categorically, "it means that we are friends and wish each other well."

"I'm your friend, too. I wish you well on the rest of your journey," she said and her eyebrows broke into the fluttery ballet of our first meeting. She dropped her eyes. Overcome by sadness, I held out my hand.

* * *

In the duty-free shop at Hanoi airport four sales assistants in crisp white shirts were standing weeping among the cognac bottles. I have no idea why they were crying, but there are times when I can be very moved by strong displays of emotion and possibly it was due to the influence of the inexplicable weeping of the four salesgirls that I found myself having to fight back the tears as the plane was swallowed up by the clouds over Hanoi and I saw the rice paddies falling away beneath me for the last time.

For some reason I was put in mind of an evening in Hanoi when, from my balcony, I watched the black silhouettes of the bats against the ruddy glow of the evening sky, flitting this way and that with the strangely aimless precision which their radar system dictates for them in the hunt for dancing swarms of insects. They were not the most elegant of flyers, with their febrile fluttering. They flew as a mouse breathes, in short bursts, as if they were the hunted, not the hunters. The way they flapped their wings made it seem as though the action did not come naturally to them. The thought struck me that I was flying in much the same way as the bats, in pent-up fear of falling, because the air was just as unnatural an element for me as it would be for a mouse.

But now I understood that at some point during my journey through Vietnam this fear had loosened its grip on me, without my being aware of it, and I realised that the reason why my fear had gone was not because I had become a better flier, but because of my instinctive feeling that to fall would also mean to come into contact with the earth and renew one's ties with it.

I had given so much thought to the weightlessness inherent in freedom and concentrated mainly on the darker potential of freedom and the corruption which freedom can degenerate into when sought late in life. But my journey through Vietnam had led me to think that freedom might also be used to become attached to people once more, with bonds of responsibility. Wherever I went I encountered trust – and I carried that trust with me as a promise to myself.